DISCARD

'As the terror attacks on the United States become history as well as politics, there is now an opportunity for greater critical thinking on the representation of the event. In this timely and engaging book, David Holloway provides an impressive synchronic account of the meaning and importance of 9/11. It deserves to be widely read by scholars and postgraduates occupying positions in diverse disciplinary locations.'

Tim Dunne, Professor of International Relations, University of Exeter

Titles of related interest from McGill-Queen's University Press.

After the Terror by Ted Honderich

Critique of Security by Mark Neocleous

Reigns of Terror by Patricia Marchak

Satanic Purses: Money, Myth, and Misinformation in the War on Terror by R.T. Naylor

Security and Defence in the Terrorist Era by Elinor C. Sloan

Cultures of the War on Terror

Cultures of the War on Terror

Empire, Ideology, and the Remaking of 9/11

David Holloway

McGill-Queen's University Press
Montreal & Kingston • Ithaca

For Jenny, Calum and Ethan

ISBN 978-07735-3483-4 (cloth)
ISBN 978-0-7735-3484-1 (paper)

Legal deposit third quarter 2008
Bibliothèque nationale du Québec

Published simultaneously outside North America by Edinburgh University Press

Library and Archives Canada Cataloguing in Publication

Holloway, David, 1967-
    Cultures of the War on Terror : empire, ideology, and the
remaking of 9/11 / by David Holloway.

Includes bibliographical references and index.
ISBN 978-0-7735-3483-4 (bound).–ISBN 978-0-7735-3484-1 (pbk.)

    1. Politics and culture–United States. 2. September 11 Terrorist
Attacks, 2001, in mass media. 3. War on Terrorism, 2001- , in mass
media. 4. Iraq War, 2003- –Mass media and the war. 5. United States–
Politics and government–2001-. I. Title.

HV6432.H652 2008   973.931   C2008-902115-0

Typeset in Janson and Helvetica by
Servis Filmsetting Ltd, Manchester, and
printed and bound in Great Britain by
CPI Antony Rowe, Chippenham, Wilts

Contents

List of Illustrations   viii
Acknowledgements   x

   Introduction   1
1. History   7
2. Politics   31
3. Mass Media   58
4. Cinema   81
5. Literature   107
6. Photography and Visual Art   129
   Conclusion   154

Appendix A: Timeline   159
Appendix B: Synoptic biographies   167
Annotated bibliography of further reading and texts cited   172
Index   188

List of Illustrations

Fig. I.1   9/11 World Trade Center Attacks. Onlookers watch
            as Manhattan's Financial District is engulfed by
            smoke from the collapse of the World Trade
            Center's South Tower after being struck by a plane.
            Smoke billows from the top of the North Tower,
            which was also hit by a commercial airplane shortly
            before the attack on the South Tower.   2
Fig. I.2   Ground Zero.   3
Fig. 2.1   Richard Clarke promotes his book, *Against All
            Enemies*, in Germany, during June 2004.   32
Fig. 2.2   Thousands march up Pennsylvania Avenue towards
            the Capitol in Washington, DC, during anti-war
            demonstrations on 25 October 2003.   33
Fig. 2.3   Condoleezza Rice testifies before the 9/11
            Commission on Capitol Hill, 8 April 2004.   42
Fig. 2.4   American anti-war activist, dressed as an Abu Ghraib
            prisoner, stands among crosses at Camp Casey, near
            the Texas ranch of President George W. Bush during
            November 2005. The camp was named for activist
            Cindy Sheehan's son, Casey, who was killed in Iraq.   52
Fig. 3.1   CentCom, Doha, 2 April 2003. US Army Brigadier
            General Vincent Brooks briefs journalists on the
            rescue of Jessica Lynch, who can be seen on the
            screen behind Brooks. Video footage of the rescue
            was shown to reporters during the press conference.   70
Fig. 3.2   President Bush on the *USS Abraham Lincoln*, 1 May
            2003.   72
Fig. 3.3   Harold Perrineau, Dominic Monaghan, Evangeline
            Lilly and Matthew Fox of the television show, *Lost*,
            in California, September 2004.   77

Fig. 4.1   Director M. Night Shyamalan, and actors Bryce
            Dallas Howard, Adrien Brody and Joaquin Phoenix,
            at the world premiere of *The Village*, July 2004, in
            New York.   89
Fig. 4.2   'Sublime' terror in Spielberg's Cold War re-make,
            War of the Worlds.   93
Fig. 4.3   'This guy could be like Mossadegh in '52 in Iran'.
            Alexander Siddig as Prince Nasir Al-Subaai, in the
            Stephen Gaghan directed political thriller, *Syriana*,
            made by the Participant production company.   98
Fig. 4.4   Michael Moore, photographed by Marcel Hartmann,
            May 2004, Paris.   105
Fig. 5.1   Philip Roth in New York, May 2007.   109
Fig. 5.2   Frédéric Beigbeder.   119
Fig. 6.1   19 September 2001. A young woman looks at one of
            the many displays which sprang up spontaneously
            after the attacks of September 11, with photos of the
            missing, in New York.   130
Fig. 6.2   *here is new york*. Visitors view photographs in the *here
            is new york* gallery in SoHo, New York, during
            January 2002.   134
Fig. 6.3   A visitor to the 2006 Whitney Biennial, New York,
            looks at Richard Serra's *Stop Bush*.   143
Fig. 6.4   *Tribute in Light*, Ground Zero.   145
Fig. 6.5   In June 2004, an Iranian couple walks past mural
            paintings depicting scenes of the torture of Iraqi
            prisoners by US soldiers at the Abu Ghraib prison
            near Baghdad, on a major highway in the Iranian
            capital Tehran. This photo was part of the exhibition
            *Inconvenient Evidence: Iraqi Prison Photographs from
            Abu Ghraib*.   149

Acknowledgements

A lot of people have helped in many different ways with this book. Particular thanks to John Beck, Paul Bridges, Neil Campbell, Josie Chapman, Robin Chapman, Julie Coxon, James Dale, Colin Dyter, Sarah Edwards, Richard Golland, Helena Grice, Mike Gunn, Jenny Holloway, Calum Holloway, Ethan Holloway, Simon Justice, Alasdair Kean, Jane Keeling, David Manley, Helen Oakley, Liz Oldfield, Simon Philo, Nicola Ramsey, Jenny Robinson, Ruth Willats, Tim Woods.

Introduction

Continuity and Crisis

When Islamist insurgents hijacked four commercial airliners on September 11 2001 and crashed them into the World Trade Center in New York and the Pentagon in Washington, DC, destroying the Trade Center and killing almost 3,000 people, the attacks were widely described as a moment of historical rupture, an epochal event that drew a clear line through world history, dividing what came after 9/11 from what went before (Figures I.1 and I.2). Yet in many ways the feeling that everything changed on 9/11 was an illusion. Even in the United States, life for many continued much as it always had. Nor was the danger posed by al-Qaeda on 9/11 a new or surprising development. Twice in the preceding five years, first in August 1996, and again in February 1998, Osama bin Laden had issued public declarations of *jihad* (holy war) against the United States. In June 1996, in an attack in which bin Laden has often been implicated, the US military barracks at the Khobar Towers near Dhahran, Saudi Arabia, was blown up by a truck bomb, killing nineteen Americans and wounding hundreds more. The bombing of the US embassies in Kenya and Tanzania in August 1998, in which twelve Americans and 291 Africans died, was also carried out by al-Qaeda fighters. There were portents of worse to come. In June 1999, the US temporarily closed six of its embassies across western Africa, citing bin Laden-related threats. For the same reason, in December, on the eve of the first new year of the new millennium, the State Department warned Americans abroad to avoid large public gatherings. Back home in Seattle, the mayor cancelled the city's millennium celebrations altogether. Then, in October 2000, in the most audacious anti-American attack yet, suicide bombers blew a hole in the side of the destroyer *USS Cole* while the ship was moored at Aden, in the Yemen, killing seventeen American sailors.

Catastrophic though they were, the 9/11 attacks were just one incident in a much bigger, transnational Islamist insurgency, whose immediate antecedents were the international brigades of Muslim fighters

1

Figure I.1 9/11 World Trade Center Attacks. Onlookers watch as Manhattan's Financial District is engulfed by smoke from the collapse of the World Trade Center's South Tower after being struck by a plane. Smoke billows from the top of the North Tower, which was also hit by a commercial airplane shortly before the attack on the South Tower.
© Seth Cohen/Bettmann/Corbis.

that expelled the Soviet Union from Afghanistan in the 1980s after a guerrilla war lasting a decade. These men fought in conflicts around the world during the 1990s – notably in the Balkans, and in the Russian republic of Chechnya. By 2001, al-Qaeda-linked attacks against Americans were just one part of a burgeoning insurgency that was global in scope and significantly emboldened by its Afghan successes. During the early years of the war on terror, Islamist insurgencies were under way in Afghanistan, Iran, Iraq, Palestine, Lebanon, Pakistan, Saudi Arabia, Kashmir, Egypt, Tajikistan, Uzbekistan, Dagestan, the Philippines, Indonesia, eastern India, Malaysia and the Yemen, with portents of similar activism to come in Kyrgyzstan and western China. There were also prospects for increasing Islamist militancy in states across East Asia, mainland Europe and North America. In Africa, al-Qaeda was active in Sudan, Somalia, Morocco, South Africa, Libya, Algeria, Mauritania, Nigeria, Madagascar, Uganda, Ethiopia and Eritrea (Anonymous [Scheuer] 2002, 2004). 9/11 was long in the making, and the pre-9/11 and post-9/11 worlds were broadly continuous not discontinuous,

Figure I.2 Ground Zero.
© Yoni Brook/Corbis.

however much it suited politicians to claim that the attacks came out of the blue, and that 'night fell on a different world' (Bush 2001) on the evening of September 11.

Another way to gauge the extent of an historical break or rupture is to look for the new cultural and intellectual paradigms, or the radical departures in old ones, prompted by the apparently disjunctive event. Contemporary discussions about the causes and outcomes of 9/11, however, were usually couched in explanatory frameworks, terminologies and styles, which had deep roots in American or Western cultural and intellectual history. At times there was an undeniably strong revisionist current in contemporary thought and culture. Yet wherever one looked in the post-9/11 era what was most striking was the absence of clean breaks. It is important to emphasise this, because the idea that 9/11 was a moment when 'everything changed' quickly became established in official discourse, where it played directly to partisan political agendas in Washington which had argued for some time for a systematic review of foreign policy and national security strategy to ensure that the transition to a post-Cold War order characterised by American primacy would be managed successfully. When the Bush administration published its *National Security Strategy* (NSS) in the autumn of 2002, historical rupture on 9/11 was precisely the case it argued in defence of the 'Bush Doctrine' of pre-emptive war, unilateral policy-making and 'regime change' in 'rogue states'. Representation of 9/11 as the moment when everything changed became the ideological lynchpin of the 'war on terror', a phrase the Bush administration used to refer to policy-making offered as responses to the 9/11 attacks – the wars the US waged in Afghanistan and Iraq, the federal legislation enacted in the name of 'homeland' defence and the challenges the administration posed to existing frameworks of federal and international law in the pursuit of 'war on terror' goals.

The idea of a war on terror was itself a representation of events, a rhetorical construction, a series of stories about 9/11 and about America's place in the world. As the historian Andrew Bacevich observed, terror 'was not the source of opposition to the United States, but only one especially malignant expression' of it. Terror was 'a tactic, not an enemy' (Bacevich 2002: 240, 231). Declaring a war on terror, Bacevich noted, 'obscured the political root of the confrontation' and 'made it easier to deflect public attention from evidence suggesting that it was America's quasi-imperial role that was provoking resistance – and would continue to do so' (ibid.: 231). Declaring a war without limits on an amorphous abstraction like 'terror' also meant that 9/11 could be represented as evidence in a political narrative primed for war and 'regime change' in Iraq, a genuine *cause célèbre* among groups of 'neo-conservative' policy advocates and political think-tanks in Washington during the late 1990s. The 9/11 Commission, the CIA, even the President himself, eventually acknowledged that no credible evidence had been found linking Saddam Hussein with the 9/11 attacks; and in many ways it was difficult to think of a more unlikely pairing than the pious insurgent Osama bin Laden and the dictator of a secular state who waged war on the Islamic revolution in Iran throughout the 1990s. Nevertheless, throughout 2002 and 2003, in a concerted campaign the President and senior administration figures repeatedly associated 9/11 with Iraq, in speeches, briefings, press conferences and other public statements, regularly referring to the danger Saddam posed by citing 9/11 as an example of the damage 'rogue states' could inflict on Americans if their influence went unchecked. Richard A. Clarke, who resigned as the administration's anti-terrorism chief in March 2003, observed that attacking Iraq in response to 9/11 'would be like our invading Mexico after the Japanese attacked us at Pearl Harbor' (Clarke 2004: 31). Nevertheless, by January 2003, a Knight Ridder poll suggested that 44 per cent of Americans believed 'some' or 'most' of the 9/11 hijackers were Iraqis; a *New York Times*/CBS poll carried out in March showed that 45 per cent of Americans believed Saddam was 'personally involved' in 9/11; and by August, a *Washington Post* poll found that an incredible 69 per cent of Americans believed Saddam Hussein probably played some part in the attacks (Feldmann 2003; Kornblut and Bender 2003). From the very beginning, '9/11' and the 'war on terror' were so appropriated by storytelling and mythmaking that the events themselves became more or less indivisible from their representations, or simulations, in political rhetoric, mass media spectacle and the panoply of other representational forms that made the events feel pervasive at the time – films, novels, photographs, paintings, TV drama, specialist academic debates and other forms of public culture and war on terror kitsch.

This book offers a cultural and ideological history of some of these forms between 9/11 and the mid-term Congressional elections of 2006 (a significant turning point for the Bush administration, and for the broader representation of the war on terror as a period of domestic 'crisis'). The book is an ideological history in the sense that it examines ideas, and the uses to which ideas were put, to debate, legitimise, qualify, contest or repress contemporary discussion about the causes, consequences and broader 'meanings' of 9/11 and the war on terror. And it is a cultural history in the sense that it views 'culture' (meaning representation) as the forum or social space in which these debates were played out. In a period when many Americans felt remote from centres of real political power, culture often functioned as a vital resource for citizens attempting to make sense of momentous historical events that often seemed beyond their influence or control. This book traces some of the ways in which culture worked in this fashion for contemporary Americans.

Another defining sensibility of the post-9/11 period was the feeling that history meant the living of trauma and crisis. 9/11 and the war on terror were described as a national security crisis, an imperial crisis, a crisis in capitalist democracy and governance, a crisis in the relationship between the US and Europe, multiple crises in the frameworks and institutions of international law and order (notably the UN and NATO), as well as a series of military and humanitarian crises, and a crisis in Islam. There was also a tangible sense that a period of political crisis was unfolding at home. The most damaging allegation was that the executive branch – the Bush administration – had lied to the American people about Iraqi involvement in 9/11, and then lied again about the existence of weapons of mass destruction in Iraq to justify, as a matter of national security, a war that many contemporaries described as an exercise in imperialism. But after 9/11 it wasn't just the executive branch that seemed to fail. Congress, the Supreme Court, the CIA, the military and the FBI were all attacked, either for acting unconstitutionally or for failing to do the job the Constitution assigned to them. An incompetent executive, it was alleged, engaged in wilful deception of the people and exceeded its constitutional powers – partly because some of the powers it arrogated to itself were unconstitutional and partly because Congress sometimes failed in its institutional role as a check and balance on executive authority. An imperialist foreign policy brought 'blowback' and quagmire. There was catastrophic failure in US intelligence agencies. For much of the period, different state agencies and institutions were at loggerheads. The 'crisis in the republic' after 9/11 was more a sensibility, a feeling in the air, than an actual political crisis. At no point were state institutions or agencies ever in jeopardy. Yet the domestic 'crisis' sensibility of the early war on terror amounted to more than just popular disagreement with the Bush administration or disenchantment with mainstream politics. The feeling that republican institutions and processes were under attack, or that they were being prevented from working as they should, was widespread after 9/11. The manner in which this 'crisis' was resolved, almost ritualistically, in a distinctive American political cycle of catharsis and renewal, is another main theme in this story.

1 History

From the 'Clash of Civilizations' to 'New Empire Revisionism'

American citizens looking to the historiography and intellectual history of the early war on terror for evidence that 9/11 was a moment of historical rupture may have been disappointed by what they found. While the post-9/11 period prompted new nuances in existing historiographies and intellectual traditions, some of them surprising, a more obvious trend was the revitalisation of established approaches and traditions that had languished since the end of the Cold War either below the radar of mass public exposure or beyond the bounds of political and intellectual 'respectability'. The result was an immediate and almost seamless blending of debates about foreign policy and national security into the mainstream of contemporary American culture wars.

One explanation for 9/11 and the war on terror that rapidly became common coinage in the US and the West, often in reduced form as popular cliché and mass media soundbite, suggested that Islam and the West were engaged in a 'clash of civilisations'. The idea had a variety of sources in the West, including 'Orientalist' stereotypes about the exotic 'otherness' of Easterners embedded in elite and popular cultures. After 9/11 the concept was most often associated with an essay entitled 'The Clash of Civilizations?' by Samuel P. Huntington, which was first published in the academic journal *Foreign Affairs* in 1993, and then expanded to book-length in *The Clash of Civilizations and the Remaking of World Order* (1997). Sometimes apocalyptic in tone, 'The Clash of Civilizations?' concluded that in the immediate future 'a West at the peak of its power' would be confronted by 'non-Wests that increasingly have the desire, the will and the resources to shape the world in non-Western ways' (Huntington 1996a: 5; see also Huntington 1996b, 1998, 2001). Huntington also found that 'a central focus of conflict for the immediate future' would be between the West and Islam (Huntington 1996a: 24).[1]

The Huntington thesis provoked a broad spectrum of academic debate in the 1990s, but after 9/11 the idea of a clash of civilisations went mainstream. Sometimes it was appropriated to serve agendas other than those explicitly addressed in Huntington's essay. Sometimes it was caricatured. More often it was plagiarised, usually unwittingly, by voices that had assimilated some of the argument from other sources, but were unaware of its provenance. Writing in his op-ed column for the *Los Angeles Times*, the popular historian Niall Ferguson compared 'The Clash of Civilizations?' to George Kennan's epochal 1947 essay 'The Sources of Soviet Conduct' (1947), a document often described as the blueprint for US 'containment' of the Soviet Union during the Cold War. As Ferguson wrote, after 9/11 Huntington's model seemed to make sense of 'an impressively high proportion of the news' (Ferguson 2006).

The emerging historiography of the time, however, was largely at odds with much of the Huntington thesis. Pundits and politicians who referred to Huntington in Western media often did so awkwardly, with caveats and reservations, as if unsure how far they agreed with him or as if unable to sift the bits of the Huntington thesis they liked from the bits that they did not. In his *Los Angeles Times* piece, Ferguson eulogised 'The Clash of Civilizations?': 'As works of academic prophecy go', he wrote, 'this has been a real winner'. But he also cautioned readers about the concept's 'seductive simplicity', conceding that conflicts in the Middle East had 'little to do' with civilisation identity (ibid.). Explanations for 9/11 had an ambiguous, almost apologetic Huntingtonian inflection at higher levels too. Ten days after 9/11, President Bush told Congress and a worldwide TV audience that the 9/11 bombers 'hate our freedoms' and 'way of life', 'our freedom of religion, our freedom of speech, our freedom to vote and assemble and disagree with each other'. It sounded like a clash of civilisations, but in the same speech the president also described al-Qaeda as 'a fringe form of Islamic extremism that has been rejected by Muslim scholars and the vast majority of Muslim clerics; a fringe movement that perverts the peaceful teachings of Islam' (Bush 2001).

Like all exercises in futurology, the Huntington thesis left itself hostage to the complex and unpredictable outcomes of emerging trends and unexpected events. It was the essay's assumptions about what produces history, though – assumptions that went to the core of Huntington's argument – that were most problematic. Huntington proposed that world politics was entering a new phase, where the primary causes of conflict would no longer be ideological or economic, but 'civilizational', and where

> The great divisions among humankind and the dominating source of conflict will be cultural. Nation states will remain the most powerful

actors in world affairs, but the principal conflicts of global politics will occur between nations and groups of different civilizations. The clash of civilizations will dominate global politics. The fault lines between civilizations will be the battle lines of the future. (ibid.: 1)

'Differences in culture and religion', Huntington wrote, '*create* differences over policy issues, ranging from human rights to immigration to trade and commerce to the environment' (Huntington 1996a: 7; emphasis added). Readers familiar with Huntington – writing in *Foreign Affairs*, Fouad Ajami referred to him as 'one of the most influential and brilliant students of the state and its national interest' (Ajami 1996: 27) – sometimes struggled to reconcile 'The Clash of Civilizations?' with his earlier work. Though Huntington conceded that nation-states would remain 'the most powerful actors in world affairs' (Huntington 1996a: 1), the repositioning of policy-making, diplomacy and national security strategy as an outgrowth or ciphering of 'civilizational' values, pushed political administrations and the apparatus of nation-states to the margins of historical discussion (see Ajami 1996; Weeks 1996). Broad historical flows and specific historical events were described as the expression of civilisational 'essences' – qualities that were intrinsic, fixed and more or less predetermined. Civilisational differences, Huntington wrote, 'will not soon disappear. They are far more fundamental than differences among political ideologies and political regimes' – they are 'not only real; they are basic'. Because of this, clashes between civilisations also seemed intractable. Whereas in the Cold War 'the key question was "Which side are you on?" and people could and did choose sides and change sides', in conflicts between civilisations the question was 'What are you?' and the answer to that, Huntington asserted, was 'a given that cannot be changed' (Huntington 1996a: 4, 5).

As it made the transition from specialised academic debate to popular currency, old concerns about the limitations of the Huntington thesis also came into the mainstream. One critic commented on Huntington's 'frustration with … complexity', his disregard for 'complicities and ambiguities', describing 'The Clash of Civilizations?' as a simplistic analysis in which 'the crooked and meandering alleyways of the world' were artificially 'straightened out' (Ajami 1996: 28, 31, 27). Another spoke for many when suggesting that Huntington's civilisations were 'pseudo-civilizations', to be feared 'for the same reason that Nils Bohr admonished us to fear ghosts: We see them, and we know they are not there!' (Piel 1996: 55). If they existed at all, his critics argued, 'civilisations' overlapped one another to a far greater extent than allowed for in 'The Clash of Civilizations?' and could not be homogenised in the ways that Huntington proposed. Civilisations were conflicted entities, divided and contested from within by a multiplicity of competing causes, identities and struggles (see Bartley 1996: Binyan 1996; Kirkpatrick 1996; Mahbubani 1996). Far from being givens, the 'common objective elements' that Huntington identified as facilitators of civilisational bonding – 'language, history, religion, customs, institutions' – were all constructed, conflicted and contingent things (Huntington 1996a: 3).

If Huntington foresaw an apocalyptic future shaped by global culture wars, he was in no doubt as to whose essential values should prevail. 'The Clash of Civilizations?' sounded decidedly American-centric at times, and concluded with a mapping of priorities for the consolidation and expansion of 'Western' global hegemony in the decades ahead. Given the absence of competing 'Western' hegemons, Huntington clearly meant American hegemony. However, he also had in mind a particular kind of American hegemony. In a response to his critics published in *Foreign Affairs* in the 1990s, Huntington attacked as un-American the idea of 'special rights (affirmative action and similar measures) for blacks and other groups', reserving particular scorn for what he called the 'parallel movement' of intellectuals and politicians pushing an 'ideology of "multiculturalism"', which he criticised for rewriting American history 'from the viewpoint of non-European groups' (Huntington 1996b: 61). Huntington's distaste for multiculturalism and his anxiety about the impact of (as he saw it) alien groups rights politics on indigenous traditions of individual rights-based republican democracy, located his defence of the 'clash of civilisations' thesis in the centre-ground of contemporary culture wars debates. Published originally during the high watermark of early culture wars controversy in the 1990s, at times the Huntington thesis looked like a tendentious projection onto the world stage of conflicts within contemporary America, one that struggled to put the alarming heterogeneity of a multicultural US back in the box by appealing to identity at 'the broadest level of identification' (Huntington 1996a: 3; see also Huntington 2004).

Nevertheless, the idea of a 'clash of civilisations' was popular after 9/11, partly because it made for a reassuring abstraction of contemporary events and partly because it implied that 9/11 and the wars in Afghanistan and Iraq were the working through of broadly predetermined outcomes. The suggestion that suicide bombers attacked the World Trade Center because of 'who we are', rather than because of the policy-making of US political administrations since the 1950s, made it easier for citizens to live with the realities of war, not least because it dovetailed so neatly with official explanations of events coming from the White House and Downing Street. As an exercise in popular historiography, the idea of a clash of civilisations lent itself well to a period when the drive to legitimise foreign policy adventurism placed a premium on appeals to patriotism and to the sacrifices required of citizens in the name of national security – abstractions that required Americans to make conscious acts of self-identification with collective entities bigger than themselves. The Huntington thesis served this purpose admirably, verging on outright romanticism in the appeals it made to an essential selfhood rooted in collective, 'blood'-based notions of identity. The implication that history was the working through of engrained civilisational destinies gave Huntington's prose an epic edge that sometimes slid his style into full-blown apocalyptic mythology. 'Civilizations disappear and are buried in the sands of time', he wrote. 'In Eurasia the great historic fault lines between civilizations are once more aflame' and 'Islam has bloody borders' (Huntington 1996a: 3, 12).

Momentous geopolitical events that are described as inevitable or predetermined, like events hailed as moments of historical origin or rupture, are often better understood as an accretion of multiple causes and effects that overlap and intersect over longer periods of time. In many respects 9/11 and the war on terror were textbook examples of this, each deriving from a plurality of existing conflicts and contexts that converged during the 1990s: the legacies of older Western imperialisms in Central Asia and the Middle East; the 'imperial' economics of US foreign policy since the Second World War (WW2); the legacies of Cold War diplomacy; the lingering consequences of the first Gulf War; contemporary struggles within Islam and Islamism; the ongoing Arab/Israeli conflict; and other struggles between Islamist insurgents and state authorities around the world. Each of these different but interrelated contexts and conflicts contributed in vital ways to the shaping of 9/11 and the war on terror.

The multiple conflicts converging in this period often sounded intractable in contemporary commentary, such were the intricacies and subterranean histories knotting them all together. Each problem seemed interwoven with multiple other complications, each malfeasance or resentment seemed to compound or rekindle another, and any putative cause or consequence seemed freighted with a deck of additional prompts and outcomes, not all of them intentional, predictable or immediately apparent. With so many overlapping and unstable factors in play, an abstraction like 'clash of civilisations' was attractive because, like all soundbites, it reduced complex and opaque historical forces to a more manageable form – one that was the easier to grasp for being grounded in instantly recognisable culture wars cliché. Yet as a 'master term' explaining contemporary events, the clash of civilisations concept was flawed, not least because of what it left out or ignored, and what it pushed to the margins of the narratives it told.

If it is to be persuasive, historical narrative that explains 9/11 and the war on terror by stressing a particular 'master term' or 'overdetermining instance' – a principal driver of events, one that influences some or all of the other factors involved – must do at least two further things. It must find ways of recognising the multiplicity of interlocking conflicts and contexts shaping events; and it must also acknowledge their 'relative autonomy', the meanings and histories these contexts enjoy outside and beyond their involvement in the shaping of 'American' history alone. One approach that attempted this after 9/11 took the form of a broad-based revisionist assessment of US foreign policy and national security strategy since the Second World War, and was grounded in the study of American 'empire'. This revisionism drew on existing models and schools of thought, and hardly constituted a coherent movement, for the principal contributors were too diverse politically and too disparate in the intellectual approaches and professional backgrounds they brought to bear. Partly because of this very diversity, however, the revisionists' willingness to rethink US 'hegemony' in the loaded terms of 'empire' and 'imperialism' produced a discourse that had considerable elasticity, bringing a number of the key historical contexts already noted in this book into orbit around the 'overdetermining' concept of American empire.

Debate about the existence and forms of an American empire had resurfaced at the end of the Cold War, and had continued through the 1990s as a specialism in Western universities in international relations theory, contemporary history courses and cultural studies departments. Lodged harmlessly enough in the intellectual subsoil of the Western academy, or dispersed into small pockets of radicalism that remained generally peripheral to mainstream political discourse, debate about American empire in the 1990s made only sporadic and limited impacts on popular discussions about America's role in the world. After 9/11 the climate changed dramatically. The concept of American empire often occupied the centre-ground in discussion about the causes and consequences of 9/11, and about the underlying motivations and historical drivers of the war on terror. The Bush administration denied that America had an empire to maintain or enlarge. But after 9/11, on this and related issues, the administration looked increasingly out of step. Pundits, analysts and policy-makers began referring to America as 'the homelands'. Newspaper articles and popular histories compared the

US to classical Rome and nineteenth-century Britain, describing 'empire denial' as a contemporary American pathology. After 9/11 commentators of many political stripes and persuasions suddenly agreed that something that could legitimately be described as an American 'empire' did exist after all. Paradoxically, because it was such a broad and conflicted church, post-9/11 empire revisionism sometimes looked like the closest a deeply divided period came to a consensus explanation for contemporary events.

One of the more startling developments was the emergence of an affirmative discourse of American empire, in which Western historians and other intellectuals sought to define US policy as imperialist and to defend American imperialism by theorising it as a provider of global 'public goods'. One figure who declared himself 'fundamentally in favour of empire' was Niall Ferguson, whose *Colossus: The Rise and Fall of The American Empire* claimed that 'many parts of the world would benefit from a period of American rule'. Some countries, Ferguson observed, 'will not correct themselves. They require the imposition of some kind of external authority' (Ferguson 2004: 24, 2). The pay-off to 'rogue' and 'failed' states for imperial intervention in their internal affairs, Ferguson argued, would include tangible public goods such as schools, hospitals, transport and communications infrastructures. More important would be the intangible public goods of 'order' and 'stability' in global systems which Ferguson anticipated would flow from an appropriately administered American empire. These goods seemed primarily economic in character, including 'free international exchange of commodities, labor and capital', and other conditions 'without which markets cannot function – peace and order, the rule of law, noncorrupt administration, stable fiscal and monetary policies' (ibid.: 2). Yet the case Ferguson built for a more vigorous American imperialism in *Colossus* was characteristic of much affirmative empire revisionism in the immediate post-9/11 years in that it preferred to talk about political initiatives and national security rather than economic interests as the principal factors at play in 'imperial' US policy.

In particular, affirmative empire revisionism tended to agree that the post-Cold War political geography of 'rogue' and 'failed' states had proved itself beyond the administrative reach of established multilateral institutions like the United Nations (UN). By definition, affirmative revisionists contended, the UN could not deal with threats from groups or states that had placed themselves beyond the writ of international law (see Chapter 2). As the only political forum where member states could compensate for their lack of influence in global affairs relative to the US, Ferguson argued, the UN had been hijacked by the sectional interests of weaker states. This proposition, which was also an article of faith in contemporary neoconservative doctrine, became a staple of affirmative empire revisionism in the early years of the war on terror. Given the vacuum in international authority caused by serial failings at the UN, affirmative revisionists argued, America was the only agency capable of intervening in the affairs of 'rogue' and 'failed' states to protect its own national security and to maintain global order. The economist Deepak Lal dismissed the UN as a 'remnant of the old international order', predicting 'a long drawn-out death by perpetual neglect or opportunistic utilization in the interests of the imperium' (Lal 2004: 79).

Despite its comments on the UN, Lal's *In Praise of Empires* was actually a notable exception to affirmative empire revisionism's tendency to deflect attention away from American economic interests and into debates about politics and national security. Rather than tidying economic factors to the margins of his discussion, Lal grounded his *apologia* for American empire in a vigorous defence of capitalist globalisation. Globalisation, Lal argued, was not new: it had been 'a cyclical phenomenon of history for millennia', and throughout history 'the order provided by empires has been essential for the working of the benign processes of globalization, which promote prosperity'. 'Most of the world since civilization began', Lal contended, had lived 'under empires'. Centres of imperial power came and went as empires rose and fell. But empire and imperialism were historical norms for Lal, not aberrations – they were 'natural throughout human history' (ibid.: xix, 42, xxiv). The twenty-first-century American empire was a vital phase in the globalisation project, the coming to fruition of a second integrated Liberal International Economic Order (LIEO) to follow the first one administered by the British empire in the nineteenth century. Describing imperialism as 'natural' seemed an odd move for a developmental economist to make, and *In Praise of Empires* was a thoroughly doctrinaire book, whose faith in capitalism as an agent of universal prosperity and global uplift recalled earlier post-Cold War tracts like Francis Fukuyama's *The End of History and the Last Man* (1992) and particularly Thomas Friedman's *The Lexus and the Olive Tree* (1999). The principal barrier to the success of the American LIEO, Lal argued, was that it wasn't *laissez-faire* enough. Globalisation's discontents were not caused by too much market 'liberalisation', but by too little. All forms of state intervention were 'faulty', he said, because the 'correct' economic principle was truly unfettered capitalism, and whereas globalisation itself was not ideological, 'criticisms' of globalisation were (Lal 2004: 111, 113, xix).

The most influential essay of the early revisionist vanguard was Michael Ignatieff's 'The American Empire (Get Used to It)' (2003a), a troubled affirmation of what Ignatieff called American 'empire lite', first published in the Sunday *New York Times* Magazine on 5 January 2003, a source not much noted for its frank examination of American imperialism.[2] After 9/11, Ignatieff was the first established public intellectual in the West to offer an affirmative, essay-length reading of American empire in such a prestigious popular source. 'The American Empire (Get Used to It)' was also a key moment in the intellectual history of the war on terror because its publication coincided with final preparations for the invasion of Iraq and the Bush administration's failure to secure explicit authorisation for war at the UN. In the coming months, journalists, political analysts, ex-administration officials, civil servants and members of the US Congress and British Parliament would all suggest that the decision to invade Iraq had already been made. But its coinciding with the mobilisation for war meant that Ignatieff's essay was published at a pivotal moment in terms of public debate about war on terror policy, and the issues Ignatieff identified as key debating points cropped up repeatedly in subsequent studies. 'The American Empire (Get Used to It)' wasn't just timely, it quickly became canonical too.

The American 'empire lite', Ignatieff claimed, heralded 'a form of imperial rule for a postimperial age'. Empire lite was 'not like empires of times past, built on colonies, conquest and the white man's burden' (Ignatieff 2003a). Ignatieff described the empire lite as 'a global hegemony whose grace notes are free markets, human rights and democracy, enforced by the most awesome military power the world has ever known'. Empire lite also meant 'laying down the rules America wants (on everything from markets to weapons of mass destruction) while exempting itself from other rules ... that go against its interest' (ibid.) It meant enforcing America's influence using 'soft power', 'influence, example, and persuasion', market power, the power to intimidate militarily without having to engage. Most important, it meant the capacity to secure consent from others by the provision of public goods – policies and outcomes that followed American interests, but that also benefited the populations or ruling elites of non-hegemonic states. According to Ignatieff, the primary public good supplied by American empire lite was order. 'Bringing order', he said, was 'the paradigmatic imperial task' (ibid.; see also Ferguson 2004; Lal 2004). This meant the US becoming the guarantor of 'peace, stability, democratization and oil supplies in a combustible region of Islamic peoples stretching from Egypt to Afghanistan' (ibid.) – which meant reshaping the Middle East according to US interests, using both soft power and military violence.

'Empire lite' also connoted a distinctive state of mind or ideological condition. In common with other major empire revisionists of the time,

Ignatieff proposed that America had acquired its empire 'in a state of deep denial' (Ignatieff 2003a; see also, Bacevich 2002; Chomsky 2004; Ferguson 2004). After 9/11, however, 'empire denial' went rapidly out of fashion with historians and public intellectuals in the West. For Ignatieff, this was a good thing. Empire denial, he argued, was not an ideology that would equip the US to secure its existing domain, let alone expand it by the arduous means of warfare and nation-building, and Ignatieff's observation that Americans would have to overcome engrained habits of 'denial' if the public goods empire provided were to flow was an important qualifier to his discussion.

One reason Ignatieff felt able to affirm the American 'empire lite' was his assumption that the causes of 'combustion' in the 'region of Islamic peoples' were Islamic and European, not American. Though he acknowledged that the 'order' the empire maintained was grounded in American self-interest and that American power had aroused 'avenging hatreds' around the world, Ignatieff all but ignored the role played in securing successive *Pax Americana* since WW2 by US backing for dictatorships, tyrannies and human rights abusers in the Middle East and Central Asia, many of whom were at war with their own Islamist constituencies. In 'The American Empire (Get Used to It)', the avenging hatreds on show at 9/11 seemed generated by a value-free abstraction, 'American power', not the uses of it. If anything, as in Huntington's clash of civilisations, 'Islamic peoples' in Ignatieff were combustible because of Western absence from Central Asia and the Middle East. In an interpretation that gathered fresh momentum after 9/11 among Western intellectuals, particularly among apologists for American empire, the real driver of Islamist 'combustion' was the inability of indigenous, postcolonial governance to embrace the gifts of political self-determination bestowed on them by the philanthropic West after WW2. 'Radical Islam would never have succeeded in winning adherents', Ignatieff suggested, 'if the Muslim countries that won independence from the European empires had been able to convert dreams of self-determination into the reality of competent, rule-abiding states' (Ignatieff 2003a). America, he wrote, 'has inherited a world scarred not just by the failures of empires past but also by the failure of nationalist movements to create and secure free states – and now, suddenly, by the desire of Islamists to build theocratic tyrannies on the ruins of failed nationalist dreams' (ibid.). Despite his explicit claims to the contrary, the 'empire lite' described by Ignatieff at times sounded very much like the old nineteenth-century imperialist notion of 'the white man's burden', with the US now labouring alone, in a unipolar world where only Americans seemed capable of sorting out the mistakes made by others, under the yoke of imperial *noblesse oblige*. Into the 'vacuum of chaos and massacre' that followed the failure of postcolonial states, Ignatieff wrote, 'a new imperialism has reluctantly stepped' (ibid.).

Affirmative empire revisionism's contention that anti-American Islamism was caused by the absence of Western influence in 'failed' states or regions seemed self-serving to say the least. It was also vigorously contested from the start by more oppositional strands of the post-9/11 empire debate which identified the 9/11 attacks as an instance of 'blowback' – war on terror shorthand for the unintended consequences of US foreign policy rebounding, or 'blowing back' upon, Americans. A key text was Chalmers Johnson's *Blowback: The Costs and Consequences of American Empire* (2002), which argued that American empire had created catastrophic anti-American resentments (Johnson 2002; see also Johnson 2004). *Blowback* was largely ignored in the US when it was first published in 2000. In print, but marginal in 'respectable' academic discourse and popular history before 9/11, it was instantly fashionable after, and like Huntington's 'clash of civilizations' the term it popularised entered the mainstream post-9/11 lexicon almost overnight.

Originally used to describe a battlefield scenario where poisonous gas is blown back on the forces deploying it, the phrase 'blowback' was first used in the application for which it became famous after 9/11 in a CIA report on the coup that the Agency helped stage in Iran in 1953. The Iran coup was the first instance of a foreign government overthrown with CIA assistance, and 1953 was often cited in 'blowback' accounts of 9/11 as something akin to an imperial year zero in post-WW2 history. The coup installed a pro-US dictatorship that reversed the democratically elected Mossadegh regime's decision to nationalise an Iranian oil industry dominated by Western energy companies. The regime that replaced Mossadegh ruled Iran for a quarter of a century with the help of one of the twentieth-century's most notorious secret police, trained by the CIA, until an Islamic revolution installed in its place the 'fundamentalism' of the Ayatollahs in 1979. In a new preface written for the 2002 edition of *Blowback*, Johnson situated the 9/11 attacks 'in a direct line of descent from events in 1979' – the year, he said, 'in which the consequences of the overthrow of the Iranian government in 1953 came due' (Johnson 2002: xii). 'Blowback' accounts proliferated after 9/11. Chomsky's *9/11* (2001) and *Hegemony or Survival* (2004), William Blum's *Rogue State* (2002), 'Anonymous's *Through Our Enemies' Eyes* (2002) and Sardar and Davies's *Why Do People Hate America?* (2003) were just some of the contemporary bestsellers that situated 9/11 as a retaliatory attack on US imperialism in Asia and the Middle East. Blum acquired a particular notoriety in

January 2006 after *Rogue State* was endorsed by Osama bin Laden in a CIA-verified audiotape. ('This is almost as good as being an Oprah book', Blum said, as *Rogue State* shot from 205,763 on Amazon.com's index of its most ordered books, to 26 [Montgomery 2006].)

In certain respects it was not surprising to see an Islamist leader endorsing a 'blowback' writer. The two public declarations of holy war issued by bin Laden in 1996 and 1998 and many of his other public pronouncements before and after 9/11 sometimes read like condensed classics of 'blowback' critique, proposing a 'defensive *jihad*' against an America denounced for 'blatant imperial arrogance'; a US bin Laden compared to 'locusts' spreading through Muslim territory 'consuming its wealth and destroying its fertility' (bin Laden 2005: 25; bin Laden 2005: 59). A number of themes recurred in bin Laden's pre-9/11 pronouncements, grouped around the issue of holy Muslim lands that were 'occupied' by 'infidel' Americans and Jews. Particularly important to bin Laden was America's 'appropriation of Saudi Arabia' (bin Laden 2005: 27) – a reference to the presence of tens of thousands of US troops who remained garrisoned in the kingdom after the end of the Gulf War (a religious outrage for Islamists, and a humiliation so close to the holy cities of Mecca and Medina). During the 1990s, bin Laden often talked about how the House of Saud's guarantee of cheap oil for the American economy – following an agreement by President Franklin Roosevelt and King Abdul Aziz Al-Saud in 1945 – had squandered resources that should have benefited Saudis, leading to an expropriation of Saudi wealth by the US and to widespread impoverishment among Muslims on the Arabian peninsula. Bin Laden also returned regularly to the subject of US policy on Iraq during the 1990s (another country hosting important Muslim holy sites), where American bombing raids continued after the Gulf War and where American-led sanctions imposed through the UN killed more than one million Iraqi civilians – in 1999, UNICEF (the United Nations Children's Fund) reported that half a million of them were children under five. In another recurring theme, bin Laden also pitched the anti-American *jihad* as blowback for US support for Israel in the ongoing Arab/Israeli conflict. The Al-Aqsa Mosque in East Jerusalem is regarded as another of Islam's holiest sites, making Israel's 'occupation' of Jerusalem, and American support for it, another Crusader atrocity in the eyes of many Muslims. For bin Laden, the US had been waging war on Islam since 1945. The declaration of a 'defensive' *jihad* signalled that Muslims were simply responding in kind.

Another important 'blowback' voice at the time, one who paid close attention to what Islamists said when they described why they were fighting, was a writer initially known only as 'Anonymous', who followed his

Through Our Enemies' Eyes (2002) with a book called *Imperial Hubris* (2004) which spent eight weeks on the *New York Times* bestsellers list in August and September 2004. 'Anonymous' turned out to be Michael Scheuer, a senior CIA official who had been head of the Agency's bin Laden unit in the 1990s. Chalmers Johnson didn't figure overtly in *Through Our Enemies' Eyes* or *Imperial Hubris* and Scheuer didn't use the term 'blowback', but his analysis sounded distinctly Johnsonian at times. American policy in Asia and the Middle East had provided 'a fertile environment for al Qaeda's efforts' (Anonymous 2002: 228), he noted, and Scheuer returned regularly to the specific instances of US policy cited as motivations for defensive *jihad* by bin Laden, warning that a US policy status quo in the Middle East would only intensify existing Islamist hostilities to America and the West. The empire's 'road to hell', Scheuer said, lay in the hubristic presumption that 'only the lunatic fringe' was drawn to bin Laden's brand of anti-American Islamism, rather than the 'broadening spectrum of Muslim society' (ibid.: 27) for whom US foreign policy was seen, *a priori*, as an attack on Islam, and for whom response by the waging of defensive *jihad* was a scriptural requirement. The Islamists' claim 'that the United States is attacking the religion, sanctities, resources, children, and dignity of Islam', Scheuer acknowledged, was 'a view increasingly held by Muslims around the world' (ibid.: 229). In speeches Bush referred to the 9/11 bombers as 'a fringe form of Islamic extremism' and the administration's *National Security Strategy* called Islamists 'the embittered few' (National Security Strategy 2002: 1). Scheuer, however, argued that 9/11 should be seen as part of 'a worldwide, religiously inspired, and professionally guided Islamist insurgency', defending itself against what its sponsors saw as a hostile alliance of Christian Crusaders and Jews – a 'worldwide version of the successful defensive jihad Muslims waged for more than a decade against Soviet forces in Afghanistan' (Anonymous 2002: xvii, 4).

Despite not using the term himself, Scheuer had an important place in the emerging 'blowback' historiography of the time, not least because of the limits he implicitly ascribed to the usefulness of the Johnson thesis. Ignatieff argued that a successful empire was one that avoided 'overstretch' by knowing and working within its capabilities. One important aspect of this meant acknowledging that 9/11 was partly the product of struggles within Islam over which the US could exert little direct influence.[3] The important point Ignatieff made about the relative autonomy of these struggles – struggles that were implicated in 9/11, but that were also internal to Islam itself – got lost in his generalising about 'the Muslim world'. The point was also often lost in 'blowback' accounts of 9/11, where the emphasis was generally on

American causes rather than Islamist ones. By instinctively identifying American history as the decisive or 'overdetermining' instance, rather than looking to the construction and internal dynamics of the insurgency itself, Scheuer implied that 'blowback' accounts ran the risk of glibly attributing 9/11 to 'one or another US action' (Anonymous 2002: 24), underestimating and misunderstanding the complex historical and cultural factors, and the relatively autonomous Islamist agencies, driving the insurgency. Scheuer attributed this tendency to what he called 'imperial hubris', an ideology of mature empire that produced a 'distorted America-centric vision of reality' characterised by 'our beliefs in the universality of our culture and values' (Ibid.: 25, 251). Put differently, and extrapolating again from Scheuer, there was a fine line between the imperial hubris that blowback accounts condemned and the imperial hubris such accounts sometimes appeared to embody, in their identification of malign US influence in every hidden corner of world affairs. Taken together, *Through Our Enemies' Eyes* and *Imperial Hubris* set out to counter such hubris by providing a detailed history of bin Laden's central role in building and co-ordinating the international networks of business, religious, political and paramilitary ties, which produced the global insurgency of which 9/11 was merely one dramatic instance.

One example of 'imperial hubris' widely heard after 9/11 was the truism that the CIA had 'created' Osama bin Laden and al-Qaeda by arming and training the guerrilla army of Afghan Muslims and international Islamic volunteers which waged *jihad* against the Soviet occupation of Afghanistan in the 1980s. While it was certainly true that the CIA used the *mujahadeen* to wage a proxy war against the Soviets, and that bin Laden's later standing as an insurgency leader owed much to his legendary service in Afghanistan, as Scheuer observed, the hubristic claim that the US had 'created' bin Laden in Afghanistan during the 1980s missed vital truths about the anti-Soviet *jihad*. In the first place, if the Soviet Union had not invaded Afghanistan in 1979 there would have been no *mujahadeen* to fight an 'American' proxy war; in the second, the Soviets were defeated in Afghanistan by an Islamist revolution, not a democratic or capitalist one. Overwhelmingly, the Afghan *jihad* was a story of Islamist and Soviet agencies, not American ones. Scheuer's emphasis on the powerful theological currents and authentic Islamist agencies flowing out of the anti-Soviet *jihad* and into the worldwide insurgency of the later 1990s and 2000s explained 9/11 by pointing to histories that were often ignored or smothered in the America-centrism of 'blowback' accounts. In particular, Scheuer stressed that the proximate causes of anti-Americanism in Muslim societies were not necessarily

American actions *per se*, but the behaviour of 'apostate' Muslim regimes – corrupt Islamic governments, as the insurgents saw it, who were supported financially, militarily or diplomatically by the US, some of which (including Egypt, Pakistan and Saudi Arabia) were at war with their own Islamist constituencies. By emphasising that Islamist anti-Americanism often stemmed from conflicts between Islamists and 'apostate' Muslim regimes, Scheuer grounded the history of 9/11 and the war on terror in struggles within Islam and Islamism, as well as in 'blowback' for American foreign policy.

These relatively autonomous internal disputes had catastrophic consequences for Americans on 9/11. Through the later 1990s, for the first time, a position emerged in radical Islamist strategy which identified US support as the principal pillar of Muslim apostasy. A grouping led by Osama bin Laden began arguing that the defeat of apostate Islam rested on driving out US influence from the affairs of Muslims. Cut the head off the snake, the theory ran, and apostate regimes that depended for their survival on American support would perish, along with Israel. For Scheuer, bin Laden's historical significance lay partly in his successful lobbying for a shift from targeting apostate governments (reflecting a Koranic requirement to tackle the 'near-enemy' first should Islam be attacked) to an 'America-first' strategy. The switch to an 'America-first' strategy was achieved only after considerable internal debate (Scheuer called it a 'struggle' [Anonymous 2002: 169]) within key Islamist organisations, notably so in the influential Egyptian groups Al-Gama'at Al-Islamiyah (IG), the largest Islamist group in Egypt, and Egyptian Islamic Jihad (EIJ), a smaller group that evolved from IG in the late 1960s and was indivisible from al-Qaeda in the post-9/11 period. In *Through Our Enemies' Eyes* Islamism was diverse and provisional, because like American foreign policy it was the product of internal debate and hegemonic struggle. Analysing 9/11 and the war on terror by concentrating on histories of ideological struggle in Islam and Islamism, returned agency, instrumentality and authenticity to Muslim actors who were often depicted at the time, in the West, as madmen raging impotently at modernity, or as ciphers acting out unanticipated consequences of American foreign policy.

It would be a mistake, however, to imagine that Scheuer's emphasis on authentic Islamist agencies made his books exercises in multiculturalism. As in Huntington's 'The Clash of Civilizations?', where the diagnosis of Islam's 'bloody borders' served the recommendation that the West pursue a redoubled hegemony over non-Western 'civilisations', so too *Imperial Hubris* and *Through Our Enemies' Eyes* featured passages where Scheuer recommended 'relentless, brutal, and, yes, bloodsoaked offensive military actions until we have annihilated the Islamists who threaten us, or so mutilate their forces, supporting populations, and physical infrastructure that they recognize continued war-making on their part is futile' (Anonymous 2004: 85). Reflecting one of the defining domestic political conflicts of the period, the CIA agent in Scheuer had an axe to grind with the Bush administration, and with senior management at Langley (see Chapter 2). But the worldview his books espoused suggested that he remained a CIA man at heart. Scheuer offered a relativist history of 9/11, one that encouraged Americans to suspend the 'innate perceptions and biases' of imperial hubris and look at their country from the point of view of America's enemies. But he did so only with a view to securing more efficiently both the destruction of the enemy and the greater goal of a new American century.

One virtue of the Johnsonian 'blowback' position was its insistence that 9/11, and the post-9/11 American empire, did not come out of the blue. The Bush administration and neocons argued that 9/11 changed everything, that the old rules no longer applied, and they differentiated between the pre- and post-9/11 worlds as though a way of life really had ended in September 2001. Johnson, Blum, Chomsky and 'Anonymous' reminded Americans who read them that 9/11 was the product of historical resentments accumulated over time by traditions of 'imperialist' foreign policy and national security strategy. The historical roots of 9/11 and empire went deep in 'blowback' historiography, and events since September 2001 existed in a continuum with events that came before.

One important non-blowback treatment of broad strategic continuities in the administration of empire, before and after 9/11, was Andrew Bacevich's *American Empire: The Reality and Consequences of US Diplomacy* (2002). Since the end of the Cold War, Bacevich argued, three successive political administrations (Bush senior, Clinton, Bush junior) had followed a foreign policy grand strategy that had convergent priorities – 'to preserve and, where both feasible and conducive to US interests, to expand an American imperium'; and to create 'an open and integrated international order based on the principles of democratic capitalism, with the United States as the ultimate guarantor of order and enforcer of norms' (Bacevich 2002: 3). 9/11, Bavevich argued, may have altered 'the tenor' of American diplomacy, but 'the essentials of US policy' remained in place (ibid.: 226). If anything, in Bacevich's estimation 9/11 reinforced existing trends, because it 'eased constraints that during the previous decade had inhibited US officials in their pursuit of greater openness (and expanded American hegemony)' (ibid.: 227). The pursuit of 'openness' in this context was a loaded term which Bacevich used to describe a form of imperialism without colonialism, where 'what mattered was not ownership or even administrative control' of resources, markets and investment opportunities, but commercial access to them (ibid.: 25) – a thoroughly Chomskyan truism, whose centrality in Bacevich's book was indicative of how much broader the parameters of 'respectable' history-writing became after 9/11.

Bacevich's argument also echoed Deepak Lal's assertion that empires define themselves primarily through the pursuit of enlarged spaces 'open' to economic penetration. Excepting the Depression of the 1930s and the Vietnam War era, Bacevich argued that the pursuit of economic openness had been 'the basis for a broad national consensus on foreign policy' in the US for a century, beginning with the economic crises of the 1890s, and culminating in the 'globalisation' of American capitalism after the Cold War (ibid.: 26). By 2001, Bacevich suggested, this consensus 'enjoyed nearly absolute acceptance' among US policymakers, and 'rendered moot old distinctions between realists and idealists, nationalists and internationalists' (ibid.: 215). As discussed in more detail in Chapter 2, many of the administration's American critics preferred to paint the Bush White House as an aberration, an exception to the rule, a detour in US political history that could be regulated and corrected by submission to the norms of due constitutional process – the will of the people embodied in Congress and the judiciary, and in domestic electoral cycles. One reason Bacevich's *American Empire* was such an important book was that it subverted this liberal orthodoxy, turning Bush into a representative figure rather than an aberration, by locating his administration firmly in the American grain.

Bacevich also emphasised the continuities binding the pre- and post-9/11 eras by drawing attention to the debts his own work owed to the older revisionist voices of American historians Charles Beard (1874–1948) and William Appleman Williams (1921–90). By revising these earlier revisionisms back to their theoretical core, discarding in the process the more sensationalist claims that had traditionally caught the eye of hostile historians, Bacevich was able to argue convincingly that the heterodoxy of Beard and Williams provided 'an essential point of departure for understanding American statecraft today' (ibid.: 23). Reviving Beard and Williams allowed Bacevich to locate his critique of American empire in a native tradition, and to do so by theorising 9/11 and the war on terror in relation to structural weaknesses in American and world capitalism. Beard and Williams both understood that foreign and domestic policy were 'parts of the same thing' (Beard 1935: 301) and that the drivers of US foreign policy were primarily economic. For

Beard, a saturation of American domestic markets after the Civil War and a lack of outlets for the investment of surplus capital presaged economic stagnation and decay, and placed economic expansionism at the centre of US grand strategy. Without a fundamental reordering of American class relations – including a wholesale redistribution of wealth – sustaining domestic growth and prosperity for the Americans who enjoyed it would require a world open to US economic penetration. Imperial foreign policy, for Beard and Williams, was thus both the product of class inequalities in American capitalism and the means by which those flaws could be addressed, without the need for an egalitarian restructuring of society at home. Updating this thesis, Bacevich argued that the war on terror showed just how successfully the broad imperial strategy of US foreign policy had survived what were commonly assumed to be dramatic moments of historical rupture, in 9/11 and the end of the Cold War. In each case, Bacevich argued, 'foreign policy remained above all an expression of domestically generated imperatives', with 'opening the world to trade and foreign investment . . . a precondition of America's own well being and therefore the centrepiece of US strategy' – a strategy 'best served by the United States occupying a position of unquestioned global pre-eminence' (Bacevich 2002: 77).

Another important example of the influence of Williams and the 'Wisconsin school' in post-9/11 empire revisionism was David Harvey's *The New Imperialism* (2003), where Harvey applied what he called his 'historical-geographical materialism' to the 'landscape of capitalistic activity' under production before and since 9/11 (Harvey 2003: 1, 95). As a Marxist, Harvey looked particularly at how capitalist 'logics' – the internal rhythms and dynamics of capitalist production and consumption, what Marx referred to as 'the laws of motion of capital' – produced geographical histories shaped distinctively by developmental trends in capitalism. As Harvey put it in *The New Imperialism*, his aim was to understand 'how a space economy [of empire] emerges out of processes of capital accumulation' (ibid.: 94).

Since capitalism was an expansionary and growth-fixated economic system, Harvey argued, wired for the never-ending accumulation of capital, it required a political correlative to which Hannah Arendt had referred as 'a never-ending accumulation of power', to protect it and to ensure its growth or 'expanded reproduction'. In effect, this meant that the history of so expansionary an economic system as capitalism must also be 'a history of hegemonies expressive of ever larger and continuously more expansive power' (ibid.: 34) – a pattern also traced by the sociologist Giovanni Arrighi in his comparative approach to the history of successive hegemonies established by the Italian city-states, the Dutch, the British and the US (Arrighi 1994; see also Arrighi and Silver 1999). As Harvey put it, 'any hegemon, if it is to maintain its position in relation to endless [and endlessly expanding] capital accumulation, must endlessly seek to extend, expand, and intensify its power' (Harvey 2003: 35). Harvey incorporated these positions from Arendt and Arrighi into *The New Imperialism* to offer a theoretical framework for the development of American empire since the Second World War and to theorise the behaviour of American imperialism since 9/11, with particular attention to what he called the broad shift from 'consent to coercion' in the administration of the empire under Bush (Harvey 2003: 183–212). The force and theoretical complexity of Harvey's own argument confined Williams to a brief mention in the footnotes. But the underlying assumptions he made about foreign policy in *The New Imperialism*, particularly its derivation in the reproduction of class hierarchies at home, were Wisconsin School assumptions. It was possible, Harvey observed, for the US to avoid imperialism 'by engaging in a massive redistribution of wealth within its borders and a redirection of capital flows into the production and renewal of physical and social infrastructures'. But, as he also observed, this would mean 'an internal reorganization of class power relations and transformative measures affecting social relations of a sort that the United States has refused systematically to contemplate ever since the Civil War' (ibid.: 75, 76). This being the case, privately accumulated capital that could find no profitable opportunity for reinvestment in the US had little choice but to create investment opportunities abroad. Harvey's understanding of the broad mechanics of the twenty-first-century American empire was Williamsian to the core.

By emphasising the link between class conflict at home and empire abroad, *The New Imperialism* brought a cutting edge to Bacevich's revival of Beard and Williams. What made *The New Imperialism* really significant, though, was its theorising of the war on terror as a crisis in 'neoliberal' capitalism – the so-called 'Washington Consensus' capitalism of the 1980s and 1990s, built on deregulated markets, privatisation, cost-cutting, antipathy to trade unionism, downward pressures on wages, the globalising of markets and capital/labour flows, 'just-in-time' niche production and severe retrenchments in national welfare states. Under the terms of the Washington Consensus, market forces rather than military power or interventionist governments would order the world. In the optimism of a post-Cold War boom in the US, the Clinton administration viewed the globalisation of neoliberal capitalism as a panacea – a driver of democracy and economic 'liberalisation' in non-Western regions and a provider of public goods to Americans, not just in the form of 'prosperity', but also in the enhanced prospects for national security that would come with membership of an integrated global market.

This neoliberal vision of a world made secure by market forces, Harvey argued, was in trouble before 9/11. He located 9/11 historically by referring to the economist Robert Brenner, whose work on the long-term impacts of increased competition in capitalist world markets, particularly from the revitalised economies of Germany and Japan, may have dismayed even Deepak Lal. Brenner had described a developing 'long downturn' in the aggregate profitability of global capitalism since the late 1960s, identifying a scarcity of profitable outlets for the reinvestment of 'over-accumulated capital' (a problem made worse by the arrival of new competitor economies) as a key driver of longer-term capitalist decline (see Brenner 1998, 2002). For Harvey, the return of imperialism by military conquest in Iraq signalled the moment when the neoliberal vision of an America and a world made prosperous and secure by market forces (part of what Ignatieff called 'soft power') finally collapsed. On this, at least, Harvey appeared to agree with the Bush administration. During the 1990s, Bush's neoconservative supporters said, Clinton's 'wishful brand of idealism' had placed too much faith in the 'liberalizing powers of commerce' (Kaplan and Kristol 2003: 59), when commerce itself, as the Bush *National Security Strategy* put it, 'depends on the rule of law' (NSS 2002: 19). For Harvey, on the pretext of a war on terror, the war in Iraq was actually part of a wider war on Brenner's long downturn, with military power rather than market forces now creating the circumstantial order (or rule of law) necessary for the pursuit of 'national' (meaning elite) economic interests. In the Iraq war, Harvey noted, those interests included ensuring access to the world's second largest known oil reserves, and the forcing open of substantial new areas for profitable investment by privately owned American capital. In a new theorising of Marx's term 'primitive accumulation', Harvey called this 'accumulation through dispossession' – a process that he argued was intrinsic to all stages of capitalist development, not just its formative period as Marx and Rosa Luxemburg had argued. The virtue of Harvey's re-routing of old Marxian theory about primitive accumulation was that it theorised clearly the relationship between neoliberal capitalism and the shift to a more coercive and less consensual American empire after 9/11. Harvey brought 'globalisation' and the war on terror together by viewing each as a symptom of more deeply embedded contradictions in the workings of late twentieth- and early twenty-first-century capitalism.

The shift that Harvey identified as a movement from hegemony secured by consent to empire secured by coercion did not signal that unipolar American power had moved into a new era of uncontested domination of world affairs. On the contrary. If the rapid emergence of a politically diverse discourse of American empire after 9/11 was one of the more remarkable intellectual developments of the period, part of what made it so was the level of agreement on the existence of clear limits to American power and the likelihood of a dramatic scaling-back of imperial ambitions in the medium and longer term. The possibility of imperial 'overstretch' or 'overreach', an idea popularised at the end of the Cold War by the historian Paul Kennedy in his study of the decline of previous empires, *The Rise and Fall of the Great Powers* (1990), haunted even the most affirmative empire revisionists after 9/11.

One common response to the wars in Afghanistan and Iraq was that the recourse to military violence implied that in other areas of influence (diplomacy, economics, the appeal of 'American values' and other instruments of 'soft power') the US was weak. Coercion had become the imperial strategy of choice only because the US could no longer maintain or expand its empire by consent. A disproportionate dependence on unrivalled military power was just one issue in a catalogue of 'push' factors for potential American decline identified by contemporary analysts. Niall Ferguson anticipated a coming historical shift away from the unipolar order of the early post-Cold War and the likely return of traditional great power rivalries; as did contemporary 'resource wars' historiography, where the key issue was rivalry among the US, Russia, China, India, Pakistan and Iran for control over oil and gas reserves in the Caspian Sea basin (see Klare 2002, 2004; Kleveman 2003). Charles Kupchan's *The End of the American Era* identified the rise of an integrated Europe as a particular danger to US supremacy (Kupchan 2003). Empire revisionists also worried that US policy would exacerbate existing conflicts in a spiralling cycle of catastrophic blowback, at the same time as the Bush administration's preference for unilateral policy-making would inflame long-standing conflicts, or stimulate new ones, not least between the US and traditionally friendly nation-states. As the Bush administration itself acknowledged, America could not afford to keep global order on its own. 'European participation in peacekeeping, nation-building and humanitarian reconstruction' was vital, Ignatieff observed, to the strategy of maintaining and expanding the empire (Ignatieff 2003a). The dangers of unilateralism alienating Cold War friends and allies at so crucial an historical juncture were therefore profound, and critics of the Bush administration argued vigorously that American power divorced from the structures and protocols of multilateral governance became weaker and less effective, not stronger, as a result (see Chapter 2). From such a perspective, *Washington Post* columnist and prominent neoconservative Robert Kagan's influential argument in *Paradise and Power* (2003) – that an unbridgeable ideological division long in the making had opened up between Europe and the US after 9/11 – was worrying indeed. Even Lal, whose faith in the messianic power of capitalism as a panacea for global strife sounded rather old-fashioned after 9/11, worried that the neocon credo identifying American values as universal values would prove damaging and counterproductive, fostering precisely the kind of global culture wars anticipated by Huntington in 'The Clash of Civilizations?'.

Contemporary empire revisionists also saw the potential for imperial decline in domestic American weaknesses. Ignatieff's designation of the US as an 'empire lite' questioned whether an electorate conditioned by engrained patterns of empire denial had the stomach for the sacrifices demanded by efficient imperial rule. 'The burden of empire is of long duration', Ignatieff worried, 'and democracies are impatient with long-lasting burdens – none more so than America' (Ignatieff 2003a). Affirmative empire revisionism's analysis of the potential for imperial decline sometimes also revealed the elitist, class-based perspectives of its leading exponents. In a twist on Ignatieff's argument that the real threat to the empire came from the electorate's lack of moral fibre (see also Krauthammer 2004a, 2004b), Ferguson and Lal identified the danger of overstretch not in the 'laudable and attainable' (Ferguson 2004: 28) goals of American political elites, but in the competing costs of the welfare state. Americans, Ferguson said, 'like Social Security more than national security' (Ferguson 2004: 269), and both he and Lal predicted that welfare state commitments would cause a serious fiscal crisis in the US, with Ferguson reminding readers that this had been a major factor in the fall of imperial Rome. Lal's observation that the British LIEO in the nineteenth century had been weakened by 'the rise of demos (the common people)', and the claims they made for egalitarian social goods (Lal 2004: 108), threw into relief once more the ideological character of the case he built for imperialism. If the American empire fell, affirmative empire revisionism often implied, it would be the fault of the people, and of misguided politicians who pandered to the least deserving elements among them.

In Harvey's *The New Imperialism* too instability and the potential for imperial decline were inseparable from domestic weakness, though Harvey's Marxism identified the problem in the logics of capitalist economies, rather than in the egalitarian claims of groups that were exploited or marginalised by these systems. The American empire felt vulnerable in *The New Imperialism* partly because the relationship between its principal logics – a 'capitalist logic of power' and a 'territorial logic of power' – was antagonistic. The ever-expanding hegemony required for ever-expanding capital accumulation operated as a 'territorial logic' within relatively fixed territorialised space (within national borders, for example, or in non-national territory opened up by trade agreements or imperialism). These territorial logics were the result of strategic decision-making and had long-term ends. They aimed to produce the environmental equilibria that would facilitate reliable cycles of capital accumulation, and tended to be constrained by the circumstances of the state commanding them. By contrast, at what Harvey called 'the molecular level' of capitalism – the banal routines of daily capitalist accumulation and exchange, the everyday production and consumption of commodities – the 'capitalist logic of power' worked relentlessly to fragment and dissolve the 'territorial' logics deployed for its defence and reproduction. Geared endlessly towards capital accumulation, molecular capitalist logic was 'perpetually expansionary and therefore permanently disruptive of any tendency toward equilibrium' (Harvey 2003: 95). Where territorial logics were characterised by their production of relatively fixed space, capitalist production of space was eternally in flux. Competition generated damaging cycles of boom, bust and creative destruction, and 'a state of perpetual motion and chronic instability in the spatial distribution of capitalistic activities as capitalists search for superior (i.e. lower-cost) locations', producing a disordered space economy and a temporality scarred by sudden disjunctions, ruptures and reinventions of space – the antithesis of the regularity and fixity pursued by territorial logics of power. 'The geographical landscape of capitalist production, exchange, distribution, and consumption', Harvey noted, 'is never in equilibrium' (ibid.: 96). The American empire sounded highly unstable in *The New Imperialism*, the product not so much of political imperatives to export democracy and human rights or to maintain national security as of internal contradictions in an irrational, anarchic and crisis-prone economic system.

Some of the political implications of the shift from consent to coercion, and the widespread sense of 'crisis' that this shift provoked in republican political processes and institutions and in frameworks of international law, are examined in the following chapter. Many Americans during the Bush years felt that an imperialist foreign policy and sound republican governance at home were politically and ethically irreconcilable – a suspicion Chapter 2 suggests was heightened, when the public goods envisaged by admirers of American empire simply evaporated, like Saddam Hussein's weapons of mass destruction, in the dry desert air of Iraq after the invasion in 2003.

---

1. Actually, between the West and 'Islamic-Confucian' states. This was one of the most widely criticised aspects of the Huntington thesis (for example, see Ajami 1996: 31; Mahbubani 1996: 38).
2. Ignatieff's essay is sometimes referred to as 'The American Empire: The Burden'.
3. 9/11, Ignatieff said, 'pitched the Islamic world into the beginning of a long and bloody struggle to determine how it will be ruled and by whom: the authoritarians, the Islamists or perhaps the democrats'. The US, he cautioned, 'can help repress and contain the struggle, but even though its own security depends on the outcome, it cannot ultimately control it' (Ignatieff 2003a).

2 Politics

'Crisis' in the Republic. The Unitary Executive, the Bush Doctrine and Adversarial Review

One of the more dramatic political spectacles of the early war on terror was provided by the president's anti-terrorism 'czar', Richard A. Clarke, who resigned from his post in March 2003, then wrote a flamboyant book explaining why (Figure 2.1). Clarke's *Against All Enemies* (2004) described how the White House had ignored intelligence warnings about al-Qaeda before 9/11 and had hijacked the attacks to wage a wholly unrelated war on Iraq, fooling the American people into believing that the Iraqi regime of Saddam Hussein was implicated in 9/11. Clarke argued that the conduct of the president and senior figures in his administration amounted to a usurpation and abuse of republican high office. Justifying his resignation, he spoke of 'an obligation' to write what he knew, and of a higher loyalty 'to the citizens of the United States', which 'must take precedence over loyalty to any political machine'. In the concluding paragraphs of the coruscating preface to *Against All Enemies*, Clarke paid tribute to the 'small group of extraordinary Americans [who] created the Constitution that governs this country' and issued a challenge to his fellow citizens: 'In this era of threat and change', he wrote, 'we must all renew our pledge to protect that Constitution', not only against threats from 'foreign enemies', but also 'against those who would use the terrorist threat to assault the liberties the Constitution enshrines'. Clarke left no one in any doubt that the threat he envisaged came from the Bush administration as much as from al-Qaeda, and he called on 'my fellow citizens' to defend the Constitution 'against all enemies' (Clarke 2004: xi–xiii).

After 9/11, and in the middle of an ongoing international security crisis, with the country still at war in Afghanistan and Iraq, the spectacle of the administration's anti-terrorism chief calling the president an enemy of the people and a threat to the republic was truly sensational. Clarke's book spent eleven weeks on the *New York Times* bestsellers' lists in 2004, four of them at number one, and *Against All Enemies* reflected a political sensibility that seemed increasingly commonplace after the

Figure 2.1 Richard Clarke promotes his book, *Against All Enemies*, in Germany, during June 2004.
© Frank Rumpenhorst/epa/Corbis.

invasion of Iraq, particularly after the Abu Ghraib prison scandal came to light in spring 2004. The Iraq war provoked popular anti-war demonstrations and movements, and political debates about US foreign policy, that were unparalleled in scale and intensity since the 1960s (Figure 2.2) – debates that reached a turning point in November 2006, when dramatic midterm election results meant the Republican Party lost control of both Houses of Congress to the Democrats for the first time since 1994. The 2006 midterms looked like a damning rebuke for the White House, whose political credibility was weakened further in December with the publication of the findings of the Iraq Study Group (ISG), a bi-partisan committee established by Congress in March 2006 to investigate the state of the war in Iraq and to advise on policy options and ways ahead. The ISG report described the situations in both Afghanistan and Iraq as disastrous and advised a phased withdrawal of troops. At the time it was a significant blow for Bush, whose bid to increase troop numbers deployed to Iraq ran into trouble in Congress shortly after. In early December, a CBS poll put Bush's approval ratings at 31 per cent, their lowest since his election in 2000 (PollingReport.com 2007).

Figure 2.2 Thousands march up Pennsylvania Avenue towards the Capitol in Washington, DC, during anti-war demonstrations on 25 October 2003.
© Gregg Newton/Reuters/Corbis.

As late as the invasion of Iraq, though, high-profile figures in the US who spoke publicly against the war ran into difficulties. On 10 March 2003, the Texas-based country band, the Dixie Chicks, told an audience in London that they were ashamed Bush came from Texas. The Dixie Chicks returned home to death threats, warnings of violence against their families, public burnings of their CDs and bans on their music by stores and radio stations, which threatened to end their careers as professional musicians. A fortnight later, with the invasion of Iraq under way, the film-maker Michael Moore was widely reviled after he used his Oscar acceptance speech at the 75th Academy Awards to accuse Bush of taking the US to war under false pretences. By the 2006 midterms, and the ISG report the following month, the political climate had changed dramatically. With the Democrats controlling Congress it became common to hear Washington insiders and political pundits talking about how the president was now on the margins of debate about Iraq. By February 2007, the Dixie Chicks were winning Grammy awards again – five in all, including album of the year for *Taking the Long Way* (2006).

The charges Richard Clarke's *Against All Enemies* levied at Bush were heard regularly in the years after 9/11, with allegations that republican governance was under attack in the US becoming part of the political rhythm of the early war on terror. Sometimes these allegations stemmed from tensions, trends and debates that were already well established in American political history. Some of the interinstitutional friction characterising domestic politics after 9/11, for example – notably tensions between military commanders and their civilian leaders, and between the CIA and the White House – went back to the 1960s. In Clarke's *Against All Enemies*, and in an increasingly broad spectrum of contemporary political opinion, one of the more damaging allegations of the time was that the White House itself was preventing republican institutions and processes from working as the Constitution intended or allowed. The administration's homeland security initiatives led to early controversy over the Patriot Act, legislation framed by the White House and signed into law in October 2001, giving law enforcement agencies unprecedented powers with minimal judicial oversight. Human rights NGOs, lawyers and political activists attacked the Act for fostering a 'lack of due process and accountability' which 'violates the rights extended to all persons, citizens and non-citizens, by the Bill of Rights' (ACLU 2003). The American Civil Liberties Union (ACLU) argued that the Patriot Act cut across First, Fourth, Fifth, Sixth, Eighth and Fourteenth Amendment rights, including the rights to freedom of speech, assembly, religion and the press, the right to trial, and entitlements to due process and protection by the law (ibid.; see also Chang 2002; Cole and Dempsey 2002).

Another damaging allegation was that the executive had been 'hijacked' by sectional interests, usually identified either as a sinister cabal of neoconservative warhawks hellbent on attacking Saddam Hussein, or as corporate powerbrokers from the US energy and defence companies which did particularly well out of contracts to 'reconstruct' Afghanistan and Iraq (some of whom had close ties with President Bush and Vice-President Dick Cheney). The 'hijack' thesis sometimes sounded rather glib. The Bush Doctrine, as outlined in the 2002 *National Security Strategy* (NSS), and as practised in Iraq, did adopt a number of neocon policy positions, and the *NSS* spoke at times with a distinctly neocon turn of phrase. Nevertheless, Bush's relationship with the neocons, and the neocons' relationship with him, were always more complex than the idea of a conspiracy to 'hijack' the White House seemed to allow. After 9/11, as one contemporary account put it, 'the neocon solution seemed, to conservatives at least, to be the American solution' (Micklethwait and Wooldridge 2004: 210), and a number of neoconservative policy recommendations – 'regime change' in 'rogue states', exporting democracy, the need for more assertive uses of American power in pursuit of an expanded American hegemony – were adopted by the Bush administration. 9/11, another contemporary noted, 'elevated neocon thinking – a vigorous US nationalism – to the intellectual center. What had been a peripheral policy thrust became the dominant school of thought' (Gurtov 2006: 37; see also Micklethwait and Wooldridge 2004). This was not the same as a coup in or by the White House. There is no question that Bush's foreign policy became noticeably neoconservative after 9/11, or that 9/11 was exploited by neocon influences in and around the administration, often for ends that had little to do with 9/11. But with the exception of Paul Wolfowitz, Donald Rumsfeld's deputy at the Pentagon (2001–5), the first round of senior Bush appointees included 'no full-fledged neocons in the democratic-imperialist mode' (Micklethwait and Wooldridge 2004: 208). The Secretary of State, Colin Powell, had a reputation as an advocate of multilateral institutions and cautious uses of military power, while 'assertive nationalists' like Rumsfeld, Condoleezza Rice and Cheney may have agreed instinctively with neocons that the US needed to be more assertive in pursuits of its interests overseas (Rumsfeld, with Wolfowitz, had also signed the notorious letter sent to President Clinton by the influential neocon thinktank, the Project for the New American Century, in January 1998, in which eighteen co-signatories urged the president to pursue regime change in Iraq). But they 'had no patience with nation building, spreading democracy and the like' (ibid.: 202).

Neoconservatives reciprocated, keeping Bush at a distance too, even on the eve of the war in Iraq, a key neocon cause. In their classic neocon *apologia* for the war, *The War over Iraq: Saddam's Tyranny and America's*

Mission (2003), Lawrence Kaplan and William Kristol noted sniffily that, on the stump in 2000, 'candidate Bush placed misgivings about military intervention at the center of his foreign policy agenda'. For all its delirious praise of Bush's 'moral clarity', *The War over Iraq* also implied that the president had a recidivist foreign policy gene, one that would revert to 'nothing more than a variation of old-world *realpolitik* and an echo of Gerald Ford' if it were allowed to develop unchecked (Kaplan and Kristol 2003: 68). After the crushing blows taken by the Republican Party in the 2006 midterm elections, the neocon hegemony in the White House was challenged by a powerful coalition of old guard 'realists' led by James Baker, chairman of the ISG (who had been Bush senior's Secretary of State, 1989–93), and Brent Scowcroft, the elder Bush's National Security Adviser. As the news from Iraq grew steadily worse and the president's influence diminished in Congress, senior neocons like the former chairman of the Defence Policy Board (DPB), Richard Perle, and Kenneth Adelman, another member of the DPB, 'scurried off Bush's sinking ship', as one former senior aide to Bill Clinton, Sidney Blumenthal, put it (Blumenthal 2006a). Adelman was quoted in the press describing a 'dysfunctional' administration's 'enormous flaws' (ibid.), and the neocon suspicion of Bush, barely concealed in a classic contemporary tract like *The War over Iraq*, turned into open recrimination by the end of 2006, and a self-conscious public distancing of influential neocons from the administration. After 9/11, the opportunistic convergence between 'assertive nationalism' and neoconservatism was made easier because the two traditions shared an engrained scepticism about traditional Wilsonian commitments to the rule of law as embodied in international institutions. Agreement on this allowed neocons and assertive nationalists 'to form a marriage of convenience . . . even as they disagree[d] about what kind of commitment the United States should make to rebuilding Iraq and remaking the rest of the world' (Daalder and Lindsay 2003: 369). During Bush's second term, however, particularly after the 2006 midterms and the publication of the ISG report, it was a marriage that was at best fractious and at times appeared to have broken down altogether.

Complicity in a neoconservative 'hijacking' of republican high office was just one of the accusations directed at the Bush executive. Gore Vidal and Michael Moore referred to Bush's incumbency as a 'coup' and to his administration as a 'junta', and Philip Roth wrote a novel about a fascist takeover in the White House (see Chapter 5). Yet there was no need to look to such *outré* voices as Vidal's, or to such flights of historical fancy as Roth's, for serious political discussion about the damaging impacts of executive-led war on terror policy on the republican fabric of the American body politic. Blumenthal argued that Bush was 'the most wilfully radical president in American history' (Blumenthal 2006b: 1) because his leadership embodied the political theory of the 'unitary executive' – a view asserting 'that the President had complete authority over independent federal agencies and was not bound by congressional oversight or even law in his role as commander in chief' (ibid.: 7). In Blumenthal's account, the core value of the 'unitary executive' model adopted by the White House saw political accountability as 'a threat to executive power, not as essential to democratic governance' (ibid.: 19). Blumenthal described the Bush White House as the presidency 'construed as a monarchy', and worse, 'the full flowering of the imperial presidency as conceived by Richard Nixon' (ibid.: 8, 19). The Bush administration, Blumenthal wrote, was 'uniquely radical in its elevation of absolute executive power, dismissal of the other branches of government, contempt for the law, expansion of the power of the vice president, creation of networks of ideological cadres, rejection of accountability, stifling of internal debate, reliance on one-party rule, and overtly political use of war' (ibid.: 20).

Political outcomes like these were often seen by contemporary commentators as part of the empire debates considered in Chapter 1. Since the end of the eighteenth century, a powerful native tradition in American political history had viewed empire 'as the republic's permanent temptation and its potential nemesis' (Ignatieff 2003a). After 9/11, anxious affirmations of American empire like Michael Ignatieff's 'The American Empire (Get Used to It)' (2003a) were replete with references to the warnings of the founding fathers and other political leaders of the early republic. One that cropped up regularly was John Quincy Adams's famous warning in 1821 that if America were tempted to 'become the dictatress of the world, she would be no longer the ruler of her own spirit'. The political and intellectual tradition that identified with Adams equated empire with militarism, a shrinking purse for the provision of domestic public goods to US citizens and curbs on liberty. 9/11 added to this list of anxieties about empire a new sense of vulnerability to 'blowback' from American policy in what Ignatieff, in a striking and self-conscious imperialist conceit, called 'the frontier zones'. On the eve of the invasion of Iraq, Ignatieff predicted that the war would be 'a defining moment in America's long debate with itself about whether its overseas role as an empire threatens or strengthens its existence as a republic' (ibid.), and so it proved.

The most significant facet of the republican 'crisis' of 2001–6, however, was the affirmations of American political institutions and processes on which, paradoxically, the 'crisis' often depended for its articulation. It wasn't just Richard Clarke who appealed to the Constitution and to republican due process as the benchmarks of political legitimacy by which Bush's stewardship of the war on terror should be judged. Other vociferous critics of the White House, such as Michael Moore, wrote books suggesting that democratic elections and the Constitution would provide the political solutions to the Bush Doctrine (Moore 2002, 2003). The country singer and anti-war activist Steve Earle wrote liner notes to his 2004 album, *The Revolution Starts Now*, in which he called the Constitution 'a REVOLUTIONARY document in every sense of the word', and challenged Americans 'to defend and nurture this remarkable invention of our forefathers' by participating fully in the democratic process during election year (Earle 2004).

This containment of dissenting opinion within parameters that allowed powerful affirmations of existing political institutions and procedures to take place, as part of the process of dissent, is a familiar ritual in American political history. One striking example in the early years of the war on terror was by a Canadian resident in the US, Michael Ignatieff, an important figure in the intellectual history of the period, in his treatise on political ethics during wartime, *The Lesser Evil* (2005). Behind its anxiety about the ethics of torturing individuals in the pursuit of majoritarian interests, *The Lesser Evil* offered a hymn to 'adversarial review' – the collective term for democratic cycles of republican renewal, in which citizens sit in judgement on their leaders at the ballot box, the checks and balances of republican governance function as intended, and democracy's existing institutions 'provide a resolution' to the behaviour of governments (Ignatieff 2005: 3). This was fine, as long as Americans feeling better about their democracy was sufficient redress for the suffering of those who died, or whose lives and countries were wrecked, at the sharp end of US policy. Adversarial review allowed incompetent or iniquitous leadership to be punished, but it didn't prevent such leadership or its consequences happening in the first place. Reading Ignatieff's *The Lesser Evil* was a bit like revisiting the old debate between John Dewey and Randolph Bourne over American intervention in the First World War. Like Dewey's, Ignatieff's pragmatism in *The Lesser Evil* – he called it 'ethical realism' (Ignatieff 2005: 21) – seemed reactive and pessimistic, unable or unwilling to make political ethics a progressive intellectual agency capable of helping shape history, rather than simply reacting to it when things went wrong. Ignatieff also seemed to underestimate the extent to which the pragmatic acceptance of necessary 'lesser evils' might lead to an eroding of the same institutions he valorised as ethical fail-safes in the political process of adversarial review. While he argued that republican democracy would apply a political and ethical fix to rogue political administration, Ignatieff was less forthcoming over the problem that adversarial review, in the form of presidential elections, was also responsible for electing such administration to office. From this point of view, as for Clarke, the Bush Doctrine was essentially an aberration, not an embodiment of living traditions in American political history or a product of the political system itself. The 'crisis' in republican governance during the Bush era often seemed real enough. But because it was rhetorically contained within ideologies of adversarial review that positioned the Bush White House as a detour in authentic republican history, it was a 'crisis' that was widely assumed to be time-limited and self-correcting, and thus not really a crisis at all.

The post-9/11 period in the US was characterised by purgative rituals of adversarial review that were particularly powerful because of the disturbing evidence of political dysfunction that they had to assimilate or overcome. One far-reaching assessment of sclerosis in state institutions and process came from within Congress, in the form of the National Commission on Terrorist Attacks Upon the United States (the 9/11 Commission), whose expansive, multi-authored *The 9/11 Commission Report* (National Commission 2004a) was compared by one reviewer to the *Federalist Papers*, such was its ambition 'to foster the debate by which the country will re-imagine itself through its [federal] bureaucracy' (*Publishers Weekly* 2004). The National Commission had a self-consciously bipartisan membership of five Republicans and five Democrats, and broad terms of reference – 'Why did they do this? How was the attack planned and conceived? How did the US government fail to anticipate and prevent it? What can we do in the future to prevent similar acts of terrorism?' (National Commission 2004b: 2). The *Report* identified what it called 'operational failures' in 'organisations and systems' across government structures that had failed to adapt to the national security contexts of the post-Cold War era. In state agencies and institutions across the board, the *9/11 Commission Report* concluded, 'there were failures of imagination, policy, capabilities, and management' (ibid.: 8, 9).

One reason the 9/11 Commissioners drew attention to the *Report*'s bipartisan authorship was that it seemed symbolic of the Commission's key finding – that 'unity of purpose and unity of effort are the way we will defeat this enemy and make America safer' (ibid.: 26). The *9/11 Commission Report* focused on the inability of disparate state agencies to communicate with and within one another, on intelligence and anti-terrorism initiatives. Yet it wasn't just a lack of communication that alarmed the 9/11 Commissioners. Over and again in *The 9/11 Commission Report* the agencies and institutions themselves sounded chronically unfit for purpose. The CIA, the *Report* concluded, had neither the structure nor the operational capability to lead the intelligence war against al-Qaeda. The FBI had 'limited intelligence collection and strategic analysis capabilities, a limited capacity to share information both internally and externally, insufficient training, perceived legal barriers to sharing information, and inadequate resources' (ibid.: 13). The protocols governing national defence and civil aviation agencies NORAD (North American Aerospace Defense Command) and the FAA (the Federal Aviation Administration) were described as 'unsuited in every respect' (ibid.: 7). The *Report* also concluded that the Defense Department was hamstrung in its approach to al-Qaeda before 9/11 by the same operational handicaps that contemporary empire revisionists said were symptoms of a reluctant 'empire lite' – risk-aversion and a dependence on unreliable proxies to do the dangerous and dirty work of fighting on the ground. Congress was criticised by the 9/11 Commission for responding slowly and incoherently to the threat posed by transnational terrorism. Congressional attention to terrorism 'was episodic and splintered across several committees', Commissioners reported, and its oversight of intelligence and counterterrorism procedures was 'dysfunctional' (ibid.: 15, 25). With its further warnings about the permeable state of America's borders, immigration controls and aviation security, *The 9/11 Commission Report* must have made grim reading for Ignatieff, whose faith in the ethical legitimacy of democracy imposed by imperial military violence rested squarely on the assumption that democratic institutions and processes produced just and efficient governance.

On its first term of reference, 'Why did they do this?', the *Report* seemed thin and said disappointingly little about the rejigged grand strategy that a reordered bureaucracy might usefully pursue, if part of its aim were the prevention of future 9/11s. In a textbook example of what Michael Scheuer called 'imperial hubris' (see Chapter 1), the appeal of Osama bin Laden to Muslims was described in simplistic and dismissive terms as 'the story of eccentric and violent ideas sprouting in the fertile ground of political and social turmoil' (National Commission 2004a: 48); while the *Report*'s recommendations for preventing the continued growth of Islamist terrorism were couched in vague homilies about fighting 'extremists', developing coalitions to disrupt 'terrorism', pursuing 'economic openness' and policies that would provide 'opportunities for people to improve the lives of their families and to enhance prospects for their children's future' (National Commission 2004a: 379).

Another striking 'crisis' trend was the range of inter-institutional tensions set in train or exacerbated by 9/11 and by the White House's response to the attacks, tensions that sometimes escalated into open conflict. *The 9/11 Commission Report* commented on a lack of cohesion between security, intelligence and law enforcement agencies in the US – a situation not necessarily remedied by legislation such as the Homeland Security Act (2002), or by the US Department of Homeland Security (2003) the Act created. (These aimed to increase the cohesion of national security initiatives by creating new tiers of centralised, top-down administration when, as Elaine Scarry observed, the only effective defence of the nation on September 11 had actually come in the 'distributed and egalitarian' form of citizen activism by passengers on United Airlines Flight 93, the hijacked plane which crashed in Pennsylvania, apparently en route to Washington [Scarry 2006: 186].) More than a lack of cohesion, the extent to which different parts of the state bureaucracy were at times actively at odds with each other after 9/11 was one indicator of the degree to which the White House and Pentagon drove an agenda that was often depicted at the time as radical, authoritarian and illegal in both federal and international law.

Inter-institutional conflicts, or tension between different bodies within the state apparatus, included those between the White House and the Supreme Court over the detention of prisoners of war; between civilian and military leadership of the armed forces over military strategy in Afghanistan and Iraq; and between the CIA and the White House over allegations of catastrophic 'intelligence failure' in the lead-up to 9/11 (one of the more dramatic moments of the 9/11 Commission hearings being Condoleezza Rice's public acknowledgment that a report titled 'Bin Laden Determined to Attack America' had landed on the president's desk five weeks before the 9/11 attacks) (Figure 2.3). During 2003 and 2004, accounts were rife of how the White House and the CIA were 'at war' (see Follman 2003; Bamford 2004; Hayes 2004; Powers 2004; Sherwell 2004). Such was the administration's determination to invade Iraq that when the CIA could provide no actionable intelligence on Saddam's notional stockpiles of weapons of mass destruction, Rumsfeld even instituted what the contemporary intelligence expert Thomas Powers called 'a new CIA' at the Pentagon, the Office of Special Plans, created in September 2002 to bypass CIA analysis of raw intelligence material on Iraq (Follman 2003).

The turf war between the Defense Department and the CIA over intelligence-gathering signalled a dramatically expanded role for the Pentagon in the national security affairs of the empire, and was identified by Seymour Hersh as one of the roots of the military prison

Figure 2.3 Condoleezza Rice testifies before the 9/11 Commission on Capitol Hill, 8 April 2004.
Photo by Mark Wilson/Getty Images.

scandals at Guantánamo Bay and Abu Ghraib (Hersh 2004). Empire-building at the Pentagon also created tension with the State Department. The 'disciples of neo-Reaganism' ensconced in the Pentagon believed that the State Department was not equipped to do the dirty work of a war on terror (Gurtov 2006: 37); while over at State, in a barbed comment that was also aimed at the White House, Colin Powell's chief of staff, Lawrence Wilkerson, alleged that coercive inter-rogation and torture of military intelligence detainees laid the US open to war crimes charges (Borger 2005). Thomas Powers was just one of numerous contemporary voices claiming that the White House obses-sion with Iraq had jeopardised national security (Follman 2003), meaning that the president had betrayed the primary responsibility of the executive to protect the American people, by diverting vital CIA resources away from the war against al-Qaeda. The 'war' between the executive branch and the CIA turned particularly nasty in July 2003, when the White House leaked the identity of a covert CIA agent, Valerie Plame (a criminal act under federal law), apparently in revenge for an article in the *New York Times* by her husband, Joseph Wilson a US diplomat. Wilson had refuted claims made by the president in the 2003 State of the Union Address that Iraq had tried to buy uranium in Africa, having travelled to Niger to investigate the claim the previous year (Wilson 2003). In June 2007, Lewis ('Scooter') Libby, Cheney's chief of staff and national security adviser, a senior figure in the Bush White House, was sentenced to two and a half years in jail for perjury, having lied under oath about the circumstances of Plame's 'outing' by the administration.[1]

As one factor at play in the republican 'crisis' of the early war on terror, inter-institutional conflict between different state bodies had its most visible roots in the 'unitary executive' formulation of foreign policy and national security strategy known as the Bush Doctrine. Though its diplomatic and military applications were at times wholly radical, aspects of the Bush Doctrine had been around for some time in post-Cold War think-tanks in Washington and in policy traditions that dated from the Cold War era, and earlier. Its 'fullest elaboration', 'the most comprehensive statement of the administration's foreign policy', was the *National Security Strategy* (*NSS*) issued by the White House in Autumn 2002 (Daalder and Lindsay 2003: 370). The *NSS* tilted away from a cautiously 'realist' Cold War emphasis on protecting existing balances of power favourable to US interests ('stability'), and towards an aggressive expansion of America's influence in key regions, pitching the strategy of an expanded hegemony in an authentically pessimistic neoconservative lexicon, where 'the gravest danger to freedom [lay] at the perilous crossroads of radicalism and technology' (NSS 2002: 13, quoting Bush 2002), and where 'the enemy' was 'terrorism' – 'premeditated, politically motivated violence perpetrated against innocents' (ibid.: 5). In the wider war on terror, the *NSS* said, the US would make no distinction between terrorists and 'those who knowingly harbor or provide aid to them'. In the manner, neocons liked to imagine, of Harry Truman in 1947, pledging to support 'free peoples who are resisting attempted subjugation by armed minorities or by outside pressures', the 2002 *NSS* promised that states menaced by terrorism would receive 'the military, law enforcement, political, and financial tools necessary to finish the task' (NSS 2002: 5, 6; Truman 1947).

The ideological core of the Bush Doctrine was its neoconservative insistence that in a world transformed by post-Cold War realities and 9/11, foreign policy and national security strategy must also be reinvented. Cold War concepts of deterrence, it said, did not work against rogue states or enemies seeking martyrdom. Nor did 'realist' traditions geared towards maintaining existing balances of power make sense, when the post-Cold War context in which 'national' interests were pursued was a 'unipolar' world characterised by American primacy. As in Huntington's clash of civilisations thesis, the solution was a more vigilant and assertive American hegemony. Few prominent neocons, and no senior figures in the Bush administration, talked openly about empire. They didn't need to. The Bush Doctrine turned national security into a transnational public good that could be secured only by American global dominance and by the vigorous policing of competitor states and groups. As the *NSS* put it, 'The United States must and will maintain the capability to defeat any attempt by an enemy – whether a state or non-state actor – to impose its will on the United States, our allies, or our friends. . . . Our forces will be strong enough to dissuade potential adversaries from pursuing a military build-up in hopes of surpassing, or equalling, the power of the United States' (ibid.: 30). American power, as one contemporary estimate put it, was 'at the strategy's center' (Daalder and Lindsay 2003: 371).

Using that power after 9/11 meant challenging the legitimacy of the UN, the forum, in a powerful strand of neoconservative thought, where weak states combined to aggregate and offset their weakness, the better to promote their own influence at the expense of the legitimate interests of a unipolar US – a tendentious account of the UN that also cropped up in contemporary discourses of affirmative empire revisionism discussed in Chapter 1. The struggle that the Bush administration initiated against the UN was the defining inter-institutional conflict of the period. The *NSS* stressed that 'while the United States will constantly strive to enlist the support of the international community, we will not hesitate to act alone, if necessary' (NSS 2002: 6). The choice of language was revealing. Striving to 'enlist the support' of the international community was not the same as working within or deferring to it, and the sections of the *NSS* that dwelt on the means and ends of international 'co-operation' seemed broadly dismissive of existing international frameworks and institutions. Section III, on how to strengthen global alliances and international co-operation to defeat terrorism, was an opportunity to explain how a reformed UN might take a key role in the war on terror. But it mentioned the UN just once, and then only in the context of a reminder to international organisations 'such as the United Nations', that they shared in the obligations of postwar nation-building in Afghanistan (ibid.: 7). In section VIII, on agendas for cooperation with 'other main centers of global power' (ibid.: 25–8), the UN fared even worse, meriting not a single mention, despite the space reserved for discussion of other 'main centers' which included NATO, the EU, Russia, China and America's 'Asian alliances'. Such commitments to existing multilateral institutions as survived in the 2002 *NSS* looked more like regretful concessions to the limits of American power than a genuine enthusiasm for international co-operation – the pragmatic outcomes of constraints external to and beyond the control of the US, rather than an articulation of beliefs.[2]

While the need for the 'sustained cooperation' (ibid.: 25) of others was not at stake, the institutional and logistical forms that such political cooperation should take certainly were. Forming 'coalitions of the willing' (meaning loose, non-binding, ad hoc agreements among governments, bypassing the established forums for collective decision-making at the UN), the *NSS* asserted, would be a key strategy for confronting the emerging threats of the twenty-first century (ibid.: 11). The language suggested that such coalitions could function as an adjunct to existing international frameworks – coalitions of the willing, the *NSS* said, could 'augment' permanent institutions. Yet the tone of the rest of the document, and the executive's willingness to wage war on Iraq without a UN resolution explicitly authorising the invasion, suggested that the reverse was the case and that 'permanent' institutions should now serve as discretionary add-ons to American power. There was certainly no sense in the 2002 *NSS* that 'coalitions of the willing' should feel themselves bound by the will of the wider international community or by the institutions that embodied it (not the UN, and certainly not the International Criminal Court, which had not been recognised by previous US administrations and which was the subject of renewed attack in the 2002 *NSS*). The language of the *NSS* reflected this sense of rupture in the fabric of the existing international order, positioning the US not just in the role of 'coalition leadership' (NSS 2002: 25), but as an assertive, dynamic, activist force in world politics. America, Bush's covering letter said, would seek 'to create' a new balance of power, so as to 'extend' the post-Cold War peace. 'In the new world we have entered', it said, 'the only path to peace and security is the path of action': 'when openings arrive, we can encourage change'; 'our best defense is a good offense' (ibid.: np, 3, 6). A far cry from the cautious foreign policy realism endorsed by candidate Bush on the stump in 2000, the 2002 *NSS* fairly strained at the seams with heady neocon sloganeering like this, with 'American values' proclaimed 'right and true for every person, in every society . . . across the globe and across the ages' (ibid.: np).

Away from the frontlines in Afghanistan and Iraq, the principal political battlegrounds of the 'republican crisis' were legalistic. This was particularly true of the Bush administration's conflict with the UN, where one key debate concerned the distinction between 'pre-emptive' and 'preventive' war in international law. At times the Bush *National Security Strategy* did seem to be talking, as it claimed to be, about pre-emptive action (self-defensive action taken to address an imminent threat, or clear and present danger), promising to defend Americans and American interests 'by identifying and destroying the threat before it reaches our borders' (NSS 2002: 6). At other times the language used made it sound as though what the administration was really proposing was preventive war (war fought to prevent the emergence of threats in the future), a different thing entirely. As a matter of 'self-defence', the *NSS* said, 'America will act against such emerging threats before they are fully formed', and would do so 'even if uncertainty remains as to the time and place of the enemy's attack' (ibid.: np, 15; see also Bush 2002). The administration identified this as *pre-emption*, but seemed deliberately to be blurring the distinction with *prevention*. As contemporary commentators suggested, the distinction was crucial and not as fine as the White House wanted to imply. Pre-emptive war as self-defence was recognised as legitimate under the terms of Article 51 of the UN Charter. However, no such recognition existed in international law for the 'legally dubious doctrine of preventive war (against a remote or distant threat)' (Offner 2005: 433) – the possibility that threats may become fully formed and 'imminent' at some unknown point in the future being insufficient for legitimate grounds of self-defence under the UN Charter, where preventive war constituted instead an act of unwarranted aggression against a sovereign state (see also Chomsky 2004: 11–12; Daalder and Lindsay 2003: 372; Bacevich 2005: 411; Gurtov 2006: 41). The administration's solution to this problem, 'We must adapt the concept of imminent threat to the capabilities and objectives of today's adversaries' (NSS 2002: 15), was an open challenge to international law and the institutions that embodied it.

Another bone of contention between the 'unitary executive' and the international community that brought into focus debate about the Bush Doctrine was the detention and interrogation of prisoners of war – an issue that crystallised around discussion about the illegality of torture in federal and international law. When the veteran anarchist, activist and public intellectual Noam Chomsky gave a public talk on torture in Dublin in January 2006, the crowd that came to hear him speak was so large that 4000 people were locked out of the hall (Chrisafis 2006). Three very public scandals – over the US military prison at Guantánamo Bay in Cuba, over the abuse, torture and murder of detainees at the Abu Ghraib military prison in Iraq, and over the CIA's 'rendition' of suspects to foreign jails for coercive interrogation using what the president referred to as 'an alternative set of procedures' (Bush 2006) – prompted international protests, Supreme Court rulings and Congressional interventions that helped make political discourse about torture part of the contemporary cultural fabric. This discourse prompted exactly the kinds of 'adversarial review' championed by affirmative empire revisionists like Ignatieff as guarantors of political liberties and political ethics during wartime. The House, the Senate and the Supreme Court all attempted to rein in the rights the White House asserted to determine unilaterally where the limits fell for acceptable treatment of enemy prisoners. If anything, though, what the protracted judicial debates and Congressional procrastinations about torture would suggest was just how badly served some of the most victimised groups of America's war on terror actually were by republican procedures of adversarial review.

Abu Ghraib was a major tipping point in public opinion about the Iraq war, in America and around the world. The Bush administration called the images of hooded, naked and 'piled' Iraqi detainees – some cowering in terror from dogs, others attached to what looked like live electrodes – an aberration, the work of a few 'rotten apples' who were not representative of authentic US military culture in Iraq. On 7 May 2004, Rumsfeld apologised to Congress for the 'fundamentally un-American' scenes at Abu Ghraib. On 24 May, in a statement on US strategy in Iraq at the Army War College in Pennsylvania, the president spoke of the 'disgraceful conduct by a few American troops who dishonored our country and disregarded our values' (Rumsfeld 2004; Bush 2005). Led from the top, the 'rotten apples' line became the standard explanation for Abu Ghraib among administration officials and supporters at the time. But the testimony of soldiers involved in the scandal told a different story. Some of those put on trial alleged that they had been encouraged to soften up detainees for questioning by military interrogators. Others, like Janis Karpinski, the commanding officer of Military Police in Iraq, who was suspended after one of several internal military investigations into Abu Ghraib, invited readers of her Iraq memoir, *One Woman's Army* (2005), to conclude that direct responsibility for the scandal went up the chain of command at least as far as Rumsfeld, and possibly higher. The problems at Abu Ghraib, Karpinski said, coincided with the administrative takeover of large parts of the prison by military intelligence personnel in the autumn of 2003, and political pressure to secure 'actionable intelligence' from detainees held there for interrogation.

Karpinski's version of events fitted the template set by the classic early account of Abu Ghraib, Seymour Hersh's *Chain of Command* (2004). According to Hersh's timeline, in late 2001 or early 2002 Bush authorised a covert Defense Department 'special-access program' (SAP) to establish secret interrogation centres in allied countries, 'where harsh treatments were meted out, unconstrained by legal limits or public disclosure' (Hersh 2004: 16). The SAP authorised special forces and intelligence officers to snatch suspects anywhere in the world for interrogation in SAP prisons and to carry out targeted assassinations.

Abu Ghraib and Guantánamo Bay, it transpired, were just the tip of a much larger executive initiative to circumvent existing international protocols on detention, interrogation and torture. Far from the actions of a few rogue reservists or rotten apples, the roots of what happened at Abu Ghraib, Hersh alleged, lay 'not in the criminal inclinations of a few Army reservists, but in the reliance of George Bush and Donald Rumsfeld on secret operations and the use of coercion' in fighting terrorism (Hersh 2004: 46).

After the Afghan war, controversy over detention and interrogation focused initially on the treatment of 'prisoners of war' – a contentious phrase that the Bush administration claimed did not apply to detainees held at Guantánamo Bay. Detainees at Guantánamo, the administration said, were not 'prisoners of war' because they had not worn uniforms or carried weapons openly, and had chosen to disregard international law prohibiting the targeting of civilian populations. For these reasons, Guantánamo detainees were 'unlawful enemy combatants', not 'prisoners of war'. The distinction was vital. 'Prisoners of war' were entitled to conditions of imprisonment prescribed by the 1949 Geneva Conventions, but 'unlawful enemy combatants', the administration argued, were not. On 7 February 2002, the president signed a statement declaring that the Geneva Conventions did not apply 'to our conflict with al-Qaeda in Afghanistan or elsewhere throughout the world' (quoted in Hersh 2004: 5). Since Guantánamo was in Cuba, the administration argued, detainees were not protected by federal law either. As early as the summer of 2002, a CIA analyst visiting Guantánamo to investigate the poor quality of intelligence gathered during interrogations concluded in a privately circulated report that war crimes were being committed there. In New York, the human rights NGO Human Rights Watch (HRW) described the setting up of military commissions at Guantánamo to prosecute (and potentially execute) non-US citizens involved in the legally undefined crime of 'international terrorism' as an affront to international law and fair trial standards (HRW 2002). HRW's executive director, Kenneth Roth, compared the powers taken by the US state to tribunals 'set up by a tinpot tyrant to get rid of his political enemies' (in Norton-Taylor 2002).

In the wake of the damage caused by Guantánamo in 2002 and Abu Ghraib in 2004, debates about the position of torture in the political administration of the war on terror intensified again in 2005, when the *Washington Post* broke a story about a CIA practice known as 'extraordinary rendition', whereby individuals suspected of terrorist connections were kidnapped by US intelligence operatives and taken to prisons in other countries for interrogation. As with the controversy over

Guantánamo, discussion about rendition broadened rapidly into debate about the legitimacy of government by 'unitary executive'. An Amnesty International report, 'Below the Radar: Secret Flights to Torture and Disappearance' (April 2006), defined rendition as 'the transfer of individuals from one country to another, by means that bypass all judicial and administrative due process', the aim being to keep detainees 'away from any judicial oversight' (Amnesty International 2006: 2). Fed by a steady drip of revelations and allegations over the following months, the rendition story grew, with media reports and human rights NGOs alleging that the CIA was operating a network of secret prisons, or 'black sites', in Central Asia, Eastern Europe and the Middle East, where interrogations could proceed out of oversight by federal and international law. Afghanistan, Iraq, Syria, Jordan, Libya, Egypt, Morocco, Poland and Romania were all subsequently identified as likely locations of 'black sites'. The focus of the controversy moved to Europe when it became apparent that countries there had acted as important logistical hubs for CIA flights since 9/11, providing airspace, stopover facilities and intelligence that helped facilitate the rendition of suspects. Amnesty's 'Below the Radar' report concluded that although rendition was usually initiated by the US, it was also 'carried out with the collaboration, complicity or acquiescence of other governments' (ibid.: 2) – findings that were endorsed by the European Union's most influential human rights watchdog, the Council of Europe, which published two reports following its own investigation into what it called the 'collusion' of European states with CIA renditions (Council of Europe 2006a, 2006b).

Such 'collusion' extended the crisis posed by 'unitary executive' activism into European law too. The human rights NGO Liberty estimated that rendition contravened Article 6 of the Treaty of Nice, an EU convention obliging member states to uphold basic human rights (Harding 2005). The Council of Europe argued that renditions also ran contrary to the UN Universal Declaration of Human Rights (1948) and the European Convention on Human Rights (1950) (Grey and Cobain 2006). In addition, Amnesty's 'Below the Radar' report asserted that rendition flights breached the 'Chicago Convention' (the Convention on International Civil Aviation, 1944) which allowed private, non-commercial aircraft to overfly a country or make technical stopovers without prior notification or authorisation, but not for purposes 'inconsistent with the aims of the convention' (Amnesty International 2006: 26). Amnesty concluded that while the CIA sometimes used legitimate commercial carriers, it had also set up a series of front organisations – 'companies that exist only on paper' (ibid.: 23) – to exploit the provisions of the Chicago Convention.

Echoing the debate over semantics regarding 'enemy combatants' and 'prisoners of war', unitary executive initiatives on torture protocols were intensely legalistic. In March 2002, a Defense Department analysis asserted the president's right to override federal and international laws prohibiting torture. Other assertions in the Defense Department document included a claim that interrogators who harmed prisoners could invoke a legal claim of self-defence. In August, in an infamous memo exposed by Hersh in *Chain of Command*, the head of the Justice Department's Office of Legal Counsel, Jay Bybee, advised counsel to the White House, Alberto Gonzales, that 'certain acts may be cruel, inhuman or degrading, but still not produce pain and suffering of the requisite intensity to fall within [a legal] proscription against torture'. For an act to constitute torture in law, Bybee argued, it must inflict physical pain 'equivalent in intensity to the pain accompanying serious physical injury, such as organ failure, impairment of bodily function, or even death' (in Hersh 2004: 4–5).[3]

The administration's attempt to redefine acceptable coercive interrogation as anything short of organ failure or death was not just legalistic. In its insistence that 9/11 represented a rupture in history, a moment when everything changed (including existing conventions limiting states' pursuit of national security), the White House's attempt to subvert existing laws governing the torture of prisoners was also doctrinal – in the sense that it derived directly from the Bush Doctrine as formally outlined in documents such as the 2002 *NSS* and was defended as such by senior administration officials, including the president. In a statement she made before leaving for a difficult trip to Germany in December 2005, where political controversy had broken out over revelations that German airbases played a key role in CIA rendition flights, Condoleezza Rice defended the abduction and rendition of suspects as a vital tool in the war on terror, claiming that rendition had become a legitimate tactic of national security strategy because circumstances had changed, and 'the captured terrorists of the 21st century do not fit easily into traditional systems of criminal or military justice'. Renditions, she said, were pre-emptive strikes. They 'take terrorists out of action, and save lives' (in Goldenberg and Harding 2005; see also Bush 2006).

The Bush administration's reassurances about rotten apples and pre-emptive strikes were not enough to prevent a protracted process of adversarial review taking shape around the emotive and politically charged issues of torture, detention and rendition. The scandals surrounding American military prisons sparked a debate about *habeas corpus* rights – the right to trial and the right to appeal against unfair imprisonment, key safeguards for centuries against political authoritarianism – in which state institutions reached timid, fudged or contradictory conclusions that effectively stymied the mechanisms Ignatieff argued would ensure executive accountability in wartime. In June 2004, in the case of *Rasul v. Bush*, the Supreme Court upheld the right of detainees at Guantánamo to file *habeas corpus* petitions challenging the legality of their imprisonment, and in June 2006, in *Hamdan v. Rumsfeld*, the Court also ruled that the administration's plan for military war crimes trials for Guantánamo detainees was illegal in both federal and international law. But in April 2007 the Court appeared to contradict itself by voting narrowly against hearing appeals for the restoration of *habeas corpus* rights by two Guantánamo prisoners. Congress was equally ambivalent, passing the Detainee Treatment Act of 2005 in the teeth of vigorous opposition from Cheney (who was dubbed 'Vice President for Torture' by the *Washington Post* [2005]), which outlawed 'cruel, unusual, and inhumane treatment or punishment', as already prohibited by the Fifth, Eighth, and Fourteenth Amendments to the Constitution, and by the UN Convention Against Torture. Yet the Act applied only to prisoners held by the Defense Department, and so did not apply to the CIA. It offered no legal obstacles to the process of extraordinary rendition, and it lacked a precise definition of torture. *Harvard Human Rights Journal* called it 'a feeble and incongruous attempt to restore America's credibility as a country that does not practice or condone torture' (Harvard College 2006). Both the Detainee Treatment Act and the Military Commissions Act (passed by Congress in 2006) endorsed the White House line that 'enemy combatants' did not qualify for traditional *habeas corpus* rights. While Congress fudged the issue and a divided Supreme Court offered incoherent rulings, an Australian, 31-year-old Muslim convert with no ties to 9/11, David Hicks, became the first Guantánamo detainee to be brought before a military commission in March 2006, charged with providing material support to al-Qaeda.[4]

Torture was an important representative issue in the post-9/11 era, because it embodied the Bush Doctrine in such profound ways. Torture went to the very heart of contemporary debates about how America was governed, about how, as an empire, it 'governed' the world, and about how to reconcile the political ethics of republicanism with the exigencies of imperialism. As one example of the 'American Gulliver' unbinding itself from the 'Lilliputian' constraints of international law, the administration's position on torture embodied the Bush Doctrine's position on unilateralism; the suggestion that coercive interrogation represented 'self-defence' against hypothetical terrorist atrocities of

Figure 2.4 American anti-war activist, dressed as an Abu Ghraib prisoner, stands among crosses at Camp Casey, near the Texas ranch of President George W. Bush during November 2005. The camp was named for activist Cindy Sheehan's son, Casey, who was killed in Iraq.
© Paul Buck/epa/Corbis.

the future was a doctrinal assertion of pre-emption; and the 'collaboration, complicity or acquiescence of other governments' (Amnesty International 2006: 3) in the practice of extraordinary rendition depended on precisely the kind of loose, informal and non-binding agreements between the US and friendly states described in the *NSS* as 'coalitions of the willing'.

For these reasons, perhaps, political-legal dissent (Figure 2.4) and moral disgust were by no means the only narratives assembled out of the three great detention scandals of the 'crisis' years. Writing in his *Washington Post* column as the Abu Ghraib scandal was breaking, the prominent neocon pundit Charles Krauthammer saw the revelations from Abu Ghraib, counterintuitively, as a 'moral panic' and an opportunity to reaffirm what he called 'the moral purpose of the entire enterprise'. In Iraq, Krauthammer wrote, American military power had 'liberated 25 million people' with 'hundreds, thousands, of individual acts of beneficence and kindness by American soldiers', and with 'remarkable grace and courage' (Krauthammer 2004a, 2004b). Janis Karpinski's Abu Ghraib memoir, *One Woman's Army* (2005), went further, embedding its celebration of military violence in a broader autobiographical account of her life, entwining the Abu Ghraib story with serial affirmations of American military culture, a rapturous account of the Eisenhower republicanism of the 1950s 'American Way', and what she described as her own 'pioneering' feminism – a personal crusade she claimed had broken down doors for women in the Middle East, as well as in the military. The discursive location of torture at the heart of public debate about war on terror policy sometimes offered visceral evidence of a profound political and moral crisis in the republic. But it is important to recognise that torture also functioned as a springboard on which other, more affirmative political stories were sprung – stories about the military, about foreign policy, about national security strategy, about Bush's leadership and about the essential goodness and universality of the US. Since an event like the Abu Ghraib prison scandal, like the Bush administration, could be explained away as an aberration or mistake that could be corrected (but not caused) by the sound republican procedures of adversarial review, once the initial horror had subsided the republican 'crisis' of Abu Ghraib actually functioned for contemporary Americans like Krauthammer and Karpinski as proof of America's authentic 'moral purpose'. Whatever else it told Americans about the Bush Doctrine, as much as anything it was this remarkable alchemy of contemporary discussion about torture, its ideological turning of 'crisis' and despair into patriotic affirmations of existing institutions and processes, that made torture such a revealing and representative discourse of the times.

Echoing some of the claims made by empire revisionists, Melvyn Leffler was one of several contemporary historians who pointed out that the Bush Doctrine was far from revolutionary, identifying instances in the history of US foreign relations where the Doctrine's central tenets – hegemony, unilateralism, pre-emption, regime change – had underpinned policy-making by previous administrations (Leffler 2005; see also Bacevich 2002; Hixson 2005; Kagan 2005; Drezner 2005; Gurtov 2006). Retreading Richard Hofstadter's famous contention that American political history was characterised by its 'paranoid style' (Hofstadter 1964), Walter Hixson placed the Bush Doctrine in another native tradition, describing the post-9/11 political climate as 'merely the latest example of perceived "existential" threats provoking a perfervid discourse of good versus evil, followed by war', a tradition, he noted, that was 'deeply rooted in Euro-American modernity' (Hixson 2005: 420). If the Bush Doctrine was revolutionary, contemporaries tended to agree, it was 'a revolution not in America's foreign policy goals, but in how to achieve them' (Daalder and Lindsay 2003: 367). Where previous administrations had asserted or maintained the US's preponderance by reserving the rights to act unilaterally and pre-emptively and to effect regime change, none had tested those 'rights' so assertively, or calamitously, as Bush. While pre-emption, for example, had often been cited as a legitimate policy option by previous administrations, it 'had never before been used to initiate a full-scale war' (Gurtov 2006: 40). In Gurtov's snappy summary:

> the expansionist tendencies inherent in the Bush Doctrine are what made it both radically different from past US strategic perspectives and in company with them. Erasing the line between national defense and national security, and insisting on the right to take unilateral action against threats, were not new to US foreign policy. But stretching the boundaries of preemptive action to embrace preventive war, rejecting deterrence, demoting alliances, putting the United States on a permanent war footing, and firmly believing in the efficacy, necessity, and morality of absolute military preponderance *were* new. In a nutshell, the Bush Doctrine represented an elaboration of traditional doctrine; but in a one-superpower world, such an elaboration amounted to an unprecedented assertion of a US right to global domination. (ibid.: 48)

There was, of course, another way of looking at this. Instead of asking what could be learned about US foreign policy in the war on terror by comparing the Bush Doctrine with presidential doctrines of the past, we might ask what can be surmised about the history of US grand strategy generally, its motivations and consequences since the Second World War, if its strategic norms have historically been shaped by policy traditions that so clearly anticipate the Bush Doctrine. Bush's most vociferous critics (especially those who took the essential first step towards resolving the 'crisis' that his administration represented, by depicting him as a rogue president out of step with mainstream traditions in American political history) often viewed foreign policy and national security strategy of the past in what Robert Kagan called 'rosy hues – as unfailingly multilateral, law-abiding and UN-respecting – in order to damn Bush by comparison with this mythical past' (Kagan 2005: 415; see also Eisenberg 2005). At the very least, locating the war on terror as a culmination of existing trends helps problematise such complacent readings of American political history and sheds further light on contemporary debates about the historical development of American empire.

By the 2006 midterms, debate about the Bush Doctrine had shifted from tracing the Doctrine's roots to assessing its successes and failures. The political litmus test of the Bush Doctrine, contemporaries averred, was 'whether it enhances the security, prosperity, and liberty of the American people in the long run' (Daalder and Lindsay 2003: 373). In order to do this, affirmative empire revisionists suggested, the US had to impose and maintain global order by force in a new and substantially expanded *Pax Americana*. Bringing order, Ignatieff observed, was 'the paradigmatic imperial task' (Ignatieff 2003a). By the 2006 midterms, however, the Bush Doctrine appeared to be failing these tests. Iraq, previously a secular regional buffer against Iran, became a global sink for anti-American *jihad*, and descended at the same time into the chaos of civil war. A report by the medical journal *The Lancet* in October 2006 found that more than 650,000 Iraqis, or one in forty of the population, had died as a result of the invasion in 2003. After 'victory' in Afghanistan, the pro-American regime controlled Kabul, but in the rest of the country local power reverted to its traditional bases in tribal faction and warlordism. Political elites around the world, including those in China, India, Russia and Israel, all used the war on terror as cover for escalating their own conflicts with Islamist groups. Pro-American regimes already at war with domestic Islamist opinion in Saudi Arabia and Pakistan were further destabilised at home by their allegiance to the US, while the wars in Afghanistan and Iraq also stimulated alarming nuclear proliferation in Iran and North Korea, two hard-line anti-American states identified as members of an 'Axis of Evil' by President Bush in 2002. Oil prices too were extremely volatile after 9/11. The affirmative accounts of American empire discussed in Chapter 1 argued that the public goods flowing from the war on terror would include the provision of 'order' and 'stability' in 'unstable' regions vital to US strategic interests. After 9/11, however, a number of these regions were demonstrably more unstable than previously.

Like a self-fulfilling prophecy the Bush administration's attacks on international law also weakened further institutions and frameworks whose future already looked uncertain in the new unipolar world order at the end of the Cold War. By 2005, the historian John Ikenberry was situating Bush administration unilateralism in the context of a 'systematic erosion of the authority and capacities of international institutions and regimes in the security, economic, and political realms'. This amounted to a full-blown crisis, Ikenberry felt, in 'the global system of rule-based cooperation'. Ikenberry's 'crisis' was carefully defined as an imbalance of political supply and demand. Whereas 'the demand for cooperative mechanisms and institutionalized collective action' was growing, he said, the supply was dwindling. At the precise historical moment when the complexities and dangers of an increasingly integrated and globalised international order meant that 'the world will need more, not less, institutionalised co-operation', in Ikenberry's estimation 'almost all of the world's global and regional governance institutions' had weakened since 9/11. The crisis in international governance, he said, was generated 'primarily' by the US, where the experience of American unipolarity seemed to have created 'problems in how the United States thinks about the provision of international rules, institutions, and public goods' (Ikenberry 2005: 414–15). The irony for Ikenberry, and for other likeminded contemporaries, was that the adventurism that the Bush Doctrine authorised in the name of national security served only to weaken American influence over other groups and nation-states, while further endangering American citizens (see also Nye 2002).

Assembled rhetorically around exporting democracy with 'the ultimate goal of ending tyranny in the world' (NSS 2006: 1), the Bush Doctrine helped precipitate a 'crisis' in republican democracy at home. Alongside the narratives of political resolution to this 'crisis' that had gathered pace by the end of 2006, the Bush Doctrine helped perpetuate contemporary 'crisis' sensibilities deep into Bush's second term. What was most notable about the new *National Security Strategy* (issued in March 2006 – a new *NSS* is required annually by law, but updates to 2002 were delayed by the Iraq war) was how little had changed. The 2006 *NSS* included a chapter on issues omitted in 2002, including genocide and AIDS, and declared diplomacy to be 'our strong preference' (ibid.: 23) for tackling threats from WMD. But it also reaffirmed the 2002 statement's core principles and policy thrusts, and included a trenchant defence of the doctrine of 'pre-emptive' war.

---

1. The story about Iraq trying to buy uranium in Niger during the late 1990s also surfaced in a British government white paper on Iraqi weapons of mass destruction in September 2002, the 'September Dossier' – a document that would be the subject of intense public controversy in Britain during the 2003 Hutton Inquiry into the death of Ministry of Defence employee, David Kelly. Dr Kelly had been the source for a BBC story alleging that the Blair government had 'sexed up' the September Dossier, to make fraudulent assertions about Iraqi weapons of mass destruction.
2. The principal reason for committing time and money to 'building international relationships and institutions' (a significantly different proposition to maintaining or nurturing existing ones), was that 'we have finite political, economic, and military resources to meet our global priorities' (NSS 2002: 9).
3. For the full text of the memo, see Greenberg and Dratel (2005: 172–217). By contrast, see the definition of torture in the UN Convention against Torture and Other Cruel, Inhuman or Degrading Treatment or Punishment (1984), which states that torture includes 'any act by which severe pain or suffering, whether physical or mental, is intentionally inflicted' for the purposes of obtaining information or a confession. Under such a definition,

torture can include psychological as well as physical maltreatment, and detention without trial in solitary confinement. The same emphasis on mental as well as physical suffering pertains in the US federal anti-torture statute (1994), referred to formally as Title 18, Part I, Chapter 113C of the U.S. Code, 1994. It is notable that the Defense Department responded in a similar legalistic fashion to Bybee, when accused of using white phosphorus as a chemical weapon during the siege of Fallujah in 2004. The Pentagon split legal hairs over the definition of chemical weapons, arguing that because white phosphorus burned people but didn't poison them, it should be classified as an incendiary weapon not a chemical one, and that legal constraints on its use were therefore the provenance of the UN Protocol on Incendiary Weapons 1980, to which the US was not a signatory (Monbiot 2005). For Monbiot, use of white phosphorus in Fallujah was a war crime.

4. While Bush faced significant opposition in Congress before and after the 2006 midterms, in the weeks after 9/11 Congress was twice accused of failing in its role as an effective check and balance on executive authority. The hugely controversial Patriot Act was passed by Congress with minimal debate – the ACLU estimated that 'most' members 'did not even read the bill' (ACLU 2003) – with majorities of 357: 66 in the House, and 98: 1 in the Senate (ibid.). Congress was accused of writing blank cheques for the White House over the war in Afghanistan. Voting on a 'Joint Resolution Allowing Military Action' on 14 September 2001 went 420: 1 and 98: 0 in favour of allowing the president to wage war on an unidentified enemy.

3 Mass Media

Throttling the Life from the Republican Fourth Estate

There's a lovely moment in an early Bob Dylan song where Dylan, playing the role of the hobo troubadour in the style of Woody Guthrie, is talking about the freezing winter weather. The *New York Times*, so the song goes, said it was the coldest winter in seventeen years. Having heard that from the *Times*, Dylan's character drolly observes, he no longer felt so cold.

The old adage about not believing what's printed in the *New York Times* was revived during the war on terror, not least by the spectacle of the *Times* itself publicly apologising, in May 2004, for its coverage of the lead-up to war in Iraq. The paper acknowledged falling for 'official gullibility and hype' in its coverage of Iraq's alleged weapons of mass destruction capabilities. 'In some cases', the 26 May editorial said, 'information that was controversial then, and seems questionable now, was insufficiently qualified or allowed to stand unchallenged. Looking back, we wish we had been more aggressive in re-examining the claims as new evidence emerged – or failed to emerge' (*New York Times* 2004). It wasn't the raciest *mea culpa* of the war, and the paper hedged its apology by transferring at least some of the blame to its sources; but from the *New York Times* this was heady stuff, reflecting Media Studies commentary that was often highly critical of corporate American news outlets after 9/11.

Early evaluations of US media coverage of the 9/11 attacks were replete with critics lining up to accuse American journalism of abandoning its republican obligations in the rush to wage war on 'terror'. Waging such a war, Robert McChesney noted, would have momentous implications, including significant political and economic costs – cuts in non-military services, falling standards of living for some, the curtailing of civil liberties – as well as the cost in lives. In a democracy, he suggested, a decision with such grave consequences should be made 'with the informed consent of the governed. Otherwise, the claim to be a democratic nation is dubious, if not fraudulent' (McChesney 2002:

92). However, early accounts of how corporate news outlets in the US covered 9/11 agreed to a remarkable extent that 'the media was complicit in narrowing, rather than broadening, meaningful discourse' about the attacks, and had contributed significantly to a 'confinement of the parameters of meaningful citizen debate' about appropriate American responses (Reynolds and Barnett 2003: 101). Voices like Reynolds, Barnett and McChesney, each of whom contributed essays to the two major collections of early 9/11 Media Studies (Zelizer and Allan 2002a; Chermak et al. 2003), spoke for many contemporary media analysts who protested that corporate US media had failed to provide even an outline discussion of the contexts from which the 9/11 attacks had sprung. After 9/11 it was not surprising, Douglas Kellner observed, that Americans should close ranks; but in such extraordinary circumstances closing ranks was not a republican media's job. The job that the media should have been doing, Kellner suggested, included providing 'clarification of the historical background of the event, intelligent discussion of rational and effective responses, and debate [about] what responses would be most appropriate and successful in dealing with the problem of global terrorism' (Kellner 2003: 65). For Kellner, as for many observers, the American media failed each of these republican tests both on 9/11 and in the weeks that followed, offering instead an 'exceptionally impoverished understanding of the historical context of terrorism and war' (ibid.: 69).

Critical discussion about American mass media coverage of 9/11 and the war on terror, led by public intellectuals like Kellner and key collections like Zelizer and Allan's *Journalism After September 11*, and Chermak et al.'s *Media Representations of 9/11*, re-energised traditional Media Studies debates about appropriate relationships between journalism and state power and about the contradictory interests of a republican media following democratic agendas and a capitalist media following market ones. Since the sweeping deregulation of the industry by the Reagan administrations of the 1980s, patterns of consolidation and concentration in the corporate ownership of US media had led, it was argued after 9/11, to a relative homogenising of editorial opinion in conglomerate news outlets and to cuts in less profitable programming about international affairs and foreign news contexts – a key factor in early media descriptions of 9/11 as a baffling, inexplicable or motiveless event. 'Whereas Americans once tended to be misinformed about world politics', McChesney wrote, 'now they are uninformed', a state of affairs, he said, that highlighted 'a deep contradiction between the legitimate informational needs of a democratic society and the need for profit of the corporate media' (McChesney 2002: 99). McChesney was an established figure on the Media Studies left, but after 9/11 his comments sounded distinctly mainstream. Journalism was described in the preface to the Zelizer and Allan collection as 'the circulation system of our democracy' (Navasky 2002: xiii). For many critics, though, during the early years of the war on terror it was a system that often seemed profoundly out of step with the values of republican democracy.

One prominent debate about 9/11 coverage concerned the eroding of notional standards of objectivity and detachment in news media. The main strand of this debate borrowed allusively from established discourses of sociological and psychological 'trauma', characterising print and broadcast journalism in the US by the vanishing of 'detached vantage-points situated "outside" the crisis' (Zelizer and Allan 2002b: 1) – points from which journalists could observe and report unfolding events. By this analogy 9/11 was 'traumatic', and media accounts of the day were 'traumatised', because the scale of the event and the multiple concurrent impacts that the attacks had on life in the US turned journalists into subjective participants in, rather than objective observers of, events. 9/11 was a cataclysm of such magnitude, it was suggested, that it abolished media industry concepts such as 'critical distance' and 'observer-hood' (Rosen 2002: 27, 28), making objective reportage impossible. Early Media Studies analysis of corporate media coverage of 9/11 seemed to support these findings, suggesting that the prevailing media 'frames' applied to events on the day corresponded closely with dominant ideological 'frames' in American society at large, and that coverage of the attacks by both print and broadcast media displayed a remarkable unanimity in the meanings that they attributed to the day's events.[1]

For professional media analysts reporting on reporters, the implications of such 'traumatised' news coverage were alarming, eradicating, it appeared, the very premises on which a properly republican fourth estate should function – a conceptual distance from centres of political power; sceptical scrutiny of governmental decision-making; uninhibited channelling of information to the public; the capacity to foster debate about appropriate policy options. In one famous example, Bush's National Security Adviser and future Secretary of State Condoleezza Rice, phoned the heads of all the network TV news divisions and asked them to stop screening video statements by Osama bin Laden. The networks, as Victor Navasky put it, simply 'caved in' (Navasky 2002: xv). In another, veteran CBS news anchor Dan Rather appeared on *The Late Show With David Letterman* (CBS) and wept on air as he pledged to follow his president wherever Bush might lead. The Rather episode, and the 'traumatised' climate within American corporate media, may have captured something of the prevailing public mood. Yet the CBS switchboard still jammed with calls from outraged viewers. For many media observers and many American citizens, Rather on the Letterman show was at once the acme and the nadir of the networks' response to 9/11 (see Bird 2002; Navasky 2002; Tumber 2002; Waisbord 2002; Zelizer and Allan 2002a; Kellner 2003; Snow 2003).

First-generation Media Studies accounts of 9/11 in the US also borrowed from clinical and sociological models of trauma by describing the attacks as 'large-scale cataclysmic events that shatter a prior sense of what it means, in moral terms, to remain part of a collective' (Zelizer and Allan 2002b: 2). Describing 9/11 as a 'trauma' in this way implied a breakdown in embedded models of communal identity, particularly in symbols and signifiers of national 'American' belonging. 9/11 was widely described in the print and broadcast media of the time in precisely these terms, as a loss of American innocence or impregnability, as a turning point in American history and as a fundamental reconfiguring of what it meant to be a citizen of the United States. As nodal points for rapid flows of information in a time of crisis and as communications networks linking Americans together, corporate American media, particularly TV, played a vital role in mitigating this sudden subsidence in symbols of collective American belonging by reaffirming some of its core totems. The presidency as national *paterfamilias*, or symbolic father to the nation, for example, was one symbol of collective belonging that seemed to be jeopardised on September 11, as Bush vanished into the interior of the continent on Air Force One, and stumbled badly during the brief appearances he made in front of the cameras (see Kellner 2003; Smith 2003). By the time the president finally returned to Washington that night, to address the nation live on TV in another disconcerting appearance that did little to reassure viewers, questions were being asked about Bush's ability to lead in a crisis as commander in chief. The networks, however, were undaunted. CNN assured its audience that Bush was invisible because he was 'marshalling all the resources of the federal government'. NPR anchor Bob Edwards speculated that Bush might have left for an 'alternative White House in the Blue Ridge Mountains'. Even ABC's Peter Jennings, one of the few network anchors to question Bush's actions on 9/11, suggested on air that the president's absence could be explained by the fact that he was manning a reassuringly sci-fi sounding 'command center in the sky' (Smith 2003: 90). If 9/11 and its aftermath sometimes threatened the mythos of the commander in chief as father to the nation, network TV's engrained assumptions and reflex assertions about the statesmanlike leadership of American presidents during times of national crisis went some way towards putting those symbols back together again, even as events unfolded as live breaking news (ibid.).

This moral role played by mass media – 'moral' in the sense that it reaffirmed core signifiers of collective American belonging – was particularly pronounced in what the first generation of 9/11 Media Studies described as the uncritical patriotism propagated by corporate journalism, both on September 11 itself and in the aftermath, as momentum built for war on Afghanistan. The uncritical patriotism that flooded TV screens, radio airwaves, magazines and newsprint after 9/11 was partly a function or reflex of trauma, in the sense that it helped reconstruct the abstract collective entity threatened by 'terror' – 'America', and the things 'America' meant in the dominant media frame: freedom, civilisation, innocence, resolve, victimhood, unity and the pursuit of justice via legitimate war. One manifestation of this was the proliferation of what Silvio Waisbord called 'banal nationalism', a phrase borrowed from Michael Billig to denote a saturation of corporate mass media forms in 'everyday reminders of the nation' (Waisbord 2002: 206; see also Billig 1995). References to Pearl Harbor, constructing 9/11 as a new 'day of infamy', quickly became one of the day's most widely used media clichés. Images of US senators singing 'God Bless America' on the steps of the Capitol on the evening of 9/11 were everywhere in print and broadcast media. The image of the American flag in particular – sometimes displayed metonymically in the red, white and blue of on-screen graphics (see, for example, CNN's 'America Under Attack' graphic theme) – was instantly pervasive (Kellner 2003: 67).

Corporate media coverage of 9/11 also entailed a specific reconstruction of the meaning of 'America' as a body politic galvanised for war (see Zelizer 2002). The dominant TV frame in live breaking news coverage by the networks positioned the attacks as acts of war for which the only appropriate response was rapid and massive military retaliation (indicatively, see McChesney 2002; Waisbord 2002; Kellner 2003; Reynolds and Barnett 2003; Hoskins 2005). Reynolds and Barnett's analysis of CNN's breaking news coverage of 9/11, which considered combinations of keywords, visual images, graphics inserted onto the top and bottom of the screen and opinions offered by CNN's 'expert' sources, found the word 'war' repeated 234 times in the first twelve hours of coverage, or once every three minutes on average. These included references to Pearl Harbor, statements to the effect that war had been declared on American values not American policies, and repeated suggestions that only by waging war could America construct a meaningful response to the day's events. Compounding the repetition of these spoken references, Reynolds and Barnett also highlighted the network's 'arousing' presentation of repeated and looped footage of the attacks, a visual frame they suggested leant emotional credence to expert sources' description of the destruction as *a priori* acts of war.

One question that was widely asked in the first generation of 9/11 Media Studies was why the 'trauma' of 9/11 hadn't promoted a 'civic' or 'constitutional patriotism' which might have prioritised embedded American values other than nationalism primed for war – versions of patriotism, for example, that might have emphasised the republican role of the media as a scrutinising check and balance on government; or a patriotism that insisted on the plurality of responses to 9/11 that seemed incumbent on a republican fourth estate. The opting for a hawkish, nationalist, warmongering patriotism, it was suggested, vitiated these republican commitments with 'important consequences for democratic life' (Waisbord 2002: 216).

One widely noted answer to this question was the limited range of sources on which the media relied for expert comment and analysis. This was particularly problematic on network television, where breaking live coverage of 9/11 turned almost exclusively to figures from within the military, political and intelligence establishments. Many of those interviewed had close links with US defence industries and a clear interest in advocating military solutions to the crisis (McChesney 2002: 97; Kellner 2003: 54–5). As McChesney argued, the preference for establishment figures as expert sources reflected an institutionally engrained discourse identifying media 'professionalism' with respectful access to figures in or close to centres of state power. This discourse placed disproportionate weight on 'official or credentialed sources', and tended to ignore alternative or popular ones. According to conventional news values in corporate American media, McChesney noted, 'When a journalist reports what official sources are saying, or debating, she is professional. When she steps outside this range of official debate to provide alternative perspectives or to raise issues those in power prefer not to discuss, she is no longer being professional' (McChesney 2002: 95). For McChesney this code constituted an abnegation of the media's responsibility to monitor those in power and hold them accountable once elected to office. Reynolds' and Barnett's breakdown of the first twelve hours of CNN's live coverage of 9/11 seemed to illustrate McChesney's point exactly, finding that CNN 'relied almost exclusively on current and former government officials to provide interpretation of the day's events and to effectively frame what had happened and what would happen as a result' (Reynolds and Barnett 2003: 91). During those first twelve hours, they noted, CNN did not interview a single 'official' source with any political affiliation other than to the two main parties. Having established that the spectrum of political opinion on the day's events was limited to Republican and Democratic Party sources, and having found that these sources were 'unified', CNN decided that 'the entire country was unified', discounting alternative or dissenting viewpoints that might have fostered a more inclusive debate about why the attacks had taken place and about the range of appropriate American responses to them. Not once during those twelve hours, Reynolds and Barnett noted, 'did anyone, source or journalist, suggest that an option other than supporting the president would exist' (ibid.: 95, 94).

The debate about sources in corporate news was also significant because of the limitations it revealed in the theoretical modelling of 9/11 coverage as 'trauma' journalism. Contextualising 9/11 media in models adapted from studies of psychological and sociological 'trauma' quickly became a defining paradigm in early 9/11 Media Studies, but it was problematic on several levels. The proposition that media coverage lacked critical distance on those in power and an informed perspective on America's place in the world because journalists were traumatised by 9/11 was particularly problematic, with its implicit claim that objective 'observerhood' unconstrained by ideology had been the normal order of things in US media, until these professional standards were displaced by 'terror'. In many ways 9/11 didn't so much effect a shift in corporate media practices as reveal existing ones in heightened and more transparent forms. Contemporary critics using the 'trauma' model to discuss 9/11 media would often have agreed with this. Almost by definition, however, the 'trauma' figure seemed to downplay the extent to which 9/11 coverage was the product of more deeply rooted tendencies and trends in the organisation of corporate news gathering and presentation in the US.

Explanations of 9/11 as a trauma inflicted on journalists also ran the risk of underestimating the extent to which journalists themselves helped construct the event as trauma. The flooding of the media sphere with 'banal' signifiers of national belonging, displayed alongside visual, written and spoken accounts of the attacks, extended participation in 9/11 to all Americans, anywhere, who had access to print, broadcast or alternative electronic media. One contemporary observer even described 9/11 as a media 'fabrication', in the sense that its construction as a pervasive and universal trauma was possible only because saturation media coverage opened 9/11 to universal participation by national and global audiences, irrespective of their remoteness from New York or Washington (Breithaupt 2003). As Breithaupt put it, 'The media are the apparatus that make possible the repetition of events, that amplify the magnitude of events, that offer events as an experience to those who were not present, and that bridge spatial and temporal orders (such as the past and present)' (ibid.: 68). Saturation media coverage of 9/11, in a society saturated by media, proliferated participation in 9/11, helping construct the attacks as trauma by collapsing the distinctions between those who experienced the attacks at first hand and those traumatised by images of them, and between those traumatised in real time and those traumatised after the fact in media replay time. When the World Trade Center towers collapsed, the scale of the audience facilitated by twenty-first-century mass media meant that the event was 'real' on the day for millions of Americans, as well as countless billions around the world, and then endlessly 'real' again and again, through the constant recycling of images that had long since ceased to be conventionally newsworthy, in the days, weeks, months and years ahead.

A number of the debates shaping early 9/11 Media Studies spilled over into discussion of how the US media covered the war in Iraq. As with 9/11, early discussion focused on issues arising from the problematic idea of reporters' objectivity or detachment in wartime, and the extent to which media coverage reflected or was influenced by agendas set by state authorities. As had been the case with major American conflicts since Vietnam, the Iraq war was widely described at the time as a 'media war', a war fought not just with cruise missiles, car bombs and rocket-propelled grenades, but also with images; a conflict in which opposing sides made extensive use of corporate and alternative media to circulate communications and propaganda among large numbers of people in both friendly and 'enemy' populations.

The White House's and Pentagon's attempts to manage the news agenda on Iraq encompassed a variety of initiatives, from vigorous attempts to confine or spin the contexts in which the media could report the war to fabrication of news stories and direct intimidation by military violence. It also involved an extensive and controversial programme of 'embedding' reporters with troops on the ground – a programme that included military training camps for journalists in the US, administered directly by the Pentagon. The Pentagon and White House also made direct use of global media to construct what one critic referred to at the time as an 'actuarial gaze' – ways of looking at the world that promoted risk assessment strategies by America's enemies that would be favourable to US interests, in images that were designed to intimidate, by using threatening, often ethnocentric, visual imagery (Feldman 2005). One example of the 'actuarial gaze' was the Bush administration's use of global media platforms to threaten Saddam Hussein and the Iraqi people. When he appeared on television on 17 March 2003 to deliver a final ultimatum to Saddam, instructing him to leave Iraq within 48 hours in what was effectively a declaration of war, Bush took the opportunity to speak directly to ordinary Iraqis. 'Many Iraqis can hear me tonight in a translated broadcast', he said, 'and I have a message for them'. Both the message and the medium – footage of the President of the United States threatening Iraqis, broadcast to a global audience – were 'actuarial'. 'Your fate', Bush said, speaking straight to camera, with pauses and emphases on key words, 'will depend on your actions. And it will be no defence to say "I was just following orders"'. Actuarial use of the media was not just the provenance of Americans. Iraqi insurgents, suicide bombers, Osama bin Laden and leaders in other Islamist groups – notably kidnappers in Iraq – all made extensive use of video to construct self-consciously 'actuarial' footage, which was then publicised worldwide via favoured media outlets (notably the Al Jazeera satellite television station in Qatar). In Western print and broadcast media and on the internet, DIY footage showing 'martyrdom' statements by suicide bombers, Western hostages pleading for their lives, and insurgency leaders addressing Western politicians and their electorates, became one commonplace rhythm of the media war during the early war on terror.

The idea of a media war may not have been new, but the intensity with which state agencies sought to administer the news agenda on Iraq was unprecedented. With the proliferation of 'new' or 'alternative' media, particularly the internet and Arab satellite TV (both of which, by 2003, had become mainstream suppliers of news to large numbers of people), managing the news in wartime was harder than it had ever been. Both the Pentagon and White House approached press conferences and media briefings as opportunities to spin events aggressively in their favour to global audiences, and in many respects media access to the Iraq war was more extensively policed than any previous American conflict. This did not mean that the US military or the Bush administration were always successful in persuading the media to report the lines that the Pentagon and White House wanted them to report. Journalists were often highly aware of the confined contexts in which they were being encouraged to discuss events and were often resistant to the restrictions imposed on them – the practice of 'embedding' reporters with troops, in particular, often produced invasion journalism that was as much about the military's attempts to regulate the reporting of the war as it was about the war itself (see Katovsky and Carlson 2003; Hoskins 2004; Lewis and Brookes 2004; Tumber 2004).

Even the most self-conscious of embeds produced journalism that called into question the flow of 'objective' republican reportage to citizens. Exposed at first hand to the rigours of frontline combat, embedded reporters often inserted themselves into the stories they filed, offering personalised and highly subjective accounts of the circumstances of the troops with whom they travelled. Stories from embedded reporters usually focused on tightly circumscribed contexts – the military world, the personal experience of the reporter and a handful of troops, 'the here-and-now . . . and the recent past' (Hoskins 2004: 63). In this way the system reproduced intensely rendered fragments of war and impressionistic accounts of military travel through and between combat zones – 'spectacle' images that were Hollywoodesque in their ability to conjure heightened, vicarious experiences of war, but which 'served to compress media coverage into a series of disconnected snapshots', providing compelling 'infotainment' television, but 'little opportunity for sustained critical media or public discourse to emerge on the overall waging of the war and its longer-term consequences' (ibid.: 75).

As Philip Taylor noted at the time, military news management during war has often been characterised 'more by media co-operation than by military-media conflict', with reporters accustomed to gaining access to events in return for restrictions on what they can and cannot say (Taylor 2004: 231). This was true of the embed system in Iraq too, though the terms of the deal seemed loaded more heavily than ever against journalists. The 'deal' proposed by the Pentagon gave embedded journalists first-hand access to scenes of combat and conquest, with the proviso that the only safe place for them to be was under the watchful eye and operational control of the US military. For Hoskins, the Pentagon's adoption of the embed system as its only approved mode for reporting the war, and the routinising of 24-hour contact between the military and the media, flagged 'diminishing prospects for objective and detached reporting' (Hoskins 2004: 61). Simply put, it was harder for journalists to be objective or detached in the reports they sent home when they ate, slept and worked alongside troops on whom they depended for their lives in a war zone.

Other accounts identified issues that brought the embed system into conflict with the freedom of the press. An independent report on embedded journalism during the invasion of Iraq, commissioned by the BBC and conducted by researchers at the University of Cardiff, rejected claims that embedded journalism was shaped overtly by 'interference and censorship', but did identify 'significant areas of concern' in embedded media culture (Lewis et al. 2004). Among these significant concerns, the report observed that during the invasion and early occupation of Iraq the refusal of Western media to show graphic or violent images had 'profound' ideological consequences, with embedded reporters 'forced by current constraints to produce a kind of coverage which may, for some, make war appear more acceptable'. Worryingly, the Cardiff researchers also found that the welcome extended to embedded reporters 'was accompanied by a greater disregard for the welfare of independent journalists – particularly by US forces' (ibid.).

During the invasion of Iraq, US forces took what looked like carefully orchestrated military action against journalists working for news organisations publicly identified as hostile to US interests by senior figures in the Bush administration. On 8 April 2003, American planes fired two missiles at Al Jazeera's offices in Baghdad, killing the reporter Tareq Ayyoub and wounding his cameraman, in a bombing that prompted the station's immediate withdrawal from the country. On the same day, the Baghdad studios of Abu Dhabi TV were also bombed. The attacks on Al Jazeera and Abu Dhabi TV raised questions about a third controversial incident on the same day, the shelling of the Palestine Hotel – well known as a base for journalists covering the invasion – by a tank from the US Army's 3rd Infantry Division. Two cameramen, Taras Protsyuk from Reuters and José Couso, a cameraman from the Spanish TV station Telecinco, were killed. A Pentagon report on the incident published in November 2004 denied 'fault or negligence' on the part of the army (USAFCC 2004). Nevertheless, the Army's findings had already been contested by an inquiry conducted by the Committee to Protect Journalists (CPJ) – an independent, non-profit-making organisation that monitors press freedoms around the world – which found that senior military officers who were aware that the hotel was filled with journalists had not conveyed this information to troops on the ground (Campagna and Roumani 2003). The Pentagon's report, it noted, left open the question of 'why troops were not made aware of the presence of journalists at the hotel' (CPJ 2004). Other concerns were raised over the Army's handling of its report, which was completed as early as June 2003 but not made public until November 2004, when a Freedom of Information Act request filed by the CPJ forced the Pentagon's hand. When the report was finally released, the identities of the investigating officers, the names of troops involved in the incident and other information about military manoeuvres in Baghdad on 8 April had all been heavily censored. The report did find time, however, to reiterate the Pentagon's line about the vulnerability of non-embedded media workers. As an exercise in the republican accountability of state institutions it left a lot to be desired.[2]

Away from the fighting too the Pentagon devoted significant time, money and personnel to managing the news agenda on Iraq. One institution that figured prominently was the reputedly 'million-dollar' media facility operated by the military at CentCom (US Central Command, US military headquarters in the Middle East) in the Gulf state of Qatar. Designed to centralise flows of information from the military to the media in a controlled military environment, the media centre at CentCom became the conduit through which official military briefings and statements on the prosecution of the war were released to reporters. CentCom also allowed for private, informal meetings between journalists and troops employed to liaise with the media to push the military's line on any given issue. Since it was based in Qatar, CentCom had the added advantage, for the Pentagon, of keeping some of the world's best-known journalists at a healthy distance from direct access to what was happening on the ground in Iraq.

During the invasion, managing the news at CentCom also meant inventing the news, then feeding it to a captive US media whose preference for soundbites and sensationalism made it hungry for drama and tales of American heroism. On 2 April 2003, journalists at CentCom were called in the middle of the night to be briefed on the story of Jessica Lynch, a servicewoman from the US Army's 570th Ordnance Maintenance Company who was captured by Iraqi soldiers and 'rescued' from a hospital by US special forces (Figure 3.1). The rescue had been filmed by participating troops and the footage released to the media with accounts of a daring raid conducted under fire. It was reported by the military that Lynch herself had sustained serious bullet and stab wounds. CentCom spun it as a story about a wounded American innocent, the heroism of soldiers who would not leave a comrade behind and the actions of a courageous Iraqi lawyer who had reported Lynch's whereabouts to US forces at great personal risk, and thrown himself, instinctively it seemed, behind the occupation. Unsurprisingly, with so many compelling narrative elements jostling for space, the tale instantly became part of American war on terror mythography. Such was Lynch's fame during the Bush years that her newsworthiness even outlived her tour of duty in Iraq, with reporters filing follow-up stories about her return to civilian life, her pregnancy and her progress at West Virginia University, where she enrolled as a student in 2005 (indicatively, see CBS 2005; USA Today 2006).

The most significant thing about the Jessica Lynch story was its timing. The Americans were still to take Baghdad, the invasion seemed bogged down and for reporters assigned to CentCom the limited quantity and quality of information flowing from the military had been frustrating. The Jessica Lynch story seemed too good to be true, and so it proved. Few of the details of the episode subsequently provided by Iraqi witnesses corresponded with the version in the five minutes of edited

Figure 3.1 CentCom, Doha, 2 April 2003. US Army Brigadier General Vincent Brooks briefs journalists on the rescue of Jessica Lynch, who can be seen on the screen behind Brooks. Video footage of the rescue was shown to reporters during the press conference.
© Reuters/Corbis.

tape provided by the military, which declined to produce the rest of the footage when challenged. It soon appeared that Iraqi troops stationed around the hospital from which Lynch was rescued had already fled their positions before the Americans arrived, and that her injuries, which included neither bullet nor stab wounds, had been sustained not as a result of combat or assault during captivity, but in a road traffic accident. 'We heard the noise of helicopters', said Dr Anmar Uday, one of the doctors at the hospital to which Lynch was taken by her captors. 'We were surprised. Why do this? There was no military, there were no soldiers in the hospital. It was like a Hollywood film. They cried "Go, go, go," with guns and blanks and the sound of explosions. They made a show – an action movie like Sylvester Stallone or Jackie Chan, with jumping and shouting, breaking down doors' (in Kampfner 2003). On 15 May 2003, barely six weeks after the Lynch story broke, one British broadsheet described the episode as 'one of the most stunning pieces of news management yet conceived', providing 'a remarkable insight into the real influence of Hollywood producers on the Pentagon's media managers' (ibid.).

The Jessica Lynch episode was not an isolated incident. Staging spectacular events for media (i.e. public) consumption was an important tool in the media war fought by the Pentagon and White House. Sometimes, particularly if the pictures were good enough, reporters appeared happy to co-operate. When US troops entered Baghdad, the toppling of Saddam's statue in Firdus Square on 9 April (the day after the bombing of Al Jazeera, Abhu Dhabi TV and the Palestine Hotel) provided some of the truly iconic images of the war, offering symbolic confirmation that 'regime change' had taken place. Photos, footage and most written or spoken accounts from Western reporters depicted the toppling of the statue as a spontaneous act by a crowd of Iraqis who were grateful for their liberation and who were assisted by US troops who happened to be passing. These were the 'frames' that dominated embedded American and British news coverage of the event, accompanied by close shots of the crowds celebrating, the statue falling, the troops assisting. Filmed from further away and from a different angle, however, as in Jehane Noujaim's acclaimed documentary about Al Jazeera, *Control Room* (2004), the pictures told a different story. A relatively small group of predominantly young men – in *Control Room* a senior Al Jazeera journalist claimed they were not Iraqis – were shepherded into the square by a column of American troops who came prepared for the task at hand. Three weeks later, in another example of the administration's fondness for news management by spectacular fabrication, Bush appeared on the flight deck of the aircraft carrier *USS Abraham Lincoln*, in full pilot's gear, to announce that the war was over and to provide the world's media with images of a warrior president returning safely from battle, having led his troops heroically from the front (Figure 3.2). Bush's role in the stunt was compared at the time, usually satirically, to that of fictional US President Thomas Whitmore in Roland Emmerich's Hollywood blockbuster, *Independence Day* (1996). The intended effect was spoiled further when it became clear that the *Lincoln* was lying off the California coastline at the time of Bush's dramatic touchdown, nowhere near the war.

The White House's and Pentagon's penchant for over-scripted media stunts, and CentCom's attempts to foist them on reporters at the expense of hard news from a properly accountable, republican military, alienated some journalists and devalued the military briefing as a form of newsgathering (Hoskins 2004: 71). Part of the media's frustration at CentCom was their dual awareness that they were being managed and manipulated, but were relatively powerless to intervene in or redirect the agendas being set for them. For many journalists who spent

Figure 3.2 President Bush on the *USS Abraham Lincoln*, 1 May 2003.
© Reuters/Corbis.

time at CentCom during 2003, all that could be learned there, it
seemed, was that the Pentagon had spent a million dollars on a facility
designed to tell the world's media as little as possible about the war, at
as great a distance as seemed feasible from it, in an environment where
the military gave itself the best possible shot at controlling the unpredictable flows of information generated during armed conflict.
CentCom was an attempt to throttle the life from a functionally republican fourth estate during a time of national and international crisis, and
within its own limited frame of reference it was successful at doing this.
Yet the frame of reference was sometimes difficult to contain in Qatar.
Journalists' awareness that their presence at CentCom made them
peripheral to the war promoted press resentments as well as news management. One consequence of the military's co-ordinated attempts to
control information flows was that news management itself sometimes
became the story. When the PBS TV network produced a series of the
current affairs show *Frontline* looking at the pressures on contemporary
news media in spring 2007, PBS publicity material described the
content of episodes 1 and 2 as 'the key cases and fundamental principles in the battles between the administration and the press' (PBS
2007a). Interviewed for the *Frontline* series, the veteran investigative
reporter Carl Bernstein described the Bush administration as
'Nixonian in character, in its willingness to manipulate the press', and
attributed to the White House and the office of the vice president a
campaign of 'disinformation, misinformation and unwillingness to tell

the truth' that went beyond even Nixon. The administration's attempts at controlling the news, Bernstein added, were 'something that I have never witnessed before on this scale' (PBS 2007b).

One reason that the Pentagon and White House went to such lengths to centralise and manage the flow of information to the media during the Iraq war was the exponential growth of the internet. Containing information flows in an age when new media forms proliferated endlessly the outlets through which accounts of the war could be packaged and accessed presented the Pentagon with new problems. The rush of net traffic from the US to Al Jazeera's English-language website, for example, when it launched on 24 March 2003, four days after the invasion began, was another story about media that was widely covered in contemporary Western news outlets. The first generation of post-9/11 Media Studies often contrasted the narrow parameters and 'banal nationalism' of corporate US media with the willingness of web users to explore dissonant or dissenting points of view. 'In the global information space dominated by Anglo-American multinational media organizations that traditionally can be relied upon to support "our wars"', one commentator noted, the internet allowed 'an alternative voice to be heard' (Taylor 2004: 241).

Alternative news sites flourished after 9/11, but it was dangerous to generalise about their 'alternative' news content just because they were on the internet. The web's ability to make vast quantities of information instantly available to users has often been taken as evidence of its potential or actual role as a subversive popular technology. Yet 'even a glance', as one contemporary put it, at the roster of names behind some of the major US news sites (AOL Time Warner, General Electric, Microsoft, Walt Disney, Viacom) made it obvious that what counted as 'news' about 9/11 and the war on terror would be 'constrained within the limits of corporate culture' (Allan 2002: 136). Major corporate news providers organised dedicated 9/11 websites linked from their institution's homepages, archiving 9/11 using the same frames that dominated their coverage in the traditional print and broadcast outlets to which the websites belonged. In the corporate archiving of 9/11 in cyberspace, one research group concluded, 'explanatory accounts were predominantly missing, with an origin most generally grounded in the digitized imagining of the specific moment of aircraft impact into the World Trade Center, with no explicit connection to events that precede that moment or that day' (Brown et al. 2003: 109). Notably absent from corporate sites, Brown et al. found, was 'an open discussion of context', while interactivity on such sites was commonly understood by providers 'solely as a click' (ibid.: 114, 115).

Away from the corporate sites analysts often worried about prove-nance, noting that the diversity of sources and locations issuing 'new media' news were frequently difficult to assess for quality and accuracy (see Allan 2002: 127). Sometimes this leant a subversive *frisson* to net coverage of the war. The war in Iraq brought urgency and momentum to the kinetic contemporary fashion for 'blogging' – a trend that the *New York Times* ruefully acknowledged reflected 'a popular thirst for information that at least appears unfiltered by the anchors and editors of the traditional media' (Harmon 2003). One invasion blog, by an anonymous Iraqi who called himself Salam Pax ('peace' in Arabic and 'peace' in Latin) was widely covered in mainstream US and British media, where Pax became briefly famous as 'the Baghdad Blogger' and had excerpts from his site published in book form as *The Baghdad Blog* (2003). Before and during the invasion, Pax posted updates to a blog called *Where is Raed?* (2003–4), on the mood among Iraqi civilians in Baghdad. His status as a dissident in Saddam's Iraq meant that he kept his identity and location a secret, and speculation that *Where is Raed?* was an elaborate hoax and that Pax was actually working for the CIA or even the Ba'ath Party was rife in both internet and mainstream media outlets.

Subversive *frisson* or not, politically there was nothing particularly 'alternative' about *Where is Raed?*, at least not in the West. Pax's stance on the invasion was complex, but it chimed comfortably with the sen-timents of Western liberals who welcomed the end of Saddam's regime, but who remained ambivalent about the Bush Doctrine and about the motives of the occupation. This gave Pax a near-perfect fit with the edi-torial line of the *Guardian*, for example (one of the Western newspapers for which Pax would subsequently write a series of columns and articles about the war), whose concerned liberalism perhaps saw in *Where is Raed?* both an embodiment of their readers' own opinions on the war and the paper's wish-list of what a post-Saddam Iraqi might be – grate-ful for Western intervention but sceptical of American strategy and power projection, educated, middle-class, English-speaking, attuned to Western popular culture, reliant on corporate Western media for news (as well as other war blogs, corporate sources Pax cited included web-sites maintained by the *New York Times*, *Washington Post*, CNN, ABC News, the BBC, the *Economist*, the *Guardian* and the *Observer*). As Americans bombed Baghdad, the fascination of Western media with 'the Baghdad Blogger' seemed to be both voyeuristic and narcissistic in roughly equal measure.

Partisan politics, propaganda, evasion and narcissism were not just the preserve of news and current affairs media. On American network

TV, drama programming also sifted the meanings of 9/11 and the war on terror (see Spigel 2004), more often than not from political positions that lined up behind the war effort, or that referred to contemporary events in passing but kept them at a safe distance from more prominent narrative threads. From time to time, TV drama found itself at the leading edge of controversial and politically charged revisionist accounts of 9/11. On Showtime, the one-off drama *DC 9/11: Time of Crisis* (2003) reasserted the 'framing' of the president as global statesman and republican *paterfamilias* first peddled by the networks as breaking news on 9/11, interweaving its fictional characterisation of Bush with footage of the real president at his most scripted, ceremonial and emotive (speaking from the pulpit of the Washington National Cathedral during the memorial service for the 9/11 dead, for example, and addressing Congress on TV on 20 September). The docudrama *The Path to 9/11* (ABC 2006) dragged September 11 back into the orbit of contemporary culture wars by alleging that it was Clinton, not Bush, who was responsible for 9/11 because his administrations had ignored the threat to the US from al-Qaeda in the 1990s. ABC claimed *The Path to 9/11* was based on *The 9/11 Commission Report* (see Chapter 2), but the controversial two-part mini-series was savaged by the 9/11 commissioners, several of whom spoke publicly about how 'the outright lies in this film' were 'the opposite from' the Commission's actual findings (Kurtz 2006).

Another notable trend was the rapid accommodation of modish post-9/11 themes within established drama series such as *ER* and *The West Wing*, whose engagement with the war on terror began as early as 3 October 2001, when it aired a special 9/11 episode, 'Isaac and Ishmael', which was widely criticised at the time for an Islamophobic conflation of 'Muslim' with 'terrorist', and its 'strident defence of the national security state' (Sardar and Davies 2002: 15–38; see also Spigel 2004). Newer shows such as *Over There* (an FX series about American troops in Iraq), *Sleeper Cell* (terrorism drama from Showtime) and special forces action-drama *The Unit* (CBS), invited American TV audiences to fight the war on terror vicariously in their own homes. The black comedy-drama *Rescue Me* (FX) charted the torment of a firefighter whose closest friend died on 9/11. By early 2007, genre shows across the spectrum of TV drama – including the long-running legal drama *Law & Order* (NBC) and newer shows such as the medical drama *Grey's Anatomy* (ABC), family drama *Brothers and Sisters* (ABC) and FBI-based 'cop shows' *Criminal Minds* (CBS) and *Without a Trace* (CBS) – had all examined war on terror events 'as a subplot or subliminal theme' (Stanley 2007b). In Britain, *Spooks* (BBC) made al-Qaeda and other 'terrorist' threats to national security its main focus, ending its fifth series with an episode in which the US and UK 'abandon any attempt to tackle global warming and instead build on economic and military strength so that Britain and America can control the remaining resources' (BBC 2006). Lavish joint productions between US networks and the BBC were another notable early trend. TNT and the BBC collaborated on the terrorism/national security action drama *The Grid* (2004) and the BBC came together with HBO to make *Rome* (2005), an epic twelve-part pot-boiler dramatising, suggestively, the collapse of the Roman republic in the transition to Roman empire.

The immediacy with which terror and the war on terror became almost sublime concerns in American popular culture after 9/11 was helped along by TV drama such as these, which played an important role in the cultural (and ideological) process of normalising imperial conflict, while doing so with greater genre gravitas than conventionally accorded to sitcoms, soaps or talk-shows. Dramatising contemporary events did not always generate strong ratings. *Over There*'s direct treatment of the Iraq war, for example, fared relatively poorly with audiences not ready for programming 'that turned a war into entertainment while it was still being fought' (Stanley 2007b). Other controversial aspects of the war on terror, however, slipped easily into the mainstream of American pop culture. In a series of articles written for the *New York Times* in winter 2006 and spring 2007, the TV critic Alessandra Stanley noted that representation of torture in particular had become part of the conventional *mise en scène* of American TV drama (Stanley 2006, 2007a, 2007b). Around the same time, an interview in *The New Yorker* with David Danzig, a project director at Human Rights First, noted that whereas it used to be villains that tortured on TV, 'today, torture is often perpetrated by the heroes' (Mayer 2007). In the same feature, Jane Mayer described how a deputation from the US Military Academy at West Point, led by Brigadier-General Patrick Finnegan, met the production team of the hugely successful counter-terrorism drama *24* (Fox, 2001–) at the show's headquarters in southern California in November 2006 to ask them to stop dramatising violent acts of torture. Finnegan told *24*'s production team that 'it had become increasingly hard to convince some cadets that America had to respect the rule of law and human rights, even when terrorists did not', because of 'misperceptions' spread by the show, which Finnegan said was 'exceptionally popular' with West Point cadets. *The New Yorker* also quoted a former US Army interrogator in Iraq who claimed that Military Intelligence personnel would watch episodes of the show on DVD, 'then walk into the interrogation booths and do the same things

Figure 3.3 Harold Perrineau, Dominic Monaghan, Evangeline Lilly and Matthew Fox of the television show, *Lost*, in California, September 2004. Photo by Frederick M. Brown/Getty Images.

they've just seen' (ibid.). Mayer estimated that *24* represented the early period of the war on terror 'much as the Bush administration has defined it: as an all-consuming struggle for America's survival that demands the toughest of tactics'. The show's first five series, it was alleged, featured no fewer than 67 different scenes of torture (ibid.).[3]

Torture was also alluded to in the critically lauded *Lost* (ABC), a drama series in which survivors of a plane crash were besieged by malevolent 'Others' and bizarre, quasi-supernatural events, while stranded on a tropical desert island (Figure 3.3). When one survivor, Charlie, was discovered hanging from a tree with a hood on his head in episode 11 the allusion to Abu Ghraib was unmistakable. Another central character, Said, had a backstory showing flashbacks of his previous occupation as a torturer in Saddam Hussein's Iraq. Torture was again a theme in episodes 8 and 9, where the script seemed first to vindicate the practice as a provider of public goods (the aim being to recover life-saving medical supplies from a black marketeer), but then to change its mind when Said experienced self-recrimination and temporary exile from the community as a consequence of his actions (the information extracted under torture also proved to be false).

As well as its clear references to contemporary torture debates, series 1 of *Lost* bombarded the viewer with visual and narrative emblems that directly recalled 9/11 and evoked practices and sensibilities closely associated with the war on terror. A perplexing disaster deposited survivors in a bewildering landscape where they were surrounded by hostile 'Others'. The shapes made by plane wreckage on the beach mimicked the shattered remnants of the World Trade Center, the twisted Gothic frames and arches of Ground Zero. Before the survivors' leader, Jack, could lead effectively, he had to do what neocons said Bush must do and exorcise the influence of his father. Discovery of two old corpses that the survivors called Adam and Eve in episode 6 located the tropical post-crash landscape symbolically as Eden after the Fall, and throughout series 1 the plane crash was depicted as the traumatic founding moment of a self-contained world fundamentally changed by disaster. 'It doesn't matter who we were', Jack said in episode 3 ('Tabula Rasa'), 'three days ago we all died'. *Lost*'s formal reliance on flashback scenes did tend to problematise this claim, reminding viewers constantly that the present circumstances of the survivors were explicable as the product of past events and experience. Yet the motif of a sudden disorienting shift from one world to another, which was a recognisable part of post-9/11 US culture and a core assertion of the Bush Doctrine (see Introduction and Chapter 2), was also important in *Lost*, underwriting throughout series 1 the tension of the survivors' encounters with the bewildering alien environments of the island's interior.

Bewilderment and disorientation were key post-9/11 motifs, and figured prominently in prevailing media characterisations of 9/11 as trauma, where the events of the day were traumatic partly because they were construed as inexplicable. Post-9/11 bewilderment was never as pervasive, though, nor as apparently pleasurable, as it was in *Lost*. For fans and critics alike, the principal pleasure that the show provided came from its enigmatic refusal to explain *anything* clearly. As one contemporary fan and critic of the show suggested,

> *Lost* refuses to wear its genre references on its sleeve, preferring to allow audiences to speculate on relevant interpretive and aesthetic frameworks, and then confound our expectations through twists and reversals. Another level of unexpected pleasure comes from the show's unique storytelling structure. On the face of it, the compelling narrative questions and pleasures would appear to be predicated on the suspense of what will happen to the survivors – will they get off the island or will the 'Others' (the island's mysterious inhabitants) get them first? But the show has created equally compelling narrative enigmas in the

back story of each character – what were Kate's criminal acts and motivations? How did Locke get paralyzed (and acquire his uncanny out-
doorsman expertise)? What happened to the previous crash victims
decades before? And why were these people brought together on this
airplane and then spared in the crash? (Mittell 2005)

The rapturous association of pleasure with bewilderment in *Lost* was
not a new cultural phenomenon, but it did signal something different
and something darker than during the modishly 'postmodern' decades
of the 1980s and 1990s, when pleasure in the endless deferral of
meaning – led by vanguardist cults like deconstructionism and other
radical forms of intellectual relativism – became a new orthodoxy
among the liberal intelligentsia in the West. Considered in the context
of the contemporary events to which *Lost* regularly drew the attention
of its audience, the delight that the series took in 'not knowing' the
world seemed parochial, self-regarding, even decadent, the very
antithesis of authentically republican drama.

Heightened visually by location shooting in Hawaii – including lavish
footage of beaches, jungles, seascapes, big skies and regular soft-porn
stylings – audience pleasure in *Lost* also derived from the regularity of
the series' narrative rhythms and visual style. Though it drew on multiple genres, *Lost* provided pleasure to audiences like any conventional
genre piece by conspicuously doing what audiences expected it to do,
week by week. While it was critically lauded for its narrative complexity, structurally *Lost* was actually quite predictable. Throughout series 1,
individual episodes tended to feature stock elements, the majority or all
of which appeared every week. Episodes reliably featured detail from
the backstory of one character, relayed in flashback sequences. Usually,
the source of dramatic tension in each episode would be a trip taken into
the perilous interior of the island. *Lost* also featured regular confronta-
tions between survivors and the show's stock 'bad guy', Sawyer, and
offered characters the chance to atone for mistakes in their past with acts
of redemptive heroism or kindness in the present. While narrative
'unknowing' remained the show's hallmark, individual episodes of *Lost*
also moved conventionally enough from a disruption of equilibrium
near the beginning of each episode to a restoration of equilibrium at the
end – one recurring motif for this restoration being the presentation of
heterosexual tableaux, at or close to the end of episodes, with male and
female characters reflecting on the episode's events in the relative
domesticity of the beach encampment.

Lost garnered a large and loyal following, winning an Emmy for best
drama in 2005, and both fans and critics made hyperbolic claims on its

behalf. Yet considered, as it apparently wanted to be considered, in relation to the contemporary contexts and controversies it invoked, what
was most notable about *Lost* was not its pleasing narrative complexity
or its sometimes spectacular visual delights. What was most notable
was its political timidity, its veering from a thoroughly decadent pleasure in how bewildering the world is, to a self-regarding satisfaction
with gesture politics that made reference to contemporary issues and
events, but stubbornly refused to do anything substantive with them.
Even the torture episodes seemed gestural and clumsy, 'quoting' the
issue in a manner that was just perfunctory enough to betray the show's
actual disinterest in the debates it invoked. In this respect the series
outdid even Hollywood, to whose production values *Lost* clearly
aspired. But Hollywood's preference for what the following chapter
calls 'allegory lite' representations of 9/11 and the war on terror at least
allowed audiences to begin exploring contemporary debates by objec-
tifying them in other circumstances and scenarios. In this way, usually
despite itself, Hollywood sometimes managed to provide a critical distance on contemporary events that often seemed missing in the 'traumatised' forms of corporate print and broadcast journalism.

---

1. Where 'frames' refers to the contexts in which stories are set and the meanings that are attributed to them by news providers. 'Frame analysis' may also
   look at the contexts and meanings excluded from a given 'frame'.
2. According to the CPJ, between the invasion in March 2003 and the end of
   2005, fifty-five journalists were killed on duty in Iraq 'as a result of a hostile
   action such as reprisal for his or her work, or crossfire'. The majority (thirty-
   six) of those killed were Iraqis. Around a quarter (thirteen) of those who died
   were killed by the US military, with another seven dying in 'acts of war' perpetrated by unconfirmed sources. A further twenty-one media workers,
   twenty of whom were Iraqi (drivers, guards and other staff supporting the
   work of journalists) were killed during the same period (CPJ 2006).
3. Mayer's source for this data was The Parents' Television Council, a non-par-
   tisan watchdog group. In 2005, the Assembly of Turkish Americans
   Association warned that *24*'s depiction of a fanatical Turkish Islamist would
   encourage violence against Turkish-Americans, and Fox found itself in the
   unusual position of having to screen 'positive images' of Muslims during ad-
   breaks to counter allegations about the show's content. In the UK, Iqbal
   Sacranie, secretary general of the Muslim Council of Britain, reported *24* to
   the UK's media regulator, Ofcom, for breaching broadcasting rules governing representation of ethnic minorities (Doward 2005).

4 Cinema

'Allegory Lite', and the movie Hollywood Refused to Make

One of several remakes of classic Cold War Hollywood films after 9/11 *The Manchurian Candidate* (2004) presented American audiences with what it called 'regime change in our country'. Jonathan Demme's remake of one of the most famous political allegories in Hollywood history replaced the original's fable about communist subversion and McCarthyism in the 1950s with a narrative in which the 'enemy within' became corporate capitalism, whose brainwashed stooge, ex-Gulf War serviceman Raymond Shaw, secures a vice presidential nomination on the back of a military record falsified by his controllers, a sinister transnational corporation called Manchurian Global.

In a notable deviation from the original Cold War version of *The Manchurian Candidate* (1962), where the aim of the conspiracy was to secure communist control over American political institutions, in the remake the hijacking of the republic was also an explicitly economic adventure. Indeed, one of the film's more challenging aims seemed to be to rewrite American history as imperialist history – an end to which the film began working, poetically at least, as early as its opening sequence, where American soldiers playing cards during the first Gulf War brandished fistfuls of dollars in a tank, introduced by a reworking of Creedence Clearwater Revival's famous song about the Vietnam War as class war, 'Fortunate Son' (1969). *The Manchurian Candidate* used its opening sequence to recast the recent American past as a history of corporate expansionism enforced by military and political power. As one character noted, Manchurian Global was 'not just a cor-poration', it was 'a goddam geopolitical extension of policy for every President since Nixon'. Filmed in an unsettling visual style which saw protagonists repeatedly glare straight into the camera (and thus right at audiences), often in close-up, at the time it was difficult to imagine a more edgy Hollywood treatment of the contemporary 'republican crisis' theme, or of the territory staked out by post-9/11 empire revisionists (see Chapters 1 and 2). Hollywood, it was often said by contemporaries, had been 'politicised' by 9/11 and the war on terror, and *The Manchurian Candidate* was widely reviewed on its release as a leading example of this new radical temper. One typical review called the film 'an unambiguous attack on the current American administration' (Hoberman 2004).[1]

There were, however, significant problems with this assessment. Technically, films that were often cited as leading statements of Hollywood's new radicalism, like Michael Moore's polemical documentary *Fahrenheit 9/11* (2004) or Participant Productions films *Syriana* (2005) and *Good Night, and Good Luck* (2005), were funded by independent companies, not Hollywood conglomerates (though many of the people involved were Hollywood industry insiders). More significant, perhaps, the small minority of filmmakers who did become 'a central component of global opposition to Bush's war with Iraq' generally traced their politicisation to the failures of Clintonian liberalism or the emergence of anti-globalisation movements in the 1990s, rather than to 9/11 or the war on terror (Dickenson 2006: 107). If Hollywood appeared to be politicised after 9/11, this was often because the Bush administration's response helped heighten existing trends among Hollywood liberals, not because the 9/11 attacks functioned as a moment of radical epiphany that changed the face of mainstream Hollywood film.

On closer inspection, films that were assumed to be indicative of a new Hollywood radicalism often adhered to conventional aesthetic patterns that reflected incoherent – but quite traditional – Hollywood political commitments. While *The Manchurian Candidate*, for example, invited viewers to collude in an 'allegorical' attack on corrupt imperialist governance by the Bush administration, it also went out of its way to encourage other 'readings' that seemed equally plausible given the elements that the film supplied, and other pleasures, any of which could displace or supersede the political allegory for audiences – the genre thrills of the political/conspiracy thriller; the star power of Denzel Washington, Meryl Streep, Jon Voight or Liev Schreiber; the film's edgy cinematography; its nods to the original version or deviations from it; a running *Robocop*-style sub-commentary on the pernicious social impacts of technological mass media; and so on. Amidst such competing attractions, the 'allegorical' links between Manchurian Global's hijacking of the republic and the Bush administration seemed ill-defined, if not wilfully incoherent. In 2004, a Presidential election year, many Republican voters might easily have associated *The Manchurian Candidate*'s story of a war hero with a fraudulent military record with the Democratic candidate, John Kerry, rather than with

George Bush.[2] Raymond Shaw's political party was in opposition, not in the White House. When he talked about policy, he sometimes sounded more like a Democrat than a right-wing Republican. For good measure, the filmmakers also turned the character of Eleanor Shaw (Raymond's mother, a key figure in the conspiracy) into a woman who looked uncannily like Hillary Clinton.

The incoherence of *The Manchurian Candidate*'s allegory about war on terror governance embodied a distinctive Hollywood storytelling mode referred to in this chapter as 'allegory lite' – a commercial aesthetic so packed with different hooks pitched at different audience groups that a degree of aesthetic and narrative fragmentation has become intrinsic to the way Hollywood tells stories today, particularly in the blockbuster (see Maltby 2003). The aesthetic style of allegory lite that supplies Hollywood's principal narrative mode for films about controversial subjects is pure capitalist utilitarianism, performing the tricky commercial manoeuvre of appealing simultaneously to multiple audiences, alienating as few customers as possible, while transferring responsibility for any 'politicising' of films to viewers themselves. In Hollywood allegory lite, controversial issues can be safely addressed because they must be 'read off' other stories by the viewer; while the 'allegory' is sufficiently loose or 'lite', and the other attractions on offer are sufficiently compelling or diverse, that viewers can enjoy the film without needing to engage at all with the risky 'other story' it tells. In these respects, allegory lite representations of 9/11 and the war on terror corresponded closely at times to what Richard Maltby, following Thomas Cripps, once described as Hollywood's 'conscience liberalism' – a filmmaking practice that gestures towards political conflict and controversy, but only to marginalise, obscure, override or resolve it, helping generate maximum audience share by depoliticising what begin as ostensibly political interventions (see Maltby 2003: 268–308).

Hollywood's commercial preference for 'conscience liberalism' allegory lite made for evasive filmmaking about 9/11 and the war on terror. For much of the 'crisis' era Hollywood tended to plug into contemporary debates, or at least it allowed audiences to do so, by telling stories that were ostensibly 'about' other things. *The Alamo* (2004), *The Village* (2004), *The Manchurian Candidate* (2004), *Black Hawk Down* (2001), *War of the Worlds* (2005), *Kingdom of Heaven* (2005), as well as a quasi-independent movie like Participant Productions' *Good Night, and Good Luck* (2005), were just some of the contemporary films that functioned as allegory lite representations of 9/11 and the war on terror, and were widely reviewed on release in precisely these terms. Five years after 9/11, Hollywood had made films showing sci-fi Martian armies, nineteenth-century Mexican armies and twelfth-century Crusader armies, all of them signposted to audiences as 'allegory lite' representations of twenty-first-century US militarism. It had also made films about other American wars (for example, *Black Hawk Down* and *Jarhead* [2005]); but it had made none about Fallujah, Abu Ghraib, Tora Bora or Guantánamo Bay.

Early allegory lite treatments of 9/11 and the war on terror by Hollywood produced politically incoherent films, whose latent value as cultural nodal points for republican debate and exchange was usually shortcircuited by the commercial utilitarianism of the form. While aesthetically innovative and politically adventurous filmmaking about contemporary events was plentiful on Western screens, almost all of it was made by independents or by non-American companies and crews, and it was usually shown – exceptions like Michael Moore and Participant Productions aside – to small audiences in art cinemas, not mass audiences in multiplexes. One of the early critical highlights was *11'09"01*, a portmanteau film made by eleven directors from around the world, each of whom contributed short films of their own that came together in a series of powerful collective statements about empire and the 9/11 attacks (see Conclusion). The British director Michael Winterbottom's *The Road to Guantánamo* (2006) used an ambitious mix of docudrama and 'modern horror story' (Young 2006) to film the grim tale of the 'Tipton Three', three innocent British men tortured and held for two years without charge at the Guantánamo Bay prison camp in Cuba. Another highlight was *Paradise Now* by the Palestinian director Hany Abu-Assad, partly because it carried off with such panache a story about suicide bombers that was often attempted with less verve and ambition in the West (see the film *Syriana*, the TV drama *Sleeper Cell* or John Updike's novel *Terrorist*). *Paradise Now* presented suicide bombing as an authentic part of a culture of occupation imposed by Israel on the West Bank, but still found room to examine contradictions in the political and moral philosophy of the Intifada. In the shadow of *Fahrenheit 9/11*, independent political documentary also thrived in Western cinemas after 9/11 and rapidly evolved its own war on terror sub-genres. Political documentary about media, for example, was a striking early trend. New Yorker Robert Greenwald – whose *Uncovered: The War on Iraq* (2004) had attacked the Bush administration's WMD case for war – also made *Outfoxed: Rupert Murdoch's War on Journalism* (2004), denouncing the ultra-conservatism of American network Fox TV. The Egyptian-American director Jehane Noujaim made *Control Room* (2004), an audacious documentary comparing news coverage of the invasion of Iraq by Al Jazeera with news management techniques and communications strategies deployed by the White House and Pentagon. *Control Room* was another early high-point of post-9/11 independent cinema, beginning with a disarming manoeuvre that placed viewers in the point of view of Iraqis waiting to be bombed – in a voiceover describing the tense mood in Baghdad, and a camera that lingered idly, just a little too long, on birds flying in flocks over city rooftops, their synchronised loops and dives prefiguring the coming of American warplanes. In 2005, classic documentaries about the Vietnam war such as *Hearts and Minds* (1974) and *Winter Soldier* (1972) also enjoyed revivals and limited re-release runs in Western cinemas. Errol Morris's new film about Vietnam, *The Fog of War* (2003), featured an astonishing, tortured performance from Robert S. McNamara, Secretary of Defense in the Kennedy and Johnson administrations, 'confessing' to camera, in an alternately intimate and claustrophobically rendered *mea culpa*, that mistakes were made by Americans in Vietnam.

Comparisons between Vietnam and Iraq became commonplace during Bush's second term. The revival of landmark documentaries like *Hearts and Minds* (a major influence on *Fahrenheit 9/11*) and *Winter Soldier*, and Errol Morris's *The Fog of War*, articulated a default 'allegory' of the war in Iraq that was distinct from Hollywood allegory lite because these films seemed to propose that imperial militarism was in the American grain, or at least that it expressed something organic, rather than something aberrant, in American political and moral culture. In this respect, the contrast with a Hollywood block-buster like *The Manchurian Candidate* could not have been more profound. Hollywood's risk-averse, commercial bottom line, and the utilitarianism of the corporate allegory lite – where political stories were individualised, displaced in time and space, and abstracted from their rootedness in systems and institutions – meant that the industry was perfectly placed to embody in aesthetics the notion of a self-correcting, time-limited republican 'crisis' after 9/11 (see Chapter 2). Viewers undeterred by the political incoherence of *The Manchurian Candidate*, and who stuck with the Bush allegory to the end, may have been reassured to discover that the corporate conspiracy ringleader, Eleanor Shaw, had a psychotic personality disorder and in all likelihood an incestuous sexual relationship with her son. If the conspiracy to hijack the republic in *The Manchurian Candidate* resembled the conspiracy to hijack the republic during the war on terror, the good news, the film reassured its audience, was that the Shaw/Bush scenario was a one-off, a deviation, an aberration or detour from the political norm, not an authentic product of capitalist-republican institutions and process or proof of continuity with an established imperial past.

Until the release of the Oliver Stone-directed *World Trade Center* in 2006, Hollywood audiences could have been forgiven for thinking that there was no war on terror and that there had never been a 9/11, so evasive or oblique were the industry's engagements with contemporary events. Though it was routinely described as a 'Hollywood' film by reviewers, the first film to tackle 9/11 head-on, *United 93* (which told the story of the passengers whose intervention caused one of the planes hijacked on September 11 to crash in Pennsylvania), was made by an independent production company, Sidney Kimmel Entertainment, and a British director, Paul Greengrass, whose pedigree was in political documentaries for British television. Much of the shooting of *United 93* took place at Pinewood Studios, London. When it finally arrived in 2006, Hollywood's first direct treatment of 9/11 hardly seemed worth the wait. *World Trade Center* was mawkish and cliché-ridden, and politically timid too, limiting its discussion of 9/11 almost entirely to Ground Zero and the family homes and workplaces of the victims (to whom Stone gave religious visions that authenticated their characterisation as martyrs on holy ground). *World Trade Center* often seemed to want to talk about the sacrifices made by working-class Americans on 9/11. Yet the film pulled audiences insistently against such a reading in its determination to individualise the historical story that it told. In this, the film displayed a conventional Hollywood preference for stories about individuals caught up in contentious historical events, rather than stories about historical events themselves. The pay-off for Stone's evacuations of history from *World Trade Center* was the glib reassurance offered at the end of the final scene, where the film implied that there really was a link between 9/11 and Iraq, a political line on the Iraq war that had been thoroughly discredited by 2006 and that was due a revival.

Before *World Trade Center*, the major Hollywood treatments of 9/11 and the war on terror were all conventionally framed as Hollywood allegory lite. One textbook case was another remake of a Cold War Hollywood classic, *The Alamo* (2004), which aimed, in the words of Disney's Michael Eisner, to 'capture the post-September 11 surge in patriotism' (in McCrisken and Pepper 2005: 207). To this end, the director, John Lee Hancock, revived Hollywood's most famous icon of the republic in peril, the Texas mission in San Antonio besieged by a Mexican army in 1836 – a trope that *The Alamo* had in common with the Ridley Scott-directed films *Black Hawk Down* and *Kingdom of Heaven*, both of which were also structured centrally upon the laying of siege by racialised 'Others' to heroic and/or martyred American/ Western forces.

By the time it was finally released in the US in April 2004, a year after the invasion of Iraq, the remade *The Alamo* seemed characterised more by a weary sense of myths worn out than by the kind of arousing patriotism envisaged by Michael Eisner. Like the classic early revisionist Western, *The Man Who Shot Liberty Valance* (1962), substantial sequences of the 2004 *The Alamo* were filmed as interiors, often in subdued lighting or at night, giving the cinematography a claustrophobic feel that contrasted markedly with the big skies, open plains and preference for epic long-shots in the John Wayne version of *The Alamo* (1960). Where Wayne played Davy Crockett to the mythic hilt, as a swaggering alpha male whose glib certitudes about America and its place in the world would soon wilt in the broad-based cultural revisionism of the 1960s, *The Alamo* (2004) seemed higher on bathos than heroic swagger. Congressman Crockett was introduced to viewers enjoying a night at the theatre, attending a play about himself, where both he and the actor playing him exchange a public greeting of 'Good evening Mr Crockett'. Arriving in San Antonio, the 'real' Crockett is then confused with the fictional 'Crockett' character in the play by a fan unable to differentiate between the man and the myth, who asks Crockett to 'say the lines'. Later, Crockett confesses to the equally 'storied' Jim Bowie that he only wears the iconic Davy Crockett hat because the 'Crockett' character in the play wears one. 'People expect things', he said to Bowie. 'Ain't it so', Bowie replied. When Crockett told a group of admirers asking for tales of 'Indian fightin' that he was 'never in but one real scrape' in his whole life, then recounted in detail an Indian massacre in which he had taken part, the next shot was of Bowie in bed and close to death, filmed from above so that the shot emphasised the hero's abjection.

The ideological complexity of contemporary Hollywood – or the political incoherence inherent in the commodity form of allegory lite – meant that attending to *The Alamo*'s neo-revisionism was only one way of watching the film. Davy Crockett was still given a scene where he shot the lapels off Mexican General Santa Anna's uniform from several hundred yards, and another in which he appeared to forestall single-handedly the decisive Mexican assault on the Alamo using just his skill with the fiddle and a good tune. Even on his knees awaiting execution, the 2004 Crockett was still able to humiliate Santa Anna in full view of his own army. By this point, viewers looking for ideological consistency or coherence in *The Alamo* (2004) must have found it difficult to tell whether Hancock and his crew wanted their Crockett to subvert the conventional Crockett myths, or just wanted him to appear a little too modest for his own good. The sequence in which Crockett fiddled the Alamo to a reprieve from imminent attack ended with rousing orchestral music, shots of beautiful big dusk skies (rare in this version) and lightning flashing around the Alamo, reaffirming the cosmic significance of the story at hand. From here the film staged a dramatic about-turn, cancelling out its earlier commentary on the fraudulence of American nationhood myths in an extended celebration of patriotic martyrdom, culminating in the redemptive slaughter of the Battle of San Jacinto, where Sam Houston's army avenge the Alamo by putting the Mexicans to the sword. Framed as extended flashbacks or empathetic reconstructions of the siege in the imagination of Houston, the film put the redemptive American agency that Houston represented at the very heart of the narrative.

One film that combined *The Alamo*'s siege motif with *The Manchurian Candidate*'s meditation on the corruption of republican governance, was an *auteur* piece directed by M. Night Shyamalan, whose previous films included *Signs* (2002), *Unbreakable* (2000) and *The Sixth Sense* (1999). Shyamalan's war on terror allegory lite, *The Village* (2004), brought a self-conscious 'art-house' gloss to a fable about a late nineteenth-century community terrorised by its leaders, who maintain communal order and happiness by inventing an elaborate mythology about malevolent creatures prowling the forest beyond the clearing where the action was set (Figure 4.1). The film's 'twist ending' revealed that the lies of the community's leaders were intended to prevent the villagers from venturing into a real, twenty-first-century world of urban violence and crime, which the leaders knew was there, but about which the younger generation, born or raised in the village, knew nothing. The village elders, the twist revealed, were psychologically damaged Americans who had withdrawn from society, the village a utopian experiment in the remote inner reaches of a twenty-first-century wildlife reserve fenced off to the general public.

Among the interwoven themes central to the film were loss of innocence and the long-term implications of traumatic experience, parochial or paranoid leadership by elites, and the roles played by myth or ideology in securing elite power, social order and collective identity. Most important, because they were the most widely observed and transparently allegorical of the film's references to the war on terror, were the debates that *The Village* staged about the limits of good governance, the legitimacy of a 'politics of fear' and the ethics of the Straussian 'noble lie'.[3] While the 'allegory' clearly worked for some viewers, it didn't have to work for audiences to enjoy the film.

Figure 4.1 Director M. Night Shyamalan, and actors Bryce Dallas Howard, Adrien Brody and Joaquin Phoenix, at the world premiere of *The Village*, July 2004, in New York.
Photo by Evan Agostini/Getty Images.

Among the multiple 'attractions' competing for the attention of audiences in *The Village*, there was a great score, striking cinematography, Bryce Dallas Howard, Joaquin Phoenix, the romance between the two, the generalised sense of nostalgia that often attaches itself to *faux*-period Hollywood film, and a range of other genre attractions to be found in a movie that combined 'horror' conventions with others borrowed from melodrama and the psychological thriller. For audiences attracted by publicity materials and reviews suggesting that it was a post-9/11 fable about the iniquities of leaders who lied to their people about weapons of mass destruction and terrorist threats, *The Village* offered other things too, not least a reassuringly aestheticised exposition of the dirty business of politics. Written, directed and co-produced by Shyamalan, *The Village* was a beguiling and at times beautiful film that looked and sounded like 'art-house' cinema. Yet as conventional, if highly crafted allegory lite, the film also placed itself at one remove from the contemporary controversies it appeared to engage, its layered displacements of the narrative 'about' war on terror governance onto other things and into *auteur* aesthetics, allowing *The Village* to deny any real political intent or commitment while still parading its 'subversive' trimmings to audiences as something akin to what Tom Wolfe once called 'radical chic'.

The Village was by no means simply an attack on Straussian leadership, though it was careful to be this as well. While Shyamalan was sometimes at pains to acknowledge that the elders presided over a dysfunctional society, one that divided leaders from the led, fostering secrecy, paranoia and a parochial isolationism that denied citizens access to vital medical technologies, at other times this society secured by political lies and 'state' terror seemed close to idyllic. In early sequences, clean and well-fed children played happily at a well. Women sweeping a porch danced and played while they worked. Well-stocked greenhouses and vegetable gardens suggested a bountiful, efficient and organic union of nature and culture. In many ways it was a vision of life and labour before the fall, governed by a 'unitary executive' (see Chapter 2) whose well-intentioned lies had produced a benign and ordered society that worked in the best interests of its citizens.

Shyamalan's 'conscience liberalism' in *The Village* was at its most affecting in the emphasis it placed on audience identifications in shaping the film's political meanings. Film theory has often argued that our 'primary' identification as viewers is with the camera, whose gaze we necessarily share. Beyond that primary identification, however, viewers also make a range of 'secondary' identifications with the characters they encounter in films, some or all of which may be made unconsciously. In *The Village*, patterns of identification were complex, partly because they were contradictory. In important scenes the film appeared quite wilful in its massaging of audience-identification with the 'government' of the community we were shown. During the scene in which viewers are first introduced to the elders gathered as a group, the elders sit in a closed circle in the village hall, discussing the community's social calendar. They smile at each other. They carry themselves like citizens rather than leaders. They appear rational and benign. Several of the women are knitting. More powerful than the characterisation, however, in constructing audience identifications with these protagonists in this scene, are the points of view that viewers are forced to adopt by cameras that place 'us' within the closed circle of seated elders, literally shoulder to shoulder with 'them', the camera giving us viewing positions that simulate our own presence as a member of the group, initiating our relationship with lying patrician leaders by positioning us sympathetically as one of them.

Yet *The Village* was also notable for its careful crafting of audience-identifications with villagers victimised by the lies of their leaders. This was particularly the case with the film's heroine, Ivy Walker, a young blind woman who embarks on a perilous quest to 'the towns' to acquire medicine for her betrothed, Lucius Hunt, who lies close to death having been stabbed by a rival for Ivy's affections, a mentally disabled villager, Noah Percy. Ivy's blindness made her the most vulnerable and exploited of *The Village*'s citizens, not just because it was she who risked death by travelling alone through the forest to the dangerous outer world of 'the towns', but also because her blindness meant she was unable to see the real twenty-first-century world beyond the forest, and so could return to the village not merely with medicines, but with the lies of the leaders substantially intact. In the allegory lite, Ivy's blindness looked like a republican token of her exploitation by elite political power, and provided a motif upon which *The Village* forged powerful audience-identifications with the character, constructing scenes and sequences where our emotional experience of the action – and our own figurative 'blindness' to the film's real story, up until the twist ending – was closely linked to hers. In one scene, where Ivy rushes panic-stricken to Lucius's house after hearing that he has been attacked, the soundtrack puts the hubbub of the village low in the mix, replacing it with an accentuation of the noises in Ivy's head – her nervy, shallow breathing, the sound of paces counted half-aloud, the tap of her cane at the top of the mix echoing like a gunshot on the wooden steps of the house, all constructing a point of view for audiences that mimicked vividly the subjective experience of a character in distress, relying on her ears rather than her eyes to navigate. The camera in this scene, positioned low to the ground in front of Ivy, looks up at her as she walks, so that we, 'blinded' again, walk backwards along the path in front of her, unable to see where we are going, with our peripheral vision also severely constrained by the camera's low-slung viewpoint.

One consequence of this to-ing and fro-ing in the massaging of audience-identifications was that the film's allegory lite was conventionally equivocal, or incoherent, in the 'political' and ethical positions it adopted, refusing to choose between leaders and led, victimisers and victims. Another factor that helped anchor this refusal to choose in the film's distinctive visual style was Shyamalan's use of static cameras filming extended shots, with single shots sometimes stretched to encompass entire scenes. *The Village* was certainly noticeable, in the context of contemporary Hollywood, for its avoidance of the rapid edits and choppy, multi-perspectival camera positionings imported from MTV in the 1980s and 1990s. The stillness of the extended single-shot scene underpinned visually the film's refusal to choose 'politically', constructing the camera as a detached, neutral or objective presence in the action, sometimes recording characters as they walked in and out of shot and interacted in front of a seemingly disinterested lens. Before the film's twist ending, where *The Village* suddenly stopped being 'about' either the late nineteenth century or 'about' war on terror governance, and instead became about something else entirely, the film's determination to avoid choosing between the 'sides' it established meant that even viewers predisposed to viewing *The Village* as a film about neoconservative political leadership may have struggled to discern what commitments, if any, the film had actually made.

Given the frequency with which visual motifs associated with 9/11 and Iraq were ostentatiously displayed in yet another Cold War remake, Steven Spielberg's *War of the Worlds* (2005), it was harder to ignore the contemporary issues to which the film's allegory lite directed audiences than it was in *The Village*. Reviewers at the time commented on Spielberg's conspicuous tweaking of previous versions of the *War of the Worlds* narrative, so that aliens who traditionally arrived from space came instead from underground, present but invisible among us like terrorist sleeper cells. The film offered a tapestry of signposted references to famous images of 9/11, exceeding by some distance the conventional gesturing towards topicality of Hollywood allegory lite. A panicked crowd in a city street fled a gigantic debris cloud. An aeroplane crashed onto a house, leaving bits of its undercarriage prominently displayed to the camera in the wreckage. American refugees flooded roads usually choked with vehicles, while collages of photos and cards mounted on streetlamps, hydrants and booths showed images of the 'missing'. Other scenes evoked the horror of 9/11 more allusively. Corpses drifted down the Hudson River. The white ash remains of pulverised buildings and human bodies, and the empty clothes of dead Americans, floated from the sky. In the opening scenes, dense thickets of American flags hung from porches and windows in working-class New Jersey.

War of the Worlds was not unique in its willingness to refer to contemporary events in Hollywood allegory lite. But it was notable for the extent to which it paraded these references so ostentatiously to audiences. Even with all its ideological baggage, a film like *The Alamo* could still be enjoyed and understood as 'just' a Western or war film, *The Village* as a *faux*-period romance, psychological thriller or horror film. However, the care with which *War of the Worlds* was steeped in the visual iconography of 9/11, and the extent to which it forced audiences to re-experience 9/11 empathetically through encounters with that imagery, made it much harder to concentrate on other aspects of the film. 'Is it the terrorists?' asked the hero, Ray's, daughter, during the

Figure 4.2 'Sublime' terror in Spielberg's Cold War re-make, *War of the Worlds*.
© Paramount Pictures/ZUMA/Corbis.

first Martian assault. 'What is it?' his son repeated, 'Is it terrorists?' Ray's answer to his children was 'No, this came from someplace else'. But Spielberg's relentless recycling of 9/11 imagery in the film seemed to tell a different story. More than any other Hollywood film of the Bush era, *War of the Worlds* tapped and exploited popular anxiety about terrorism, and helped reproduce it in the process as a palpable and insistent reality in everyday life (Figure 4.2). In Spielberg's *War of the Worlds* 'terror' was sublime (in the Romantic sense, meaning the experiences of dread and awe felt viscerally through the senses when in the presence of omnipotent power), partly because the film was anchored in such overwhelming CGI (computer-generated imagery) spectacle. Sublimity and 'spectacle' have been part of the *War of the Worlds* narrative since H. G. Wells. But the spectacular dimensions of the story had never been so fully realised, nor the terror that they embody made so sublime, as in the punishing visual and aural CGI assaults of the Spielberg version, and the tumultuous colour palette through which the traumatic emotional core of the movie expressed itself – landscapes, cities and big skies awash with violent eruptions of colour that extended both the look of the 1953 film and what Wells called the 'lurid' palette of the novel (Wells 2005: 45).

Repeating the Darwinian inflection of previous versions of the *War of the Worlds* story, in Spielberg's remake the world was an environment to be survived, a world to which Americans must adapt rather than one that could be moulded to suit their interests, or upon which Americans might impose themselves arbitrarily at will. As in Wells's novel, in Spielberg's remake 'we' survived because, although we were lower on the food chain than the Martians, we were better adapted to living here than they were. (The invincible Martian military machine is eventually stopped in its tracks by common Earth bacteria.) The understated heroism of the central protagonist, Ray, cut against such a conclusion, but the Wellsian logic of the film implied that 'our' survival was less a matter of civilisational superiority, and more an accident or contingency of the unfitness and environmental maladaptation of others. Darwin was important in a variety of post-9/11 contexts, in domestic 'culture wars' debates over 'creationism' and 'intelligent design', and in contemporary war on terror culture such as Ian McEwan's novel *Saturday* (discussed in Chapter 5) or the ABC TV drama *Lost* (discussed in Chapter 6). Darwinian themes were particularly important in *War of the Worlds* because they provided the grounds on which – contrary to the story's suggestion of a war between different worlds – the film asserted an ontological continuity between Americans and the army of occupation against which they were pitted. Since both 'they' and 'we' participated in a common Darwinian struggle for survival, the story was less about a cosmic clash of civilisations than about struggle within a single universe shaped by universally applicable laws of nature. Intellectually, that is, the film adhered to earlier versions of the story by placing 'men' (Americans) and Martians (invaders/occupiers) within the same evolutionary continuum.

This Darwinian aspect of the *War of the Worlds* story has always been important, because its blurring of the distinction between 'us' and 'them' has traditionally allowed the story to function explicitly as social criticism, with the object of our fear, loathing or desire (the alien, the Other, the invader and occupier) often embodying alarming truths about our own society that are sublimated, or turned into more palatable forms, by projecting them onto the Martians. In Spielberg's updated allegory lite, the narrative's archetypal tendency to force a blurring of 'us' and 'them' may have manifested itself, for some viewers, as a projection of anxiety (or pleasure) about US foreign policy in Afghanistan and Iraq onto the indiscriminate super-technology of the Martian war-machine – not least because the spectacular CGI destruction wrought by the army of occupation was so thrilling that it may have been hard for some Western audiences to think of the film as being about 'terrorism' alone. If, in *War of the Worlds*, audiences were repeatedly encouraged to renew their historical identification as victims of 9/11, American audiences were also asked to identify themselves, like the Americans on screen, as victims of military invasion and conquest; an identification assisted by the film's projection of US military might onto alien invaders, a displacement that turned American audiences into victims of their 'own' sublime battery of ultra hi-tech weapons of mass destruction.

One factor that may have motivated this 'double jeopardy' pattern of audience identifications in *War of the Worlds* was non-diegetic. While the Pentagon briefed the media, and the media briefed Americans and the rest of the world, about 'smart' weapons technology and laser-guided munitions, during the Afghan and Iraq wars the US military was bedevilled by eyewitness accounts detailing heavy casualties and deaths among civilian populations caused by 'coalition' attacks. Senior officials from the Bush administration appeared regularly on network newscasts to denounce as propagandist Al Jazeera's footage of dead and dying Iraqi civilians. Nevertheless, one feature of the war on terror during 2005, the year in which *War of the Worlds* was released, was the succession of reports by Western NGOs that placed Iraqi deaths directly caused by the invasion at between 25,000 and 100,000, with a figure closer to 200,000 offered as a speculative upper limit by the authors of a 2005 *Lancet* report. By October 2006, *The Lancet* had increased its estimate to 655,000, or one in forty Iraqis.

The possibility that American audiences might 'identify' on some conscious or unconscious level with Spielberg's hi-tech military invaders was enhanced by the muted presence of the US military in the film. American troops were present throughout the later stages of the film, but exerted no real influence on the action. When birds collected on the hood of one of the Martian fighting machines, revealing the disease that was killing them, it was Ray, not a soldier, who alerted the army. More than forty-five minutes passed before US military forces even appeared on screen, and there were no military protagonists as such in Spielberg's version, the film's conflation of two of Wells's characters, the artilleryman and the clergyman, into a new one (the survivalist paedophile) downgrading further the already marginal presence of the military in Spielberg's *mise-en-scène*. In a New Hollywood genre hybrid like *War of the Worlds* (a family melodrama sci-fi alien invasion blockbuster war film), this disconnection between the American people and the military was significant because it left a vacuum at the heart of the film where more straightforward audience identifications with US military power might conventionally have taken shape.

After 9/11, Hollywood's willingness to associate Americans with the 'otherness' of the enemy sometimes brought a surprising edginess to its films. In *War of the Worlds* this made for a complex (or incoherent) set of audience-identifications with both invaders and invaded. In *The Alamo* it made for equally complicated (or incoherent) audience-relationships with the 'son of a bitch dictator' Santa Anna, a folkoric bogeyman from American history to rival Osama bin Laden and Saddam Hussein. For some audiences, the political contexts of the time may have helped make the nineteenth-century Mexican general a plausible Saddam – and, more importantly perhaps, Saddam a plausible Santa Anna. Yet in the allegory lite of *The Alamo* (2004), Santa Anna was also plausibly 'American' at times. Described as the 'Napoleon of the West', an imperialist leader of an imperial army, Santa Anna practised something akin to 'Shock and Awe', and his battlecraft disregarded conventional rules of engagement. One brief but memorable shot reproduced the familiar visual effect of footage from cameras mounted in the nose cones of US 'smart' munitions on a Mexican cannonball as it arced towards the Alamo. In Ridley Scott's blockbuster about the twelfth-century Crusades, *Kingdom of Heaven*, Western characters again assumed traits more often associated with Western stereotypes of Islamist insurgents or Arab dictators (bellicose fanaticism, doctrinaire religiosity, extreme and irrational violence). At times this helped clarify matters. In *Kingdom of Heaven*, Western audiences knew who the 'bad' Westerners were because they acted like 'Muslims'. But this political incoherence at the heart of the film also seemed to complicate audience-identifications and confuse audience responses to the war on terror issues encoded in the film, by making barbarism a Western value as well as a 'Muslim' one.

'Independent' filmmaking by the Hollywood insiders funded by Participant Productions – the production company financed by Jeff Skol, the billionaire co-founder of eBay, to make progressive, campaigning cinema – also used allegory lite to explore war on terror themes. Unusually for a twenty-first-century production company whose films enjoyed mass distribution in the US, Participant measured its political and aesthetic aims against one another, announcing that its goal was to make 'compelling entertainment that will raise awareness about important social issues, educate audiences and inspire them to take action', a challenging understanding of what a republican culture might aim to be or do (Participate.net 2005a). Participant film *Good Night, and Good Luck* retold the story of current affairs TV show *See It Now*'s (CBS) clash with McCarthyism in the 1950s, but worked hard to establish its engagement with post-9/11 issues. The lessons for the present it derived from the past were primarily political. Authoritarianism cannot be tolerated in a republic. The best way to fight attacks on the Constitution is by defending constitutional rights. Courage, and a free press, are required in the face of demagoguery. When it referred to American TV's 'allergy to unpleasant or disturbing information' and its aversion to 'subjects that may well determine the future of this country', *Good Night, and Good Luck* must have sounded familiar and prescient to many post-9/11 Americans. The closing sequence of the film even dramatised the section from Edward R. Murrow's famous 'wires and lights in a box' speech to the Radio-Television News Directors Association and Foundation in 1958, when Murrow called for American TV to conduct 'a thoroughgoing study of American policy in the Middle East'.

Participant films were linked to a website called Participate.net – a virtual community of 'actors, filmmakers, issue experts, moviegoers, and activists from all over the world' (Participate.net 2005a) – and to specific political campaigns. *Good Night, and Good Luck* was linked to a campaign called 'Report It Now', whose campaign materials also left little doubt about the film's contemporary relevance. 'In our current climate of fear, stifled dissent, homogenized newscasts, and a cowed press', the website noted, 'it has become ever more crucial to engage in critical debate and truth-seeking' (Participate.net 2005b). Via the links established with 'Report It Now', and the script's regular reminders that threats to First Amendment rights came from factors like the influence of capitalist advertising on media as much as from mavericks like Joe McCarthy, *Good Night, and Good Luck* went some way beyond the conventional narrative constraints of Hollywood 'allegory lite'.

Where *Good Night, and Good Luck* warned Americans to heed political lessons from the past, *Syriana* engaged directly with the sharp end of twenty-first-century US foreign policy in the Middle East. The film's most radical claim was that Arab dictatorships and Islamic states could only be democratised by the development of progressive indigenous reform movements that the US had often worked hard to contain or shut down. 'This guy could be like Mossadegh in '52 in Iran', one character said, comparing *Syriana*'s Prince Nasir to the Iranian president toppled in a CIA-supported coup in 1953, after Mossadegh had threatened to nationalise American and British oil interests in Iran (Figure 4.3) (see Chapter 1). Disappointingly, *Syriana* then fudged the issue by prevaricating over the kinds of Arab nationalism that would be appropriate, Nasir's agenda settling in the end for a programme that allowed for foreign ownership of 'Syrianian' national resources.

Where Hollywood allegory lite was characterised by evasion and sublimation of 'issues', a Participant movie like *Syriana* seemed hobbled by the sheer variety of complex subjects that it tried to take on board. The film's discussion of blowback, suicide bombing, oil, American attitudes

Figure 4.3 'This guy could be like Mossadegh in '52 in Iran'. Alexander Siddig as Prince Nasir Al-Subaai, in the Stephen Gaghan directed political thriller, *Syriana*, made by the Participant production company.
© Glen Wilson/ Warner Bros./Bureau L.A. Collection/Corbis.

to Arab nationalism, class power, migrant labour, neoconservatism and the weakness of superpower hegemony grounded in violence made for heady but sometimes opaque filmmaking. Purposefully dense, it seemed, *Syriana* was a film that demanded the close attention of the viewer, but didn't always reward it. One reviewer spoke for many when he described the 'weird absence of . . . political light' in *Syriana*, and the 'blank, uncompelling tangle' at the heart of the film (Bradshaw 2006). One tense scene towards the end, where veteran CIA agent, Bob Barnes, met the powerful Washington lawyer acting for corporate energy interests, Dean Whiting, in a diner, could have been a *tour de force* of political cinema – the moment when the film finally brought key protagonists together, so as to make explicit a concept of the state in which the functioning of the intelligence community abroad was indelibly linked to the reproduction of class power at home. This seemed to be part of what *Syriana* was trying to say, but instead the scene looked like it had been lifted from *The X-Files*. The danger in *Syriana* was that so smart and complex a film may have left many viewers with vague confirmations of half-formed truisms – 'it's all about oil', 'power corrupts', 'terrorists are ingénues exploited by fanatics', 'the rich live in a different world from the rest of us' – but with little that was solid enough to chew. In this respect at least, *Syriana* often looked more like conventional Hollywood fare than its makers presumably intended.

Perhaps the best way of illustrating the limits beyond which Hollywood conscience liberalism would not go during the 'crisis' years of the early war on terror is to look in detail at the film Hollywood eventually refused to make. In the end, *Fahrenheit 9/11* was produced and distributed by a consortium of independent companies, one of which (Fellowship Adventure Group) was founded especially for the purpose, after Disney, alarmed at the film's explicit political content, withdrew its funding and prevented its Miramax subsidiary from distributing it under the Miramax brand name.

The public furore over *Fahrenheit 9/11* when it was finally released placed Moore at the centre of debates about 'crisis' in republican political institutions and process (see Chapter 2). In *Fahrenheit 9/11*, 'the people' and the Bush administration were relentlessly at odds, pushed firmly apart by the conflicting interests they embodied. In one scene, a distraught war mother from Michigan, Lila Lipscomb, whose son was killed in Iraq, was filmed outside the White House against a backdrop provided by security barricades erected after 9/11, whose visual effect was to split the screen across the middle, putting the White House and 'the people' on different sides of a barrier that divided them irreconcilably. In an earlier scene, a sequence of eleven intimate one-shots portrayed senior administration officials as a rogue's gallery or freak-show that had usurped republican high office. Bush looked vacant, distracted, deranged, shifting spasmodically around his seat. Cheney was inscrutable, the closeness of the shot capturing the hint of a smirk. Ashcroft was part-joker, part-narcissist, part-schoolyard bully. Wolfowitz famously licked his comb before straightening his hair. In another scene, Moore recycled the famous footage showing Bush in a classroom at the Emma Booker Elementary School in Sarasota, Florida, where the president was engaged in a photo-opportunity on the morning of 9/11 – the children grouped round his feet and the president bewildered and inert, forming a tableau that emphasised Bush's failure as a figurative 'father' to the nation.

The president's abnegation of executive duties, and the unitary executive's erosion of republican process, were constant, insistent, damning refrains in *Fahrenheit 9/11*. The film reserved its most poignant polemic for what it depicted as the betrayals of young American servicemen and women sent to Iraq. Nowhere was *Fahrenheit 9/11*'s dissent so avowedly republican than in the sequences where Moore accused the administration of abnegating its duty of care to citizens enlisting in its armies. For Moore, the military service of young Americans in Iraq wasn't conducted in the national interest, but in the interests of a self-serving corporate-political elite for whom regime change meant new markets and fresh investment opportunities. In the later sections of the film that dealt explicitly with Iraq, Moore's representation of the occupation as militarised incursions of American capital paid for by ordinary working people brought the film close to some of the revisionist Wisconsin School accounts of American empire offered by contemporary historians (see Chapter 1). Moore was careful not to use inflammatory terms like 'imperialism' and 'class war'. However, powerful sequences, such as those showing army recruiters preying like a post-industrial press-gang on African American kids with no meaningful prospects in the devastated economy of Flint, Michigan, displayed Moore's keen eye for motifs rooted in folk-memory and popular culture, and left audiences in little doubt that imperial policy overseas functioned as an outgrowth and expression of entrenched class antagonisms at home.

Much of what was said in *Fahrenheit 9/11* had already been well covered elsewhere, but Moore's film took the issues to a mass audience in an election year, at a time when the audience was there to receive them. Aesthetically too, *Fahrenheit 9/11* was a *tour de force*. Top heavy, perhaps, and tiresome in the untheorised attention it gave to the Bush family's connections with the Al Sauds, the film was nonetheless remarkable for its welding of Moore's talent for polemical editing to his extensive borrowings from fictional films and TV shows (including classics like *The Magnificent Seven* and *Dragnet*), a technique that meant *Fahrenheit 9/11*'s politics were often embedded in a rich inter-textual tapestry of American popular culture.

Partly for this reason, and partly because of its overtly polemical tone, *Fahrenheit 9/11* stretched conventional definitions of documentary. Less interested in recording facts than in evoking 'core truths', and more concerned with 'performing' reality than with mimesis, *Fahrenheit 9/11* looked and sounded like a highly evolved form of what contemporary commentators had begun referring to as 'performative' documentary – a film mode 'as much concerned with representing reality' as more traditional documentary forms, but which was also 'more aware of the inevitable falsification or subjectification such representation entails' (Bruzzi 2000: 155). *Fahrenheit 9/11* was 'performative' partly because it drew attention so willingly to the processes of its own construction, emphasising that, like all film forms, the documentary is an artifice, a manufactured and storied product assembled from sundry acts of creative labour – not an unproblematic mirror held up to an unmediated 'reality'. Owing to the sheer amount of visual material and soundtrack music *Fahrenheit 9/11* quoted, and because so much of what was quoted came from such instantly recognisable sources, the seams stitching one bit of *Fahrenheit 9/11* to the next bit – and the arbitrary processes of editing and authorship doing the stitching – were never far from view. Due to the multiple parts he performed, both within the diegesis as protagonist (where he starred in the roles of activist, filmmaker, interviewer, comedian and celebrity), and outside it as director and editor, Moore also remained highly visible and audible as a pressure 'authoring' the action throughout much of the film. Some viewers may have felt that there were limits to *Fahrenheit 9/11*'s 'performativity'. At times Moore's polemical tone made the film look more like the substitution of one absolutist understanding of what was 'real' (Moore's) for another (Bush's). But performativity in documentary film, as Stella Bruzzi suggests, does not preclude the expression of partisan politics. Quite the opposite. One effect of stressing the necessarily fabricated, narrative-based nature of all representation, including documentary film, is that the political treatise or propagandist statement becomes no less 'real' or 'truthful' than the most notionally detached, objective or observational film form.

Fahrenheit 9/11's 'performative documentary' styles also borrowed from techniques used in Hollywood fiction film, harnessing melodramatic 'characterisation' – and the network of audience attachments and identifications melodrama makes possible – to the production of political sentiment in audiences. Melodrama, film critics have argued, is Hollywood's 'fundamental mode' and one of its principal attractions as a commodity, offering audiences the chance to experience a range of emotions in heightened or exaggerated form (Williams 1998; see also Gledhill 1987; Byars 1991; Maltby 2003). Melodrama attains this goal with 'stories of family trauma, pathos, and heightened emotionalism . . . a presentation of sensational events, a moral didacticism, and a determined attempt to provoke a sequence of emotional responses in the audience' (Maltby 2003: 101–2). All these genre elements were applied in spades to Moore's dramatisation of the Lila Lipscomb story in the final act of *Fahrenheit 9/11*, with Lila 'characterised' as the model republican citizen cruelly betrayed by her president. If the melodrama did its job, by the time that Lila tearfully read to the camera her son's last letter from Iraq, and then broke down outside the White House, the pain at her loss felt too much to bear because viewers identified with her, and so shared vicariously in part of that pain.

Moore's appropriation of Hollywood's 'fundamental mode' demonstrated again his savvy use of pop culture and his instinct for what was radical or progressive in it. For all its sledgehammer aesthetics and moments of occasionally simplistic conspiracy theory, *Fahrenheit 9/11* wore its understanding of what it meant to make activist films more lightly, and with a more intuitive grasp of the filmmaker's tools best suited to activist work, than films like *Syriana* or *Good Night, and Good Luck*. Like Moore's earlier films *Roger and Me* and *Bowling for Columbine*, *Fahrenheit 9/11* was particularly adept at constructing a populist perspective on current events, summoning a diverse and inclusive range of witnesses to speak against the Bush administration. Collectively, the soldiers, families of soldiers, conscientious objectors, schoolkids, writers, pundits and analysts, FBI agents and policemen, politicians, bereaved victims of 9/11, 'senior' and other concerned citizens speaking to camera in *Fahrenheit 9/11*, formed a decentralised republic of voices arrayed against Bush. The film called them 'the American people'.

This merging of Moore's voice and the voice of the film with 'the people', meant that Moore's extravagant performances of himself were also implicitly 'performances' of a more public realm – performances, as it were, of the obligations that citizens owe to the world beyond themselves, in return for the protections afforded them by their membership of public space. The opening sentence of Moore's *Stupid White Men*, 'I am a citizen of the United States of America' (Moore 2002: 1), was a very knowing introductory line in a book that repeatedly discussed the responsibilities that come with the rights of citizenship, a book that would also eventually form the basis for significant sections of *Fahrenheit 9/11*. At the end of *Stupid White Men*, Moore observed that 'giving a few hours . . . each week to be *citizens*' was 'the highest honor to hold in a democracy' (ibid.: 256, Moore's italics). In this respect the political logic driving the film was quite traditional, with the movie often looking and sounding more like an old-fashioned treatise on virtuous republican citizenship than a revolutionary essay on class war.

Whatever else it was, *Fahrenheit 9/11* often looked like Moore's giving of those 'few hours', a portrait of the citizen as activist that enabled the activist-citizenship of its interviewees, and that solicited it in its audience – not least in the spaces Moore cleared in the film for audiences to involve themselves, or at least to feel involved, in his populist denunciations of the Bush administration. For a film that was often so didactic and packed, and that included sequences where the first-time viewer occasionally staggered through blizzards of information and comment, *Fahrenheit 9/11* was also, as one critic put it, 'often reflectively slow and . . . not afraid of silence' (Berger 2004). In its busier sequences, the film's extensive sampling of American popular culture (films, TV shows, music, celebrities, an interview with Britney Spears) maximised the points at which a mass audience could engage with the issues that it raised. Another notable facet of *Fahrenheit 9/11* was the frequency with which it posed questions directly to its audience: 'Was something else going on?' 'Will they ever trust us again?' 'What was he thinking in that chair?' 'What kind of president was he?' 'Was it all just a dream?' 'How does someone like Bush get away with something like this?' 'Was he wondering if maybe he should have shown up to work more often?' 'Why didn't Bush want the press and the public to see Bath's name on his military records?' Moore tended to answer these questions himself, of course. They were rhetorical, but they also helped solicit the participation of audiences in the construction of the film's meanings, so that when Moore made the leaps of political imagination out of which the film was built, the audience was able to make those leaps with him.

If Moore's republican disquisition on the duties and obligations of the virtuous citizen and filmmaker had more in common with Jefferson or Thoreau than Marx, his fondness for stunts that combined participatory democracy with play and mockery of the state also suggested that the immediate intellectual influences shaping *Fahrenheit 9/11* came from the 1960s. Riding round Congress in an ice cream van reading the Patriot Act through a loudhailer was in the same recognisable lineage of theatrical protest as attempts to levitate the Pentagon in 1967, or the 'Festival of Life' outside the Democratic Party's national convention in Chicago the following year, where Yippies (the Youth International Party) nominated a pig called Pigasus as their candidate for president. The delight Moore took in filming state functionaries condemning themselves with their own words or deeds also recalled the countercultural New Left's delight in the comedic ironies by which 'the system' could be made to reveal its own brutalism or irrationality. In the 1960s, Yippies scattered dollar bills from the balcony of the Stock Exchange on Wall Street and then photographed the unseemly scrambling of the brokers below. In *Fahrenheit 9/11*, Moore showed us footage of Donald Rumsfeld talking about the 'care' and 'humanity' with which US troops were prosecuting the Iraq war against shots of the corpses of Iraqi children.

Fahrenheit 9/11 played to packed cinemas across the US, even in solidly Republican states, taking more than $100 million at the box office in its first six weeks (almost half of what was taken by *Harry Potter and the Prisoner of Azkaban* in a comparable period the same summer [Berger 2004]). In certain respects *Fahrenheit 9/11* was also a quite traditional, and in the context of contemporary political debate quite conventional, articulation of the 'republican crisis' sensibility. Moore's characterisation of himself, Lila Lipscomb and other dissenting voices as proud patriots, his misguided faith that the 2004 elections would see the American people dispose of Bush, and his committed defence of the Constitution (a document that the contemporary empire revisionist, David Harvey, described as 'bourgeois to the core' [Harvey 2003: 47]), all suggested that the crisis lay not in the institutions themselves so much as their current incumbents. In *Fahrenheit 9/11*, Moore's faith that the institutions and values of republican democracy would see off Bush fed his representation of the administration as a rogue's gallery or freakshow, an aberration in a system that was fundamentally sound. The film's representation of the Bush administration as freakish and aberrant, and its populist valorising of existing institutions as the route back to a normative and equitable political culture, were typical of a lot of liberal war on terror commentary, in that the film fetishised the American political system, separating it off from the broader structures of capitalist power in which representative democracy is enmeshed. A knock-on effect of this in *Fahrenheit 9/11* was to weaken the film's contention that the war on terror was a class war at home, because it downplayed the extent to which class power radiates from the same political processes and institutions (representative democracy and the US Constitution) that Moore identified as political solutions to the un-American aberration of the Bush administration. In part this was itself a function of a more general problem in *Fahrenheit 9/11*, and in Moore's books – a populist conception of class conflict as 'the people' versus 'the corporate-political elite', which lent itself to Moore's fetishising of existing institutions, and which prevented *Fahrenheit 9/11* from unpacking more fully the reciprocal relationships it identified between class hierarchies at home and 'imperialist' foreign policy abroad.

For all its flaws, though, *Fahrenheit 9/11* was a brave film, probably the most important film of the era, by an American filmmaker who was prepared to put his head above the parapet over Iraq from the very start, at a time when public figures who did so risked vilification, or worse (see Chapter 2). Moore (Figure 4.4) drew almost as much hostility from the antiwar 'left' as he did from pro-Bush constituencies; but his willingness to do the dirty, difficult and dangerous work of public dissent during wartime threw into stark relief again the kinds of films that Hollywood was making after 9/11, and the kinds of films it refused to make.

---

1. Co-produced by the Democratic Party activist Scott Rudin, *The Manchurian Candidate* was made by Paramount Pictures, whose head of production,

Figure 4.4 Michael Moore, photographed by Marcel Hartmann, May 2004, Paris.
© Marcel Hartmann/Corbis.

Sherry Lansing, was a well-known contributor to the campaign to elect Democrat Senator, John Kerry, as president in 2004 (Hoberman 2004).
2. John Kerry's record of military service in Vietnam, for which he was deco-rated, was attacked in the summer of 2004 by a veterans' group funded by a major Republican Party donor in Texas, Swift Boat Veterans for Truth, who produced a 60-second TV ad and a book alleging that Kerry had exaggerated

his war record and had betrayed American troops by protesting against the war when his tour of duty was over.

3. Leo Strauss was a political philosopher credited in the early war on terror as a key intellectual influence on contemporary neoconservatives (see Chapter 2). The patrician idea of the 'noble lie', whose provenance in Strauss's thought was contested, proposed that the deception of citizens by enlightened elites was virtuous because it helped secure social cohesion.

5 Literature

The 9/11 Novel

Classifying a literary genre, particularly a new or emergent one, can be a fraught process. Genres are hardly ever watertight things. They spill over into and borrow from other genres and may contain multiple 'subgenres'. Some generic examples may contain some generic elements but not others. Readers themselves may be unfamiliar with the genre that is assumed to guide their reading of a given generic text. They may disagree among themselves on the elements that count as generic, or may read through a prism that has little to do with genre as such. Yet even with these reservations, and with a fairly elastic definition of 'the 9/11 novel' in place, a striking set of themes, motifs and literary forms could be seen at work, regularly and distinctively enough to be considered generic, in the first flush of novel-length writing about 9/11 and its consequences – that is, 9/11 fiction of the 'crisis' years or the 'early 9/11 novel', from Philip Roth's *The Plot Against America* (2004) to Cormac McCarthy's *The Road* (2006).

The early 9/11 novel generalised from contemporary events a working definition of historical experience as trauma; meaning that history in general, not just 9/11, was often cast as an affliction that engulfed human agency and influence, leaving no foothold from which to fashion either effective notions of participative citizenship or art.[1] The early 9/11 novel cohered as a generic world of heightened subjectivities and interiorised or 'narcissistic' narrative voices that were often emotionally damaged, unstable or mentally ill, and that viewed both history and the ungovernable public spaces beyond the self as dangerous terrain. There were notable exceptions, but the early 9/11 novel generally understood history to be governed by random factors – contingency, opportunism and unintended consequences – rather than motivated decision-making, policy initiatives or the working through of vested interests. 9/11 novelists also questioned the capacity of language, and by extension their own novels, to construct meaningful civic engagements with contemporary events. In certain cases, in the same

way that some of the visual art discussed in Chapter 6 exhibited a preference for making art about art, the 9/11 novel sometimes seemed
more concerned with debating the responsibilities and limitations of
writers, than with writing about 9/11 itself. Some authors appeared to
want to address what they described as their art's lack of purchase on
contemporary events by experimenting with literary form, notably by
incorporating visual materials into prose narrative and by returning to
older forms of metafiction.[2] Other well-worn 'experimental' techniques included the use of multiple narrators, unreliable narrators and
narrators whose fragmented or 'stream of consciousness' styles worked
in a variety of ways to disrupt or critique older realist conventions. In
many ways, novelists' relationships with 9/11 sounded a lot like 'lost-
generation' responses to the First World War, but without the faith
often displayed by lost-generation writers that art would see them
through in the end.[3]

Thematically, like Hollywood allegory lite, 9/11 novels weren't
always directly 'about' 9/11 or its consequences. The early 9/11 novel
had a particular tendency to sublimate contemporary anxieties about
state activity, and about the state's jeopardising of the safety of its citizens, in stories about the failures of family members to protect one
another – particularly the failure of parents to protect children. During
the 'crisis' years, major 9/11 novels by Philip Roth, James Kelman and
Frédéric Beigbeder (2004), Reynolds Price, Jonathan Safran Foer and
Ian McEwan (2005), John Updike and Cormac McCarthy (2006),
and minor work by novelists including Patrick McGrath, Philip Beard
and Nick McDonnell (2005), all put either orphans or troubled children and youths, or adult sons and daughters involved in distressing
relationships with parents or 'guardian' figures (usually fathers), at
the centre of their work. A number of these writers also used child-
narrators, and drew overtly on *bildungsroman* conventions.

In Roth's *The Plot Against America*, which imagined the pioneering
aviator, folk-hero and famous American fascist Charles Lindbergh,
elected to the White House in 1940 instead of Roosevelt, the failure of
'paternal' protection took three overlapping forms – the inability of the
narrator's father to protect his family against the backwash of fascism,
a betrayal of American Jews by rabbinical authority, and attacks on the
Jewish-American community by the president himself (whose abuse of
the executive role of father to the nation was contrasted, by Roth
(Figure 5.1), with the benign paternalism of Roosevelt and the New
Deal state). Generally read by critics at the time as a loose allegory of
political authoritarianism in the Bush White House, the most intrigu-
ing strand of Roth's novel about fascists seizing power in the US was

Figure 5.1 Philip Roth in New York, May 2007.
© Orjan F. Ellingvag/ Dagbladet/Corbis.

the warnings it gave about the influence of sentimental nationalist iconography on ultra-patriotic post-9/11 versions of American nation-hood (see particularly Chapter 3). Roth's child-narrator collected stamps. One item in his collection haunted him, a set of National Parks stamps picturing romanticised Western American landscapes, in the Rocky Mountain School mode of an Albert Bierstadt or Thomas Moran. Early in the novel, against a rising tide of anti-Semitism in the US, the narrator has a dream in which the iconic 'American' landscapes on the stamps are superimposed with swastikas. The important thing was the easy segue between the two, the smoothness of the transition that seemed possible between canonical imagery of 'sublime' American landscapes closely associated with nineteenth-century ideologies of Manifest Destiny, and the bowdlerised nationalist Romanticism of the Nazis. Certain strands of fascist mythography, and certain strands of American mythography, Roth implied, were drawn from the same aes-thetic well and were different in degree, not in kind. The proposition that the potential for fascism was somehow in the American grain, an idea that was also latent in Art Spiegelman's celebrated graphic novel *In The Shadow of No Towers* (2004), put *The Plot Against America*'s dis-cussion of post-9/11 governance on dangerous ground, certainly when compared to contemporary Hollywood allegory lite (though Roth was careful to describe Lindberg's coming to power as accidental and atypical, a product of political opportunism and bad political judgement, and not an illustration of systemic flaws or engrained authoritarian tendencies). In this respect Roth's novel was quite conventional, including in its 'allegorical' sketching of Lindberg/Bush as political aberrations the same clear commitment to existing political institutions and processes that converted contemporary cries of 'crisis' in republican governance into *de facto* affirmations of Americanism.

Generic emphasis on the vulnerability of children in the 9/11 novel peaked as the 'crisis' peaked, in 2006, in Cormac McCarthy's extraordinary, Pulitzer prize-winning, *The Road*. Readers joined the novel as a father and his young son headed south across a post-apocalyptic American landscape, with winter coming on. An unexplained cataclysm had scorched the surface from the Earth, all but extinguishing human life and consigning the survivors to a hellish, Hobbesian existence, in a dead landscape where everything, everywhere, was steeped in the ashes left over from the end of the world. From the outset *The Road* was a gruelling read. McCarthy structured the narrative so as to emphasise simultaneously both the young child's awful vulnerability to the predations of the post-apocalypse (extreme cold, starvation, illness, rape, slavery, cannibalism) and the likely death of the father who protects him. By making both the child's terror and the father's awareness of the child's terror central in the narrative, and by forcing the reader to dwell upon and engage emotively with these twinned experiences, McCarthy sustained a palpable sense of dread throughout *The Road*, which was heightened at key moments in the narrative by the heartbreaking bonds of love tying father hopelessly to son and son hopelessly to father. Just as important were the ties McCarthy engineered between protagonists and readers. Contemporary reviews, internet message boards and discussion forums suggested that although the book was at the plainer end of McCarthy's prose styles, it was difficult to read because it dramatised so painfully the darker fantasies of many readers at the time of 9/11. *The Road*'s grounding in apocalyptic trauma, in the ruins of an American civilisation buried in ash, made the novel's many poetic resonances with 9/11 and the war on terror explicit and unavoidable. Read in these contexts, rather than as the consummation of one writer's *oeuvre* (though *The Road* certainly looked like this as well), the novel pushed the generic conventions of early 9/11 fiction about as far as some of them could go, partly because McCarthy extended the 9/11 novel's generic stress on the flimsiness of Western modernity into full-blown apocalypse and partly also because *The Road* fetishised, and in the process heightened to an almost unbearable degree, the genre's central concern with children/citizens divested of parental/state protection. In McCarthy's apocalypse this divestment was all deferred Gothic horror, and civil society and the state itself were literally blown away.

Bleak and Beckettian in its exposition of the repetitive and meaningless rhythms of life in a world where survival meant only suffering, *The Road* created an aesthetic world with an inner logic so profound that it apparently engulfed some readers. As in his previous work, McCarthy turned violence, domination and chaos into eternal verities, in a worldview that chimed darkly at times with the pessimistic, paranoid, master/slave psychodramas of contemporary neoconservatism. Nevertheless, *The Road* still felt like a great American novel. McCarthy dallied with literary cliché – the wasteland, civilisations in ashes, the endless road, the child as repository of goodness, hope, innocence. But this was part of the point. At a time when apocalyptic imagery seemed to proliferate almost exponentially in Western culture, often becoming merely kitsch in the process, McCarthy's real achievement in *The Road* was to evoke prevailing sensibilities with such poetic poignancy by infusing hackneyed tropes with resonant meaning and fresh emotional depth.

The Road's ability to do this with such 'American' literary themes and motifs made it the first 'great American novel' of the war on terror era. The arc from Roth's overtly politicised use of the imperilled child motif in *The Plot Against America* to its appearance in McCarthy as an illustration of allegedly universal truths was also indicative of a generic preference for the abstraction or sublimation of contemporary events in literary narrative, a tendency that quickly became established as a major self-referential theme in the fiction itself. One textbook example of this was Reynolds Price's *The Good Priest's Son*, the story of Mabry Kincaid, a 53-year-old widower, philanderer and professional art conservator returning to the South for the first time in three years, drawn back to the family home and to an unresolved conflict with the father he believes has never loved him, by his unconfirmed diagnosis of a serious, degenerative illness, and a childlike anxiety about who will care for him in his declining years. *The Good Priest's Son* opened in a plane bound for New York, diverted to Nova Scotia on the morning of 9/11 as US air space shut down; but it rapidly became a story about Kincaid's self-obsessed quest for 'parental' protection. Like a frightened child, Kincaid told everyone he met about his prospective medical condition and approached most of them (including strangers) to act as his full-time carer. Against this backdrop of an all-consuming, imagined private tragedy, *The Good Priest's Son* built a narrative point of view in which 9/11 became merely a 'local calamity' (Price 2005: 221) largely submerged in the protagonist's self-obsessed point of view.

The Good Priest's Son was complicated by the fact that the novel was aware of Kincaid's narcissistic perspective on 9/11 and appeared at times to critique it, partly by having other protagonists comment on Mabry's unreliability as a narrator. An old flame, Gwyn Williams, called him 'a self-enraptured maniac', a 'self-absorbed post-adolescent friend' and 'a narcissistic brat'. 'The whole of Western civilization', she observed, 'ended this week on native ground, and all it means to you is your own piddling business' (ibid.: 75, 77). Gwyn's overstatement threw Kincaid's narcissism into relief, confirming the suspicion that, for Price, much of what Kincaid said about 9/11 was plain wrong – notably his assertion that the attacks were meaningless to non-New Yorkers, a claim flatly contradicted by several of the novel's Carolinian protagonists. Kincaid's narcissism was also made problematic by Price's decision to use a third-person narrator, which encouraged the reader to objectify the protagonist's self-obsession as one narrative element among others, rather than adopt it as a point of view. The title of the novel too, with its parable-like overtones, encouraged readers to objectify Kincaid's story, or hold it at an emotional distance while reading, viewing it as a morality tale or an illustration of proverbial wisdom, with Mabry Kincaid as the prodigal 'good priest's son' of the title.

In this respect, *The Good Priest's Son* was a novel that put the narcissistic repression of 9/11 in storytelling at the centre of the narrative it told. The close pairing – and regular comparison – of 9/11 to the unrelated private tragedies of Mabry Kincaid meant that underlying this displacement there was often bathos, not pathos, at the heart of the novel. In the manner of a lot of contemporary post-metafiction literature, the early 9/11 novel was very self-aware, very conscious of making an inward turn at a time of public historical crisis, and quite happy to discuss the paradox that its apparent concern for 'real-world' issues often entailed a flight from direct civic engagement with them. This procedure of engaging 9/11 and the Western body politic by disengaging from them recalled the 'conscience liberalism' of Hollywood 'allegory lite' (see Chapter 4). The 9/11 novel, however, differed considerably from Hollywood and from some of the 'narcissistic' visual art discussed in Chapter 6, because its frankness about its own 'condition' allowed it to turn acts of literary repression, displacement and sublimation into key generic themes. *The Good Priest's Son* wasn't literature about literature exactly, but it was certainly writing about 9/11 that seemed stuck in a discussion with itself about the terms on which a 9/11 novel might proceed.

This tension between momentous worldly events – which often appeared explicitly only as backdrop or backstory – and the pull to narrative interiorisation was quite generic in the early 9/11 novel. Like *The Good Priest's Son*, Ian McEwan's *Saturday* also used a third-person voice to construct and objectify a self-obsessed central protagonist, the surgeon Henry Perowne. *Saturday* told the story of the Perowne family's disastrous encounter with a violent local gangster, set against a backdrop of the massive public demonstration against the looming war in Iraq in London, on 15 February 2003. McEwan packed *Saturday* with long sections of interiorised personal reflection from Perowne, often couched in the impenetrable professional jargon of the consultant neurologist. Though it used an omniscient third-person narrator, what felt most important in *Saturday* was the personality and consciousness of Perowne. Given what he was thinking about – the invasion of Iraq, the demonstration, his family, working conditions for skilled middle-class labour, London, Charles Darwin, his own insignificance in the greater scheme of things – the inward-looking propensity of the narrative was held in tension with the public and historical nature of the novel's major themes. The plot too was structured around this tension, in the intrusion of a dangerous public world – the gangster, Baxter, and his thugs – into the private domestic sanctuary of the Perowne family home.

McEwan linked the presentation of Perowne as an interiorised presence in the narrative to *Saturday*'s discussion of the disempowerment of citizens; a theme made more palatable or reassuring in the novel because it mutated, when filtered through the consciousness of Perowne, into a more abstract existential discussion about the limits of human agency and influence in a universe that was indifferent to human desire. As millions marched against the war in London and around the world, one thing about which Perowne was certain was that 'the war's going to happen, with or without the UN, whatever any government says or any mass demonstrations' (McEwan 2005: 189). Throughout the novel Perowne meditated frequently on his inability to influence situations or circumstances beyond the immediate and the local, troubled by 'the powerful currents and fine-tuning that alter fates, the close and distant influences, the accidents of character and circumstance', and 'the random ordering of the world . . . at every instant, a trillion trillion possible futures' (ibid.: 65, 128). It was 'an illusion', Perowne asserted, 'to believe himself active in the story'. In the face of war, history and the working through of cosmic laws of nature, he was 'culpable in his helplessness', but also 'helplessly culpable' (ibid.: 180, 22).

Perowne took solace in a Darwinian logic that was presented to the reader as a coherent worldview, or ideology, in the sense that it allowed him to reconcile his feeling of helplessness with his belief that Western modernity was the embodiment of a progressive, evolutionary, narrative history. As a neurosurgeon, a Darwinian and a member of the Western middle class insulated more than most from the impacts of scarcity, predation and war, Perowne embraced 'biological determinism in its purest form' (ibid.: 93), imagining human history as the outgrowth of conflicts thrown up by the working through of evolutionary laws governing natural selection. Life and the forms it took, Perowne felt, arose 'from physical laws, from war of nature, famine and death', from laws 'driven on by the blind furies of random mutation' (ibid.: 56) – laws that functioned outside human decision-making and beyond human control. Perowne's Darwinism placed people on the periphery of historical processes as a matter of natural law, characterising human agency as an energy that merely confirmed or hastened outcomes that were both random and irresistible. Because the narration granting the reader access to Perowne's inner thoughts was so effectively interiorised, Perowne's worldview seemed indivisible at times from the novel's. However, the merger of Perowne's consciousness with the worldview of the novel wasn't entirely complete, and like much post-9/11 fiction, *Saturday* also included space for the reader to adopt a more sceptical perspective on what the narrative itself said. McEwan was careful, for example, to imply that Perowne's worldview could have political consequences that included a naturalising of the coming war, or its attribution to unintended consequences, accidents and contingencies, rather than vested interests, imperial designs or the working through of other elite agendas.

The most elaborate and exaggeratedly 'narcissistic' early 9/11 novel was Jonathan Safran Foer's *Extremely Loud and Incredibly Close*, a complex fiction grounded in the narrative of Oskar Schell, a disturbed child prodigy whose father had perished in the World Trade Center. Foer also made use of two further narrators: Oskar's paternal grandparents, who as youths had survived the incineration of Dresden by allied bombers during the Second World War, and whose troubled relationship was scarred by memories of Dresden and by the grandfather's love affair with his then future wife's sister, Anna, who died in the firestorm that consumed the city.

Extremely Loud and Incredibly Close presented its discussion of 9/11 and its aftermath in literary forms that dissolved almost entirely the sense of a viable social or civic space in the fictive world. Almost everything about Foer's novel drove the attention of the reader inward, into the private agonies of the traumatised self and away from any meaningful contextualising of 9/11 in public or historical space. Both Oskar Schell and the novel he inhabited responded to trauma and to the anticipation of future catastrophe by shrinking their respective subjectivities to a defensive emotional core held at one remove from the treacherous world 'out there'. Since the novel's three narrators discussed in detail their relationships with each other and with other protagonists they knew in common, their narratives intersected repeatedly. However, the highly stylised manner in which each addressed the reader meant that the three narratives also remained distinctive and discrete, each inhabiting a distinctively different textual space. The vivid evocation of protagonists' interior states of consciousness within those private textual spaces – in language that was often abstract, fragmented and punctuated by disorienting bursts of synchronic memory – appeared to ring-fence each of the three voices, dislocating them one from another, disrupting formally any sense of a broader public realm beyond the self in the fictive world Foer created.

This interiorisation of narrative voice in *Extremely Loud and Incredibly Close* was underwritten by Foer's deft characterisation, the cadences, mannerisms, private tics and personal histories of the voices that spoke revealing themselves gradually to readers, often between the lines of what was said, or in the gaps that opened up between competing protagonists' accounts of the same situation or circumstance. The novel's interiorisation of 9/11 narrative was also carried in a series of bold formal experiments that included the use of full-page photographs and other visual images inserted into the written text. When Oskar went to the top of the Empire State Building, his visit was recorded in the words he wrote. But it was also recorded by a full-page photograph of the Empire State Building's viewing platform (Foer 2005: 246), the double-exposure of the image conveying Oskar's child-like fumbling with the camera as he struggled with his 9/11 phobia of tall buildings (ibid.: 244–5). In another passage, when Oskar alluded to the extent of his trauma by comparing himself to an elephant – proverbially, elephants 'never forget' – Foer inserted into the scene a close-up of an elephant's eyeball bulging alarmingly in its socket, the skin surrounding the eyes all wrinkled and reptilian (ibid.: 95). Since visual images like these often reiterated the emotional state of the protagonist described in language, Foer was able to generate sudden doublings of affect in the narration, plugging the reader directly into the depths of Oskar's trauma by overlapping repetitive and intensely rendered interiorised points of view in pictures as well as words (a technique that was also important in Art Spiegelman's graphic novel, *In the Shadow of No Towers* [2004]). Foer attained a similar emotional intensity by an unconventional use of page-space and typography, often in juxtaposition with other visual inserts. When Oskar eavesdropped unsuccessfully on a conversation between his mother and his psychiatrist (ibid.: 203–7), the language Foer wrote was fragmented, single words and phrases creating islands isolated in blank space on the page, so that we read as Oskar heard – with this immersion of the reader in Oskar's experience then doubled by the inclusion of a photograph of a 9/11 'jumper' falling from the World Trade Center (ibid.: 205).

Partly because of techniques like these, whose impacts geared the narrative towards the stimulation of intense and immediate emotional responses, and partly because the novel told the story of 9/11 from the point of view of a traumatised child, *Extremely Loud and Incredibly Close* verged on melodrama at times. This introduced a new level of interiorisation to the novel, putting the trauma of the suffering self at the centre of the narrative and expressing it in 'private' literary forms (letters, monologues, family confessions) that reinforced the inward-turning tone of the narrative and the concomitant repressing of historical and public spaces beyond the private self into the margins of the novel.

What was also noticeable, however, was the extent to which Foer's novel, like Price's, and like the early 9/11 novel generally, often seemed restless and dissatisfied by the narcissistic contexts in which it was confined. This source of significant textual friction in *Extremely Loud and Incredibly Close*, in a narrative that was otherwise geared smoothly towards the multiple 'resolutions' staged in the novel's closing scenes, manifested itself most obviously in a running commentary on the psychic ills and degradations of social life flowing from such damaging self-obsession. The New Yorkers Oskar encountered were invariably as damaged, scarred, unstable or fixated as he, and their experience seemed to be offered as the personification of the narrative interiorisations practised by the novel – each of them gripped, like Oskar, by private tragedy so all-consuming that they became private universes in which their victims endured blighted and asocial lives. Like George Willard in Sherwood Anderson's *Winesburg, Ohio* (1919), one of Oskar's roles in the novel was to reconnect characters made 'grotesque' by their withdrawal from the world back into social life, by integrating them into the public narrative spaces, such as they were, of the novel. As the parade of 'grotesques' regularly reminded the reader, throughout *Extremely Loud and Incredibly Close* the retreat into interiority was associated with illness, myopia, misrepresentation and misapprehension: 'when you hide your face from the world', as the grandfather put it, 'you can't see the world' (ibid.: 116). The grandfather confessed that his own withdrawal (he gave up talking after Dresden) was not therapeutic, but a 'disease' that had left him imprisoned in 'the marble of myself' (ibid.: 17, 33). The experience of 'complete privacy', he noted, was the experience of being 'surrounded by Nothing' (ibid.: 110–11).[4]

Extremely Loud and Incredibly Close's definition of private, interiorised experience as nothingness, and its suggestion that withdrawal from social, public or historical space produces only faulty vision, cleared room for the novel to evaluate its own interiorisations as ideological acts: versions of 9/11 that repressed, sublimated or otherwise 'contained' alarming narratives about empire, or 'blowback', or the Patriot Act, or any of the other historically grounded, interests-driven accounts of 9/11 that circulated in contemporary discourse after the event. The free rein Foer gave to the fantasy-life of the traumatised child-prodigy in *Extremely Loud and Incredibly Close*, evident throughout in the fractured subjectivism of Oskar's style as a narrator, but particularly pronounced when he was 'inventing things in my head', explicitly identified the novel's withdrawal into the private spaces of the child's prodigious imagination as repressive acts, flights from traumatic reality, or sublimations of it, that reinvented intolerable destructive energies (guilt, grief, anxiety, terror, self-loathing) as creative ones, in the things that Oskar 'invents'. So Oskar invents a tea kettle that whistles tunes and reads to him in his dead father's voice. He invents a 'birdseed shirt' that attaches birds to the human body, allowing people to fly should they need 'to make a quick escape' (ibid.: 1–2). He fashions jewellery for his mother in which, unbeknown to her, he has arranged beads so that they contain morse code transcriptions of his father's last phone calls from the World Trade Center – a perfect sublimation, in that it manages the act of repression by turning what can't be comfortably integrated into daily life (the father's death, Oskar's guilt at concealing the phone calls) into something ornamental, a thing to adorn and beautify the mother.

Repressing history as a function of trauma also became a major theme in the lives of the novel's other narrators. The grandfather wrote about his time with Oskar's grandmother as a life characterised by deep repression of traumatic history. 'Your mother and I never talk about the past', he confessed, in a letter never sent to Oskar's dead father, 'that's a rule' – just one rule in a highly structured, rule-governed life, lived in a state of heightened alert against damaging incursions of the past into everyday life in the present. 'Everything between us has been a rule to govern our life together', he said. 'So many rules, sometimes I can't remember what's a rule and what isn't' (ibid.: 108–9).

The structure of *Extremely Loud and Incredibly Close* also helped create a narrative atmosphere in which encounters with exaggerated attempts to repress or rewrite history became a mundane part of the reading experience. The interiorisation of narrators' voices governing the overall shape of the narrative allowed the thematic foregrounding of repression to emerge organically from within the form of the novel, saturating the narrative atmospherically in denial as a felt, readerly experience. This culminated, in the novel's concluding sequence, in a fantasy in which Oskar, with the reader's collusion, used his scrapbook/journal,

'Stuff That Happened to Me', to re-imagine 9/11, but this time running backwards, so that the collapse of the towers was reversed, and history was rewritten without the death of the father. The last fifteen pages of the novel were unnumbered photo-stills from 'Stuff that Happened to Me', showing images of a 9/11 'jumper' sequenced in such a way that, by flipping through the photos, instead of falling to the ground the figure jumped back into the building. In Oskar's reverie, on the morning of 9/11 his father took a lift from his office high in the World Trade Center to the ground floor, where he walked backwards to the subway, then home, where he 'unbrushed his teeth' and put hair on his face with a razor (ibid.: 326). The grandmother had a similar fantasy about Dresden, in which 'children pulled color from coloring books with crayons, and mothers who had lost children mended their black clothing with scissors' (ibid.: 309). In the grandmother's dream, the firestorm itself was packed back into bombs 'which rose up and into the bellies of planes whose propellers turned backward, like the second hands of the clocks across Dresden' (ibid.: 306–7). At the end of *Extremely Loud and Incredibly Close*, in the accounts of Oskar and the grandmother at least, 9/11 and the Dresden firestorm were perfectly repressed historical events, because neither event ever actually took place.

The problem here, at the end of the novel, was that with no page numbers given on the photographs, there was no explicit guidance on the order in which the images of Oskar's flip-book should be flipped. It was possible for the reader to flip the pages from back to front rather than, as Oskar wished, from front to back; so that far from reversing history and erasing 9/11, the jumper still fell from the top of the page to the bottom. This called into question Oskar's reliability as a narrator, since it made it possible for the reader to experience the end of the novel in a manner that directly contradicted his point of view. This was not the only instance in which the unreliability of Oskar's interiorised narrative seemed stressed. The numerous instances of Oskar self-harming, covering his body with bruises, suggested that while acts of willed repression may create temporary emotional equilibria for protagonists traumatised by history, they do so only by storing up a wellspring of corrosive energies that are displaced elsewhere. As the grandfather told Oskar in the novel's concluding sequence, 'Just because you bury something, you don't really *bury* it' (ibid.: 322). In this respect, the ambiguous ending to *Extremely Loud and Incredibly Close* provided by Oskar's flip-book, and the questions that it raised about his reliability as a narrator, closed the novel by drawing attention again to the acts of literary repression on which its own narrative superstructure was built.

Foer resolved the central tension in the early 9/11 novel – between

Figure 5.2 Frédéric Beigbeder.
© Christophe Russeil/Corbis KIPA.

the 'outward' pull of public history as literary theme and the 'inward' pull of interiorised narrative form – by retreating from engagement with any sense of history in the round, replacing it with a fetishisation of the traumatised private self. Frédéric Beigbeder's *Windows on the World*, which described the deaths of three fictional Americans – millionaire realtor Carthew Yorston, and his children David and Jerry – in the Windows on the World restaurant at the top of the North Tower, set off in the opposite direction (Figure 5.2). Initially, though, Beigbeder's narrative was once again directed inward, and the reader had to wade through lots of self-referential discussion about the purposes and limitations of literary 'art' in a protracted clearing of the novel's throat, during which the consequences of 9/11 for aesthetics sometimes seemed more important than the carnage of the attacks. The novel's epigraphs – with characteristic hubris, Beigbeder called them 'Lightning Rods' – addressed the obligations of the artist to represent the extremes of human experience realistically, while the title itself was also self-referential. 'Some critics claim cinema is a "window on the world"' Beigbeder noted, 'others say the novel is. Art is a window on the world' (Beigbeder 2004: 240). Using these realist descriptors as benchmarks of meaningful or useful art (art that explores and illuminates the world unflinchingly), *Windows on the World* pronounced itself a failure. 'It's impossible to write about this subject', it said. 'This thing happened, and it is impossible to relate' (ibid.: 8–9). After all, Beigbeder asked, 'what verb should one use for parking a plane in a building?' (ibid.: 93). *Windows on the World* described itself as a 'doomed' attempt to describe 'the indescribable', underscoring its pessimism about the limitations of language with the further observation that 'all books' were 'useless' (ibid.: 57, 27). The novel's recurring comparison of 9/11 to the Old Testament story of the Tower of Babel appeared to confirm Beigbeder's anxiety about what 9/11 meant for art. When God destroyed the Tower of Babel, part of the people's punishment for banding together in common revolt against divine authority was to be divided into groups separated by language. On 9/11, the novel told us, God 'set His face against New York' (ibid.: 121) and the punishment was the same, with one consequence of the loss of a common language about 9/11 being fresh confirmation, if any was needed, of the limits of literary realism. In the heat of 9/11, Carthew Yorston told readers, 'figurative paintings melt/And become abstracts' (ibid.: 151).

Windows on the World cut its narrative cloth accordingly, substituting for a single omniscient narrator (whose unifying voice might have reasserted the possibility of a consensus perspective on events, a first principle of realism) no fewer than four different narrators, each of whom was made provisional and relative by the presence of the others. In place of consensus realism, the voices of the two principal narrators – Carthew Yorston, and a characterisation of the author referred to here as 'Beigbeder' to differentiate him from the author (though a slippage between the two seemed assumed) – were supplemented by episodic chapters narrated by Yorston's dying children, David and Jerry. 'Beigbeder' referred to the novel as 'hyperrealism' (ibid.: 8), and went to some lengths to construct a narrative that would look 'hyperrealist'. In New York, 'Beigbeder' observed, sounding very like the French philosopher Jean Baudrillard, 'the skyscrapers carve out the blue like a cardboard stage set. In America, life is like a movie . . . . All Americans are actors and their houses, their cars, and their desires all seem artificial. Truth is reinvented every morning in America. It's a country that has decided to look like something on celluloid' (ibid.: 21). The novel's commentary on the limits of realism often recalled American fiction of the 1960s, and had roots that went back through 'lost-generation' modernism in the 1920s and 1930s, at least as far back as the late nineteenth century. Yet what the novel most resembled wasn't 'hyperrealism' so much as old-fashioned metafiction, its narrators too alarmed, or pessimistic, to take any decadent postmodern delight in the empty play of surfaces or endless deferrals of authentic meaning – the stories they told having too much emotional and intellectual depth, too many issues that were substantially and troublingly real, churning away beneath the surface.

Beigbeder's preference for self-referential metafiction delivered by multiple narrators enabled a process of reiteration, or doubling, in the narratives of 'Beigbeder' and Carthew Yorston. These narrators had their disagreements; but in many ways they also echoed and affirmed the other's opinions and experience. Both men were separated from partners, both had children, both saw the 1960s as the beginning of the end of Western civilisation, and both viewed 9/11 as one moment in that narrative of decline. One recorded his own death and those of his children in the restaurant at the top of the World Trade Center; the other wrote about 9/11 sitting in Le Ciel de Paris restaurant, on the 56th floor of the Tour Montparnasse. Recalling Foer's and Spiegelman's aggregation of prose and visual imagery for a doubling of emotional affect, this doubling in Beigbeder's narration (which also included occasional visual inserts) meant that, by addressing similar points of view in different registers, *Windows on the World* was able to tease out nuanced positions in ideas that were often dense and complex. At other times, as in Foer, this doubling also means that *Windows on the World* could restate and re-emphasise forcefully the issues at hand, by having narrators repeat one another in a formal encoding of overstatement or reiteration that was redolent of the highly politicised and often polemical climate of the time.

The most interesting thing about the Tower of Babel analogy in *Windows on the World* was that it opened the novel's metafictional discussion about itself into contexts that went beyond language alone. One of the principal lessons of 9/11, for Beigbeder, was that 'the immovable is movable' (Beigbeder 2004: 8); that American modernity at large – technologically, culturally, morally and ideologically (as a way of life, in other words, not just as a political or economic system) – was provisional, historical and relative, not the monolith or 'subject of history' proposed in its own mythologies. 9/11 trauma in *Windows on the World* was closely linked to shock at the sheer insubstantiality of American modernity, 'all those stone blocks so fragile', Beigbeder wrote, 'so much glass and steel transformed in an instant into a wisp of straw'. On 9/11, in *Windows on the World*, New York was 'a city of glass less substantial than a tepee' (ibid.: 116, 8, 248).

But what the novel really wanted to explore was the old premise that the tools that Western modernity devised to liberate society from nature, scarcity and domination – reason, technology, capitalism, democracy – had led to catastrophic new enslavements of the human body and mind.

Whereas classic post-9/11 essays by critics of architecture and urban design, Eric Darton and Marshall Berman, viewed the Trade Center's modernism as brutalist because the towers did not belong organically to the environment on which they were imposed, in Beigbeder's treatment the reader sensed that if the World Trade Center had not existed, then Manhattan would have been compelled to invent it, so continuous was its aesthetic logic with the angular modernity of Manhattan – the island itself 'a huge checkerboard, all the right angles, the perpendicular cubes, the adjoining squares, the intersecting rectangles, the parallel lines, the network of ridges, a whole artificial geometry in gray, black, and white' (ibid.: 14; see Darton 2002). 'Despite the immensity of the towers', Beigbeder wrote, 'there was something organic about them. This something which was more powerful than us, [which] was us all the same' (Beigbeder 2004: 247).

The point at which the 'organic' geometry of the World Trade Center became 'artificial', for Beigbeder, was the moment at which the ingenious human rationality invested in the towers became contradictory, the form that the buildings assumed converting those creative rational energies into destructive and irrational ends. In *Windows on the World*, the World Trade Center may have begun as a utopian endeavour, a 'city in the sky' (ibid.: 85) which confirmed human sovereignty over nature, but it ended with 'trembling humans huddled round a locked door surrounded by machines, pipes, deafened by the noise of the supercharged pumps and the hydraulic generators' (ibid.: 144). This 'dialectic of enlightenment' (Adorno and Horkheimer 1997) impressed itself on 'Beigbeder' at an early age. Visiting New York as a child, he felt 'physically dominated by these concrete monsters', uncomfortably aware that 'something existed that was more powerful than us', that the energy the buildings contained 'was not human' (Beigbeder 2004: 247). In *Windows on the World* the final messages of the dying were left on machines, or sent virtually by email. Little seemed left of social life that was not in some way harnessed to serve and support the irrationalities of post-industrial capitalism. Education was 'the murky depths of capitalist democracy', advertising 'the military wing of capitalism'. Before the novel even finished, Ground Zero became a 'theme-park ride' (ibid.: 70, 284, 303). Language itself, the very fabric of the novel and the writer's craft, was commodified and degraded in what 'Beigbeder' referred to as the 'brainless' corporate neologisms of the stockbrokers on whom he eavesdropped at Le Ciel de Paris (ibid.: 7). 9/11 may have killed realism (again), but language itself, for Beigbeder, was already dying or dead, just one more product of a 'system' that 'no longer runs smoothly', in a degraded and irrational civilisation geared to effect 'our own annihilation' (ibid.: 193).

If the modernity embodied in the World Trade Center put people 'above nature' (ibid.: 16), the lines dividing reason and culture from the chaotic undifferentiations of superstition and nature were continually breached in *Windows on the World*. One of the things that disturbed 'Beigbeder' most about Ground Zero was the mud, the edifice of concrete and steel 'transformed into a muddy heap', as 'man-made purity' gave way to 'natural filth' (ibid.: 129). Inside the burning towers Beigbeder imagined a return to faith, mysticism, religion, remnants of histories that came 'before', but that remained repressed within, the technological rationality of capitalist-democratic modernity. The World Trade Center, 'a temple to atheism and to international lucre', became 'a makeshift church'. Survivors exited the towers without panicking because 'they had faith in the solidity of buildings'. Anyone who thought the towers would not collapse had 'too much faith in technology'. When a piece of the fuselage of American Airlines flight 11 was shown to the public, 'Beigbeder' described it as a 'relic' displayed in a plexiglass case among other pseudo-religious 'ruined objects' from Ground Zero (ibid.: 127, 116, 148, 199).

Beigbeder's emphasis on the guiding influence of superstition and faith in late modernity complemented Roth's dissection of the roles played by romanticism and myth in ideological configurations of American nationhood. *Windows on the World*, however, while condemning 'bigoted anti-Americanism' (ibid.: 16–17), had none of Roth's optimism in the efficacy of American institutions. Nor did Beigbeder subscribe to Foer's assumption that laying bare the emotional depths of the traumatised self in art might compensate for, or cure, the degradations inflicted on selfhood by history and modernity. In *Windows on the World*, the old idea that realism could be a moral force in society, helping glue it together by depicting a world that would appear equally 'real' to all readers, however diverse, looked like just another trick of hubristic modernity. There were moments in the novel when Beigbeder, like Cormac McCarthy, appeared not to have given up completely on the possibility that human warmth and people's capacity for meaningful association might mitigate the moral wasteland of Western modernity with kindness, and with art. Carthew's final email to his lover – 'the only thing that belongs to us is our loneliness, and you interrupted mine' (eventually abbreviated to 'I loved you. C.Y.') – was defiantly humanist in the significance it attached to small acts of love hurled into the void (ibid.: 228). Likewise, the aching bond between father and son at the end, as Carthew and Jerry jumped from the top of the North Tower, meant that the novel climaxed with real, visceral, human emotion, conveyed with an economy and punch that often seemed lacking in Foer. When 'Beigbeder' described, in the plainest of language, the 'astonishing', 'mindblowing' hug from his three-year-old daughter, 'my nose in her hair', both the child and he 'overwhelmed with gratitude' (ibid.: 104), the simple, naive humanism of the moment was more moving and eloquent than anything in Foer's hyperventilating *sturm und drang*. There were also moments of redemptive black humour in *Windows on the World* – memorably, the delight the novel took in what Beigbeder termed 'apocalyptic politeness', a quaint 9/11 sensibility that he says turned New Yorkers into considerate and philanthropic citizens who helped blind people across roads and gave up their places in queues for cabs. Out of such small victories came hope. 'The end of the world makes people kind', 'Beigbeder' observed (ibid.: 195). But it was still the end of the world.

Another reason why Western modernity was already ruined in *Windows on the World* long before 9/11 was the pernicious effect of permissive liberalism on social life in advanced capitalist democracies, particularly the US. In the West, Beigbeder noted, the people are expected to 'shout from the rooftops how free we are, brag about how free we are. Die to defend that freedom'. Yet, as he also noted, 'I am not happy when I am free' (ibid.: 281). In *Windows on the World*, American and Western modernity were doomed partly because the connection made in liberal political philosophy between 'freedom' and 'happiness' no longer seemed plausible. The failure of 'raging liberalism' (ibid.: 291) as a set of cultural norms, moral values and lifestyle choices, particularly for the parenting of children, was a constant theme in *Windows on the World*, because Beigbeder identified it as a primary source of the entropy consuming Western modernity. Here, in a narrative thread that mapped directly onto established culture wars paradigms in the US, and onto contemporary debates about 'crisis' in the republic, permissive liberalism turned 'freedom' into a purely individualistic concept, robbing it of its contractual moral emphasis on obligations to others, and thus of its commitment to a broader 'civic' whole. The novel discussed how liberalism valorises both the permissive economy of desire and the acts of individualised consumption on which late capitalism depends for its reproduction as an economic system and way of life, facilitating a consumer capitalism whose logics work relentlessly to dissolve or inhibit meaningful human association, civic participation and non-commodified notions of 'freedom'. As Carthew Yorston put it, having mistaken pleasure and desire for 'freedom' instead of loneliness, 'I was incapable of living for anyone but myself' (ibid.: 274). Extrapolating from the entropy of republican culture in the US and

France a wider breakdown in the liberal humanist values of Western modernity in general, *Windows on the World* offered a penetrating dramatisation of contradictions in the 'Enlightenment project' – where freedom, Beigbeder observed, meant capitalism and liberalism, but capitalism and liberalism destroyed freedom.

Generally speaking, the early genre preference for child narrators, heightened subjectivities and interiorised or 'narcissistic' narrative voices held in check the references the 9/11 novel made to social and political conflicts in the 'homelands'. Cutting against this, another notable feature of early fiction about 9/11 was the generic prevalence of class-conscious narrators and protagonists. With the mechanics of capitalism under scrutiny in the diverse discourses of American empire that flourished after 9/11 (see Chapter 1), class again became a fashionable, self-aware theme, in the early 9/11 novel. At times Roth's *The Plot Against America* was intensely class-conscious, his descriptions of the petit-bourgeois fringes of affluent Weequahic Park – where 'there resided an occasional schoolteacher or pharmacist but otherwise few professionals' – rendering in minute detail the daily grind and social mores of lower-middle-class life in early 1940s New Jersey. Here, 'the men worked fifty, sixty, even seventy or more hours a week', while 'the women worked all the time'. It was labour, the narrator observed, 'that identified and distinguished our neighbors for me far more than religion' (Roth 2004: 3). In *Windows on the World*, Carthew Yorston complained that middle-class affluence corroded moral frameworks. Even Oskar Schell, in *Extremely Loud and Incredibly Close*, wondered momentarily whether 'maybe no one should have more than a certain amount of money until everyone had that amount of money', as an African-American servant brought him coffee on a silver tray (ibid.: 149–50).

The novels most notable for their pronounced class consciousness were by British writers. In contrast to Ian McEwan's discussion of middle-class sanctuary punctured by violent crime in *Saturday*, James Kelman's *You Have to be Careful in the Land of the Free* followed the generally dismal fortunes of Jeremiah Brown, an unskilled Scottish worker mulling over his years in America during a long night's drinking in Rapid City, South Dakota, before a scheduled flight home to Scotland the following day. Written without chapter breaks, as a single 400-page stream of interiorised consciousness, often drifting into impenetrable tangents that left gaps and holes in the narrative, at first sight Kelman's novel appeared generic enough in its inward turn. Though they cast a shadow across the whole tale, in *You Have to be Careful in the Land of the Free* 9/11 and the war on terror were referred to only sporadically – in Jeremiah's allusions to 'recent furnir [foreigner] disturbances' (Kelman

2004: 90), in the detention camp referred to as a 'Patriot Holding Center' where he worked and in the craze for so-called 'Persian betting', where Americans gambled on the survival of loved ones who booked commercial flights on US airlines.

Conventionally again, Kelman also wrote into the novel a self-referential narrative strand about writing – Jeremiah, too, was working on a novel. *You Have to be Careful in the Land of the Free*, however, was saved from the sheer interiority of a novel like *Extremely Loud and Incredibly Close* because Jeremiah's class-conscious gaze politicised absolutely everything it looked at. Jeremiah described the American Revolution as a war fought by merchants, and America as a 'good land' turned into 'a horror' by 'capitalist fuckers and their money-grabbing politico sidekicks' (ibid.: 34, 3). During his stint as a security guard at the Patriot Holding Center, where Jeremiah discovered his section 'wasnay allowed weapons of serious destruction lest we seriously destructed wur hosts', his labour was the object of rigorous surveillance by employers who had 'strategically-placed mics and cameras saturating the entire area' (ibid.: 154, 167). Kelman's reliable ear for an epithet drew the reader's attention, but the really hard work was done in the novel's constant subliminal anchoring of protagonist and narrative in class experience. Like his chronic gambling, which always offered 'that wee chance like ye could do something, change something, just fucking if ye got in front man, just a wee bit' (ibid: 129), other prominent character traits like Jeremiah's self-loathing ('I knew I was nothing, a naybody, stupit dreams maybe but nothing else' [ibid.: 69]) were presented as the direct product of working-class experience. His tendency to fantasise, for example, and so his unreliability as a narrator, were presented as the correlative of long hours of tedious, repetitive, unskilled labour, where the only way Jeremiah was able to keep his brain active was to indulge in the kind of flights of fancy that peppered his narration (ibid.: 193). Even sex, a literary archetype for the most private of experience, was overdetermined by class in *You Have to be Careful in the Land of the Free*. Nipples, Jeremiah confided, 'are wondrous creations. But for manual workers nipples are a trial. One has to sandpaper the hauns [hands] before going to bed with one's woman' (ibid.: 303).

One consequence of Kelman's 9/11 was a fracturing of what Mike Davis described in the 1990s as a 'fortressing' of contemporary urban American environments – the uses of architecture, planning and design as tools for the policing of class and ethnic segregations in built city space (see Davis 1990). Recalling his time employed as a security guard at the Patriot Holding Center, Jeremiah spent the central sections of the novel describing the subversive class politics of the 'Persian bet' (originally 'survive or perish bet', shortened to 'perishing bet', then 'Persian bet'), a form of gambling whereby bookies addressed the prohibitive cost of insurance for travellers flying with American airlines after 9/11 by offering odds on the chances of surviving a flight. 'If ye survived ye lost the bet', as Jeremiah put it, 'but if ye perished yer faimly collected the cash' (ibid.: 93). Soon, working-class Americans and 'poverty-stricken bodies on an income so far below what official government experts reckoned it took to stay alive that the term "income" was dropped' (ibid.: 119) were flooding America's airports hoping to strike it lucky, or to celebrate the safe return of loved ones. One effect of this was to contaminate spaces that urban 'fortressing' assigned to the rich. Before long, the nation's arrival and departure lounges were 'hoaching with ragged persons bearing blankets or pushing grocery carts', until even 'so-called "safe" areas were clogged full of folk', and 'executive-class' flyers faced 'lines of desperate-looking vagrant craturs staring them down' (ibid.: 121, 234). In one memorable scene, a grocery cart belonging to a celebrated cart-pusher known as 'the being' explodes in flames 'in the presence of higher-level dignitaries, right inside the goddam VIP suite, the one nearest the fast-track check-in area reserved for executive-class flights to DC'. After the 9/11 airline crisis and the Persian bet, Jeremiah concluded, 'airport terminals were no longer safe havens for people with dough' (ibid.: 232).

For all its pugnacity, wit and commitment, even Kelman's picaresque class fable seemed ambivalent about the stories it told. Jeremiah Brown's untrustworthiness as a narrator threw into relief again the early 9/11 novel's suspicion that contemporary events were somehow bigger than could be accommodated within established literary modes (particularly realism). In consequence, the 9/11 novel often seemed pessimistic about literature's ability to wrestle with civic issues in ways that would be relevant to readers. This trend was hardly a new one in contemporary fiction (see Holloway 2002). In the context of 9/11 and the war on terror, though, it was a trend that helped make 9/11 fiction one main current in a powerful contemporary culture of 'empire denial' (see Chapter 1), a culture that was challenged but never fully dislodged after September 11, even in the highly self-aware literary fictions of the 9/11 novel.

---

1. This understanding of 9/11 'trauma' as a vanishing of 'objective' or 'detached' positions from which to debate the ramifications of the attacks, and as a sclerosis in republican process, is discussed in greater detail in Chapter 3.
2. Metafiction: fictional accounts of actual events; fiction starring the author

or author-persona as a key protagonist; fiction that displays its awareness that it is a constructed fiction, making that awareness a theme in the novel; fiction that selfconsciously questions literature's relationship with the 'real'.

3. 'Lost generation' was Gertrude Stein's resonant phrase for the postwar generation of American writers, including Ernest Hemingway, e.e. cummings, Ezra Pound, Scott Fitzgerald and Hart Crane, famously canonised by Malcolm Cowley in *Exiles Return* (1934).

4. The grandmother, too, described the private spaces in their apartment as places 'where you could go and not exist' (Foer 2005: 176).

6 Photography and Visual Art

'Convulsions of empire' and 'adventures in cubism'. Visualising republican culture after 9/11

On 9/11 the pioneering internet artist Wolfgang Staehle recorded the attacks on the World Trade Center by mistake, as part of a live webcam art exhibit at the Postmasters Gallery, New York. Staehle pointed 'live' web-cameras at three locations around the world, one of which showed a panoramic view of lower Manhattan, and displayed the feeds as big-screen video projections. By the beginning of the end of the 'republican crisis' in 2006 (see Chapter 2), Staehle's accidental engagement with 9/11 looked like an increasingly persuasive metaphor for artworld responses to the attacks. If one notable trend in non-cinematic visual culture about 9/11 and the war on terror during the Bush years was the central role played by diverse forms of photography in public discussion of events, another was the relative marginality of the artworld. Professional and amateur photographers played a key role in recording 9/11, particularly at the World Trade Center, where the multiplicity of images made from every conceivable angle saturated the media sphere with such a synchronic surfeit of imagery that one contemporary commentator felt moved to label it 'a welcome adventure into cubism' (Ritchin 2002: 41). In the pictures of missing friends and relatives pinned to lampposts, newspaper stands and buildings in Manhattan (Figure 6.1), in the images broadcast globally by television, internet and traditional print media and in the major collections and books that followed, photography functioned as an overtly public culture. In this it was often notably at odds with the semi-detached, sometimes hermetic confines of the artworld, just as it was at odds with the 9/11 novel and the allusive film aesthetics of Hollywood 'allegory lite'. Even in the politicised climate of the Iraq war, when the administered 'consensus' of the immediate post-9/11 period fractured, and the rhythms of art production and exhibition had had time to metabolise the implications of the attacks, Bush era visual art often seemed remote from public discussion. Writing in the September 2004 issue of *ArtForum* magazine, the installation artist and veteran anti-Vietnam War activist Hans

Figure 6.1 19 September, 2001. A young woman looks at one of the many displays which sprang up spontaneously after the attacks of September 11, with photos of the missing, in New York.
© Stephane Ruet/Corbis Sygma.

Haacke felt moved to denounce what he called the 'escapist enterprise' of the 2004 Whitney Biennial, a reliably politicised exhibition during the 1990s, but in which 9/11 'hardly seem[ed] to have registered' (Haacke, in Griffin 2004b: 226). There were notable exceptions, but during the Bush years even art that intervened in war on terror debates often did so without the sense of explicit connection to civic process, and without the degree of public exposure, that accrued to photography almost instantaneously on 9/11.

The participation of mass audiences was central to both the critical and popular success of 9/11 exhibitions such as *here is new york* and Joe McNally's *Faces of Ground Zero* – a remarkable collection of life-size images of survivors and rescue workers that McNally made with a unique camera measuring eight feet by twelve feet, with a lens once used in a U-2 spy plane – which exhibited at Grand Central Station, New York, during January 2002. Art practitioners including Richard Serra, Jenny Holzer, Santiago Sierra and Tom Sachs produced challenging and politically charged assessments of contemporary events which also depended on a dynamic interaction with audiences, sometimes in public space. In Serra's case this meant a paintstick drawing, *Stop Bush* (2004), which was displayed in the decidedly populist forms of billboards and protest poster-art freely downloadable from the internet. Yet when compared to the million visitors said to have passed through the Manhattan exhibition space of *here is new york* during its first twelve months (Nadelson 2002a), even Serra's *Stop Bush* looked like relatively marginal art. Hamstrung sometimes by its association with elite taste and the market, and at others by an insistence that art was the antithesis of society rather than its conscience or mirror, the artworld had become 'so commodified, so precious, so out of the loop of ordinary people', that 'it was at a loss' after 9/11 to know how to respond (Charles Traub, one of the organisers of *here is new york*, in Nadelson 2002b: 69).

Generalisations like these, of course, are always unsustainable in the long run. They aim to summarise broad trends and tendencies, and are dangerous to the extent that they gloss over, or ignore altogether, the aesthetic and political complexities at work in contemporary visual culture. One important early critical account, by the art historian Francis Frascina, reminds us of a significant body of work made by New York-based artist activists during and immediately after 9/11, which 'not only documented conflicts and transformations caused by traumatic events and processes of grieving, but also provided a counter to seamless media rhetoric claiming that the events on September 11 were attacks on "civilization" or "liberty" or "the free world"' (Frascina 2003: 493). In video-making such as *9/12* by Dega Omar, and *9.11* by Indymedia, Big Noise Tactical Media and the New York City Independent Media Center, Frascina identified a radical visual culture that connected representation of the attacks to debates about 'dominant social and political forces at the heart of American governmental and corporate power' – connections that contrasted markedly with the post-9/11 recycling of Norman Rockwell paintings in the *New York Times*, or *here is new york*'s acceptance of corporate sponsorship (ibid.: 497). Yet as independent videomaking, Frascina noted, *9.11* and *9/12* always risked 'being marginalized by the very production world within which they [had] currency' (ibid.: 493), and they were not the kind of 9/11 visual culture that became canonical.

Generalisations about the 'civic' roles played by photography were equally risky. While 9/11 photography often looked like authentic republican culture, the collections that became canonical tended to avoid the potentially divisive questions raised in productions like *9.11* and *9/12*. The major 9/11 photography collections – *here is new york*, *The September 11 Photo Project*, the Magnum agency's *New York September 11*, Joel Meyerowitz's *9/11 Photo Archive* and Joe McNally's *Faces of Ground Zero* – tended to absorb nagging questions about 'governmental and

corporate power' into more emollient narratives about American victimhood and heroism, or about attacks on 'liberty' or a way of life. The
9/11 Photo Archive, a collection of several thousand images Meyerowitz
made of the recovery effort at Ground Zero, on commission from the
Museum of the City of New York, even affirmed American power explicitly, touring internationally as a small exhibit, entitled *After September 11:
Images from Ground Zero*, which was hosted by US Embassies under the
auspices of the State Department. If the 9/11 photography that became
canonical often appeared to speak with an authentic *vox populi*, its ability
to function as an authentic civic art was also usually dependent on the
extent to which it could be assimilated within official ideologies and
myth structures.[1]

The paradigmatic example of canonical 9/11 photography, *here is
new york*, quickly transcended its modest origins in a vacant shopfront
in SoHo to become, it was suggested at the time, 'the biggest photographic exhibition since the 1950s "Family of Man"' (Nadelson 2002b:
68). *here is new york* took several distinct forms, as a shopfront gallery
in SoHo, as a touring exhibit in the US, Europe and Japan, and as a
website and book. Its most important characteristic was that it was
assembled from images submitted by amateur photographers and
members of the general public as well as professionals. *here is new york's*
reputation for what the *New York Times* called 'grassroots mourning'
(Elbies 2002) derived in part from its near-mythic origins in a single
'flea market' image of the World Trade Center, taped to the window of
the vacant SoHo storefront by the New York writer Michael Shulan.
The collection, it was said, was born 'in organic fashion' (Pincus 2002),
as a crowd gathered to look at the image, and Shulan, moved by the
crowd's response, taped more photos to the window. Assisted by friends
who included Magnum agency photographer, Gilles Peress, chairman
of the photography programme at New York's School of Visual Arts,
Charles Traub, and photo-editor/curator, Alice Rose George, Shulan
issued the formal call for photographs that would result in *here is new
york*. Within days of its opening in the third week of September 2001,
up to 3500 people were visiting the show daily (Elbies 2002). By
Christmas more than 1500 photographers had contributed in excess of
4000 images, made on equipment ranging from disposable cameras to
the most expensive professional rigs. By the middle of 2003, when its
organisers no longer maintained staff or permanent premises in
Manhattan, versions of *here is new york* had exhibited in New York,
Washington, DC, Louisville, KY, Troy, NY, Houston, TX, Marietta,
OH, San Diego, CA, Tampa, FL, Chicago, IL, Boca Raton, FL and
Pomona NJ. The exhibit had also shown in Europe, in Berlin,

Stuttgart, Zurich, Dublin, Dresden, Dusseldorf, London and Paris, and in Japan.

The reverential tone of many of *here is new york*'s reviews – 'redemptive', said the *San Diego Union-Tribune* (Pincus 2002), 'order in a disordered world, beauty in the most blasted terrain', said the *Village Voice* (Aletti 2001) – certainly tells us something about the taste for public culture that was notable in the US after 9/11. If the contemporary artworld often seemed unable to accommodate this republican taste, photography was ideally placed to meet it. After 9/11, republican culture in the US found one of its most developed political and aesthetic forms in vast, citizen-authored photography collections, like *here is new york* and *The September 11 Photo Project*.

From its 'organic' origins onward, *here is new york* looked like a street-level *vox populi* that claimed 9/11 for all New Yorkers and all Americans, and that stood squarely against the event's appropriation by factions or ideologies. The cornerstone of American political culture, Shulan averred in his introduction to the book, was the principle 'that wisdom lies not in the vision and will of any one individual, or small group of individuals, but in the collective vision of us all' (Shulan 2002: 9). This republican temper also informed the way the photographs were displayed to the public in galleries. Irrespective of their origin or author, photographs were digitally scanned and reproduced on the same inkjet paper in a uniform size (11 inches by 16 inches), and sold to the public for the same price ($25), with the proceeds going to the Children Aid Society's World Trade Center Relief Fund. Exhibited (Figure 6.2), the photographs had no captions or titles, forestalling attempts to individuate images or fix 'meanings' in individual photos. Crowded close together in the exhibition space as collage, pinned on walls and bunched like Christmas cards on wires strung horizontally like washing lines, the photographs were also unframed, their physical proximity allowing each image to speak to those around it, so that a given photo acquired meaning not simply from its own authenticity as an eye-witness account, but also from its position in a virtuous republic of voices. In these ways, the exhibition space reproduced, but simultaneously subverted, traditional forms of artworld display, evoking 'alternative exhibition strategies . . . of activist art groups from the late 1970s and early 1980s' (Frascina 2003: 496). In a review for the *Village Voice*, Vince Aletti described the 'lack of hierarchy' evident in *here is new york*, calling it a show where 'the star system has no place' (Aletti 2001). For Shulan, the Prince Street exhibition space was 'a people's gallery, a place where I can put my kid's photo next to one by Gilles Peress' (in ibid.: 2001).

Figure 6.2 *here is new york*. Visitors view photographs in the *here is new york* gallery in SoHo, New York, during January 2002. © Reuters/Corbis.

here is new york's populism also informed Shulan's positioning of the exhibition in opposition to corporate media accounts. 'In order to come to grips with all of the imagery that was haunting us', Shulan said, 'it was essential, we thought, to reclaim [9/11] from the media' (in Nadelson 2002a). The contrast Shulan identified between corporate media and the demotic immediacy of *here is new york* was also picked up by reviewers. 'I overdosed on TV coverage long ago', wrote Aletti, 'but I kept looking for a picture that will make it all real, help me understand, jolt me, make me feel something besides numb' (Aletti 2001). The photographs, another reviewer wrote, show 'things television would be likely to ignore' (Pincus 2002). *here is new york*'s intimate snapshots of people caught up in immense human drama often took forms reminiscent of 'street photography', offering single frames, fleeting moments stolen from stories that were self-evidently much 'bigger' than the snapshots on show – stories that were evoked by the image, but that remained pregnant and untold within it, until 'completed' imaginatively by the viewer. This 'narrativity' was heightened by the random hanging of images in the exhibition space and the random progress of viewers through it, so that the exhibit as a whole had no conventional beginning, middle or end, and the production of meaning was heavily dependent on the imaginative participation of viewers.

Unlike the activist ethic of 'participatory democracy' on show in Michael Moore's *Fahrenheit 9/11* or in Richard Serra's *Stop Bush*, *here is new york*'s republicanism offered an immersion of the self in collective experience that some contemporaries described as therapeutic. One reviewer called *here is new york* 'a newly constituted family of the wounded' (Ritchin 2002: 44); another, 'the memorial the nation has been looking for' (Elbies 2002). Others described the therapeutic grounding of the self in collective experience that they felt while viewing the photos with others – 'you're shoulder to shoulder with dozens of other people and they're all going through the same thing', said one participating photographer, Richard Rutkowski, 'The pictures surround you, it's inescapable' (in Nadelson 2002a). For Shulan, too, *here is new york* was 'about community as much as anything, a public display of private emotions' (in Nadelson 2002b: 69). At times, the collection seemed to aspire to the same representation of imagined national community that characterised monumental photographic archives such as the FSA-OWI collections (Farm Security Administration-Office of War Information) compiled by American photographers in the 1930s and 1940s, or the legendary *Family of Man* show at the Museum of Modern Art in 1955, to which *here is new york* was sometimes compared. By refusing to individuate images, and by encouraging a self-forgetfulness in its audiences, *here is new york* certainly placed the existence of an imagined national community at the centre of its expansive republican memory of 9/11. In this respect, while the collection's street-level credentials appeared to some critics at the time to counter the prevailing 'narratives and symbols of the new patriotism' (Frascina 2003: 495), *here is new york* also functioned efficiently enough within the administered consensus of the immediate post-9/11 period, during which commentators and cultural practitioners alike often felt 'free to invoke a generalized "we" and to take for granted shared values and shared assumptions' (Schudson 2002: 40). *here is new york* sometimes seemed to assume that all civic participants in the collection (viewers, victims and photographers) had an equal stake in the attacks – presumably because embedded in the idea of a 'national' community there was also the prior assumption that all Americans had an equal stake in America.

here is new york's combination of 'cubist' narrativity with a reluctance to venture much beyond New York in its representation of 9/11 ensured that the collection studiously avoided the kind of explanatory contexts or cohesive narrative frameworks that would have allowed viewers to situate 9/11 historically or politically. While its republican 'narrativity' granted audiences a role in determining the meanings of the collection, *here is new york* came with the caveat that the important

9/11 stories, overwhelmingly, were about the suffering of Americans in New York. The collection's determination to look at events through 'the collective vision of us all' also meant that narratives made marginal by the administered consensus of the time – accounts that implicated US foreign policy in the attacks, for example, or that described the World Trade Center as a loathed symbol of the corporate ordering of public space in lower Manhattan (see Berman 2002; Darton 2002) – became by definition schismatic, factional, perhaps even unpatriotic statements.

Unable to account for the events it depicted, *here is new york* some-times seemed condemned simply to relive them. This was true in the exhibition space where, as Rutowski put it, the pictures were 'inescapable'. It was also true of the website, where, lacking flagged entry and exit points to the collection, the viewer could quickly feel similarly immersed. Attempting to bring order to 9/11 by viewing the images in the book version in linear fashion, beginning with the first page and ending with the last, was equally problematic. The book was divided into four sections, each of which was subtly distinct: section one contained only black and white images, for example; section four placed particular emphasis on images of mourning, funerals and vigils, concluding with a group of images of the World Trade Center in more 'innocent' times. Section four's emphasis on rituals of remembrance, and the structural shift out of a monochrome world back to full colour, implied a coming to terms with trauma. Yet because the book told essentially the same story four times over – the towers stand, the towers are attacked, the towers fall, the destruction is barely imaginable, the people suffer and grieve – the book version of *here is new york* looked more like a cyclical narrative of perpetual return to a traumatic primal scene than a story about resolution or closure. The photos so vividly evoked heightened moments in open-ended narratives of horror and loss that to experience the collection even by extended contemplation of a handful of photos alone was also in some measure to be overwhelmed by it. *here is new york*'s sheer size and the dizzying multiplicity of open-ended and often con-flicting stories about trauma flung simultaneously at the viewer seemed ill-suited to the kind of considered, therapeutic reflection with which contemporary reviewers often associated the collection.[2]

As discussed in Chapter 3, trauma and disorientation in representa-tions of 9/11 helped fuel a vigorous form of hawkish American nation-alism which itself became a key ideology of empire. The inferences audiences were expected to draw from *here is new york: a democracy of photographs* – that democracy was attacked on 9/11, but that democracy survived – coupled with the collection's iterative return to the scene of trauma, meant that *here is new york* had more in common with the hawkish patriotism and corporate media imagery of the time than its organisers may have wished. One important trend in 9/11 photography which also figured prominently in *here is new york*, was for images showing people watching the day's events unfold (see Figures 1.1, 6.1 and 6.2) – a trend Barbie Zelizer described in an important early essay on the uses of 9/11 photography in the media (Zelizer 2002). Photographs that framed 'the act of seeing as an integral part of the coverage' (Zelizer 2002: 57) featured heavily in *here is new york* in an aesthetic that Zelizer compared to photographs of observers looking at concentration camps made at the end of the Second World War. Photographs showing Americans witnessing 9/11, she suggested, had a similar effect to the concentration camp images, reminding viewers about 'the importance of responding to the tragedy', a message that 'made it easier to mobilize support for the US military and political response in Afghanistan' (Zelizer 2002: 62).

By contrast, any discussion of how visual art represented 9/11 and the war on terror at the time is complicated by the fact that artworld treatments of events were often highly self-referential. This meant that, like the early 9/11 novel, much of the art that looked as if it was tackling events head-on often did so obliquely, sometimes more as a by-product of questions about artistic autonomy or about the universal truthfulness of art in traumatic and contested times. Often this meant a visual and critical vernacular shaped by a preference for art that was about art; or at least for art that was concerned with debating appropriate artistic responses to historical and political events, rather than for art that was explicitly about the events themselves. Only seldom did it mean art that subordinated itself to the imaginative rendition of 9/11 and the war on terror as historical, political or economic realities.

One useful place to begin exploring these trends was the September 2004 issue of *ArtForum* magazine, whose centrepiece was a special section titled 'The Art of Politics', featuring critical essays by intellectuals and notable artworld figures including Martha Rosler, Arthur Danto and the associate curator at the Institute of Contemporary Art, Bennett Simpson. The 'Art of Politics' section also featured specially commissioned artwork from fourteen contemporary artists, including Richard Serra's *Stop Bush* (2004) (a reworking of the iconic, cruciform 'hooded man' image in the Abu Ghraib prison photographs), and reproductions of work by others including Isa Genzken, Tom Sachs, James Rosenquist, Santiago Sierra, Lawrence Weiner, Laylah Ali and Jonathan Horowitz. Contextualising itself squarely within what Simpson called 'the convulsions of Empire lately witnessed around the world' (Simpson

2004: 223), *ArtForum*'s special section took as its theme the new politicisation that some contributors felt had framed artistic responses to the post-9/11 era – a trend that Rosler worried was actually a transient fashion for 'commitment' that might contaminate authentic political art with kitsch (Rosler 2004). The art and art criticism published in the September 2004 *ArtForum* was an effective primer for 'crisis' era art 'about' contemporary events, partly because it demonstrated summarily several of the broader tendencies shaping artworld responses at the time; and partly because, in what they chose to include as exemplary 'politicised' art, the editors at *ArtForum* inevitably established an early post-9/11 canon of sorts.[3]

The editor Tim Griffin's introductory text to the 'Art of Politics' special section was laid out against a print of Robert Mapplethorpe's *American Flag* (1977) on the facing page – Mapplethorpe's flag tattered and rending almost audibly, sunshine backlighting the fifty stars as if the fabric, in a gesture of solidarity with a new generation of flag-burners, was about to self-combust. Wondering, in his introduction, whether 'the times' may be 'forcing us to a completely new set of ideas about what an artist was and what an artist did' (Griffin 2004a: 204), Griffin acknowledged that *ArtForum*'s discussion of politics had been forced on the magazine and that it was a regrettable symptom of the times. With Mapplethorpe's flag in the periphery of the reader's vision, Griffin wrote of 'a deep-seated resistance we felt to the very pairing of art and politics', or even 'the pairing of art and its social context'. The 'Art of Politics' issue, he noted, had proved 'by far the most challenging to be assembled by the current editorial group at *ArtForum*' (ibid.: 205).

It wasn't the most auspicious start, but Griffin may have felt quite reassured by some of the artwork that the magazine commissioned for 'The Art of Politics'. Isa Genzken's submission came from her *Empire/Vampire, Who Kills Death* series of assemblage pieces, sculpted 'combinations of found objects – action figures, plastic vessels, and various elements of consumer detritus – arranged on pedestals in architecturally inspired, post destruction scenes' (Zwirner Gallery 2005). Genzken began work on *Empire/Vampire* shortly after 9/11. The series, parts of which were exhibited at the Carnegie International exhibition of 2004/5, was described in the Carnegie catalogue as 'directly confront[ing] the themes of architecture, power and terror' (Carnegie International 2004), and echoed a well-worked narrative of twentieth-century modernism renewed by 9/11, in which 'humanity can be felled by the very buildings we construct to shelter us'. In *Empire/Vampire*, 'ruins of architecture and the built environment [were] peopled with fragments trying to navigate the devastation', the materials that Genzken used seemingly 'scavenged from the detritus of some post-apocalyptic landscape' (ibid.).

The example of Genzken's work photographed for *ArtForum* certainly resonated with themes of 'architecture, power and terror'. To the rear of the plinth on which her materials were assembled, Genzken placed an upturned print of Kurt Hulton's famous photograph *Grand Central Station* (1934), tipped onto its side through ninety degrees, then superimposed on a perforated mesh screen wrapping the plinth. A sinister figure imposing itself on the right-hand foreground posed menacingly over other figures prone on the plinth. Heaped around the bodies was an array of found-object motifs suggesting shelter or protection abruptly withdrawn – shoes lost or discarded, a hat, tiny dolls, the umbrella that dominated the piece, its stalk rising out of the assemblage, its metal spokes twisted out of shape, the protective dome of the umbrella destroyed by a sudden gust, an explosive blast or falling debris.

However, Genzken's treatment of 9/11 was hardly 'direct' or 'confrontational'. Too much of the energy in her *Empire/Vampire* assemblages seemed directed back inward, channelled into statements about the self or the artist, rather than opening outward into the kind of civic engagements that viewers might have expected to find in art about the administration ('power') and destruction ('terror') of public space ('architecture'). As Genzken told the photographer Wolfgang Tillmans in 2005, her recent work had been 'to do with the inner view'. 'That's why the formal in my recent works is daring in a way', she told Tillmans, 'because there is little to hold on to, little one can tie things to. Except for a sense that I have when I am actually engaged in the process of construction' (Genzken and Tillmans 2005). Rather than applying herself and her art to the momentous public events of 9/11 and their aftermath, Genzken's romantic-sounding modernism seemed to work the other way around, ostentatiously placing art and the artist at the epicentre of the felt trauma, as if the real meaning of 9/11 was the opportunity it gave sculptors to emote abstractly about the attack's implications for artists. *Empire/Vampire* was 'about' power, terror and architecture, but only as abstractions, not as lived experiences or political problems. Its more tangible commitment was to explore art's redemptive potential to express the inexpressable about 9/11. The series, she said, was about getting 'a different reaction from the "already known"' – a statement that fell only just short of describing popular accounts of 9/11 as banal, and that by valorising the novel emotional response or unique feeling again placed private selfhood and art (rather than public space or the socio-political ramifications of trauma) at the centre of Genzken's work.

Genzken's major themes meant that *Empire/Vampire, Who Kills Death* retained at least a trace of a public world with which her art could engage. But many of the artists who submitted to 'The Art of Politics' *ArtForum* used the opportunity of a global industry platform to disseminate work that seemed muted in ambition and scope – partly because its abstraction meant that it often commented only allusively on contemporary events, and partly because when it did address pressing public issues head-on, it did so in a manner that often looked clichéd or credulous. A number of the submissions looked hackneyed, among them Laylah Ali's invitation to confront the horrors of war and terrorism through the *faux-naif* pictorial imagination of a child, and Trisha Donnelly's paralleling of US foreign policy with Nazi expansionism (Donnelly painted the date '1939' in the top left-hand corner of an otherwise blank page). Other submissions that were text-heavy or composed primarily of written words (see Lawrence Weiner's *Invitation to the Dance* or Barbara Kruger's *Untitled*) performed the 9/11 novel's conceit about the limitations of language in reverse, implying that contemporary events had exhausted art's facility for dealing with history visually. Such findings tended to enhance further the feeling that whereas photography often did difficult civic work after 9/11 (albeit with questionable ideological outcomes), 'the art community seemed to hesitate, to flutter around the events' (Nadelson 2002b: 69), concerning itself more with 9/11's implications for art than with the alarming historical ramifications of the attacks themselves. Jeremy Deller's untitled contribution even did this by inviting the viewer to contrast the republican authority of the photograph after 9/11 with the relative marginality of the artworld. Deller offered a plain white background on which plain black text read 'A photograph of Donald Rumsfeld shaking hands with Saddam Hussein, Baghdad, December 20, 1983' (a famous photograph taken when Rumsfeld was Reagan's special envoy to Baghdad, in a period when Saddam was backed by the Reagan administrations as a buffer against the Islamic revolution in Iran).

The self-regarding reticence of some of the artwork published in the September 2004 *ArtForum* was mirrored in the critical essays included in 'The Art of Politics', several of which took issue with Griffin's editorial premise that 9/11 and the war on terror had brought about a revival of committed political art. Attacking curators who celebrated a 'frivolously empty riff . . . on '60s collectivism', Martha Rosler complained that too many 'whimsical activities' were being treated as tokens of 'social transformation' (Rosler 2004: 218) – comments echoed by Arthur Danto, for whom the dominant artworld tone since 9/11 had been 'nostalgia for a certain activism that had vanished from the scene'. 'It seemed strange to me, given the political reality of the Bush years', Danto wrote, 'that young artists could do no better than envy artists of the 1960s for the forthrightness of their protests', and stranger still 'that they expressed their own immediate political concerns obliquely' (Danto 2004: 206). The problem, ironically, was summarised best by Griffin himself, who observed that major post-9/11 exhibitions – even those with a 'political' pedigree exhibiting primarily American work – had 'operated primarily within the formalized systems of art, never quite penetrating a broader social sphere' (Griffin 2004a: 205).

Despite or, in the problematic discourse of the avant-garde, *because* of its relative marginality to public discussion, the artworld did at times produce an engaged visual culture of remarkable aesthetic power and political/intellectual nuance, particularly in representations of the Iraq war. Here the September 2004 *ArtForum* was again exemplary, including alongside work that 'fluttered' around events submissions that merged artistic production with a vigorous republican activism against the war. The magazine's front cover carried a reproduction of Tom Sachs' nine-foot diameter reproduction of the Seal of the President of the United States, a replica Sachs made from synthetic polymer paint and hand-cut plywood. Like Isa Genzken, Sachs invited his audience to look for hidden verities submerged within the familiar – the banner unfurling from the beak of the eagle, for example, with its famous motto *E Pluribus Unum* ('Out of Many, One') reconsidered in the context of Bennett Simpson's 'convulsions of Empire'. Unlike Genzken, the truths secreted in the everyday in Sachs' *Presidential Seal* (2004) were transparently grounded in an historical world of power politics and imperial histories. Understated in design and execution despite its size, *Presidential Seal*'s mimetic quality meant that it derived its impact largely from the associations sparked in viewers when the Seal was encountered in unfamiliar surroundings, or when viewers came across it unexpectedly and were forced, perhaps for the first time, to confront and question the iconography out of which it was built. Before it was displayed on the cover of *ArtForum*, *Presidential Seal* was included in Sachs' interactive installation *Nutsy's*, at the Bohen Foundation gallery, Manhattan (November 2002–February 2003), where Sachs commented on the importance of drugs and alcohol in American popular culture. In that context, *Presidential Seal* 'appropriated a logo of perhaps the largest commercial entity in the world, America itself, and critically associated this brand with the economics of drug and alcohol distribution' (Gladman 2003). Against the back-drop of Iraq on the cover of *ArtForum*, where it functioned effectively as cover art to 'The Art of Politics' special section, *Presidential Seal* sparked other possible meanings. The clutch of thirteen arrows grasped by the eagle in its left talon – the original symbolism referring to the thirteen European colonies on the eastern seaboard of the United States – put stories about colonialism, empire and anti-imperial revolt at the centre of the piece. Sometimes stylised as cruise missiles or nuclear warheads in protest-image appropriations of the Seal, the faith-ful reproduction of the arrows in Sachs' work actually added to the political charge of the piece, making twenty-first-century 'convulsions of Empire' continuous with much older narratives of imperialism on the north American continent.

Displayed on the cover of *ArtForum* there was something very knowing about Sachs' mimesis in *Presidential Seal*, its spartan refusal to interpret or narrate this familiar emblem of state power compelling audiences themselves to extrapolate meanings from the semiotic rich-ness of the Seal (with its arrows, olive branch, eagle, banner, flag, '*E Pluribus Unum*'). *Presidential Seal* was confrontational in a way that Genzken's *Empire/Vampire* was not, because it depended so heavily on interaction with its audience. Unsettling viewers by making familiar iconographies of power look new, strange or just different, Sachs encouraged a dialogue between audience and object: 'Why has he copied the Seal?' 'Is it exactly the same?' 'What does it mean?' 'What do those arrows mean?' 'Why *hasn't* he turned the arrows into cruise missiles?' At the same time, Sachs' exacting mimesis also collapsed the distinction between the object (the Seal) and its representation (*Presidential Seal*), so that what viewers were asked to interrogate was US state power itself, not just its abstraction in art.

One group of Western art objects that consistently threatened to escape the formalised systems and institutions of the artworld derived from another collection of photographs – the explosive images made on digital cameras by US military police reservists at the Abu Ghraib mil-itary intelligence prison in Iraq, photographs that sparked a major scandal when they came to public attention in April and May 2004. In their reproduction as part of other 'art' objects, and by their reactiva-tions of the original photos in art, imaginative reworkings of Abu Ghraib imagery were the closest the artworld came during the 'crisis' years to a coherent and consistently public visual culture of the kind realised by photography. In part this was because the issues invoked in such art – the illegal detention, 'rendition' and torture of prisoners by Americans – went to the very heart of national and international debate

Figure 6.3 A visitor to the 2006 Whitney Biennial, New York, looks at Richard Serra's *Stop Bush*.
© Seth Wenig/Reuters/Corbis.

about the Bush Doctrine (see Chapter 2). The extent to which art derived from the Abu Ghraib photographs offered ambitious interventions in war on terror debates was also often dependent on its display in public (as opposed to gallery) space. One better known example of this, also reproduced in the September 2004 *ArtForum*, was Richard Serra's *Stop Bush* (Figure 6.3), a stylised but instantly recognisable paintstick reworking of the image of the hooded prisoner from Abu Ghraib, standing on a box trailing wires. Absent the wires and the box, and reproduced more as a dark Gothic shadow or silhouette, Serra placed the paintstick prisoner beneath text reading 'STOP BUSH', signing the drawing 'SERRA' in the bottom right-hand corner. *Stop Bush*'s didacticism allowed little room for the kind of creative dialogue with audiences that characterised Sachs' *Presidential Seal*. But the contexts in which *Stop Bush* was displayed, disseminated and used – billboards, downloadable internet poster-art, placards carried by antiwar protestors – allowed Serra to ground his art firmly in public political practice and republican activism against the Iraq war.

Stop Bush featured prominently in the September 2004 *ArtForum*, where it functioned as an 'editorial' image to 'The Art of Politics', separated from the other contributions by its reproduction on a left-hand page preceding Griffin's introduction and the list of contributors.

Serra's 'painting' wore its commitment to a politically engaged art practice very visibly, in the visual correspondences it set up between the activism it urged and the artist doing the urging. The blockish text of the image's intention to 'STOP BUSH' echoed in the smaller but stylistically similar text of the signature, 'SERRA', in the bottom right-hand corner – a visual linking of political exhortation with artistic identity, and thus of 'politics' and 'art', that was re-emphasised in the careful repetition of a diagonal motif sloping downward from left to right, in the slogan 'STOP BUSH' at the top of the frame, in the outstretched right arm of the figure in the middle, and in the similarly slanted signature in the bottom right-hand corner. The tangible presence of the artist and the artistic labour expended in this republican call to popular political mobilisation was also emphasised in the pronounced strokes of Serra's paintstick, a departure from the clean minimalist lines of the public sculpture for which he was best known. These were replaced in *Stop Bush* by something that looked almost expressionist in style, drawing attention in every ostentatious stroke to the authentic political anger of the committed artist at work. *Stop Bush* was self-referential, but only to the extent that the 'self' to which it referred was its own status as public art, endlessly reproducible and free, and actually used by citizens in public struggles over war on terror foreign policy.

Sharing *Stop Bush*'s commitment to an art practice embedded in republican civic space, but more openly sceptical about existing institutions than Serra, Jenny Holzer's *For the City* 'light installation' (September–October 2005) projected poems and extracts from declassified government documents about Guantánamo and Abu Ghraib onto the exteriors of the New York Public Library, the Bobst Library at New York University, and three buildings in the Rockefeller Plaza in midtown Manhattan. Some of the declassified documentation Holzer projected was heavily censored, with entire paragraphs and pages of text struck out, allowing *For the City* to hold in tension its exaggerated 'publication' of previously classified material in New York public space, with a discussion of the state's capacity to circumscribe and censor such acts of civic disclosure. *For the City* was supported by the National Endowment for the Arts, the publicly funded body subjected to furious attacks and severe budget cuts by a powerful congressional coalition of conservative Republicans and the Christian Right during the 1990s. It was presented in conjunction with Creative Time, a New York-based public arts organisation whose work involves taking art 'out of galleries and museums and into the public realm', in projects that 'enrich public space and . . . everyday experience, and [that] forefront artists as key contributors to democratic society' (Creative Time 2005). Often overtly

Figure 6.4 *Tribute in Light*, Ground Zero.
Photo by Getty Images/Joshua Sheldon.

political, Creative Time had previously been involved with projects addressing domestic violence, racism and AIDS, and had worked with the New York Municipal Art Society on *Tribute in Light* – the installation of eighty-eight searchlights that beamed twin shafts of light into the night sky above Ground Zero during March/April 2002 and that was restaged on anniversaries of the 9/11 attacks (Figure 6.4). *Tribute in Light*, a collaboration between the lighting designer Paul Marantz, the artists Julian LaVerdiere and Paul Myoda, and the architects John Bennett, Gustavo Bonevardi and Richard Nash Gould, shared a medium with *For the City* (light) which Holzer suggested was 'right for these terrible events' – the projection of light enabling 'beauty [to] let you come closer than you might otherwise' to the troubling realities addressed in the art (in Wallach 2005).

Another ambitious borrowing from the Abu Ghraib photographs included in the September 2004 *ArtForum* was Santiago Sierra's installation at the Lisson Gallery, London, *Polyurethane Sprayed on the Backs of 10 Workers* (July–August 2004) – an exhibit that was limited by its confinement in a gallery setting, but that used the space to good claustrophobic effect in a work that made complex and confrontational demands of its viewers. *Polyurethane Sprayed on the Backs of 10 Workers* did exactly what its deliberately affect-less, matter-of-fact title suggested, to ten Iraqi immigrant workers Sierra hired for the purpose in west London's Iraqi community. Dressing the Iraqis in white chemical suits, and cowling them in thick black plastic sheeting reminiscent of the hoods used at Abu Ghraib, Sierra stood his subjects in a line facing a wall. Then, in another direct reference to the prison photographs, Sierra filmed himself, equipped with chemical mask and industrial spray-gun, as he covered them in polyurethane foam. When the toxic yellow mass dried and set hard around his subjects, the moulds that were produced – traces of the bodies and labour used – became the centrepiece of the Lisson installation, which also included the objects used in the production process (the spraygun, chemical canisters, clothing, the video and other equipment) scattered across the gallery space.

Risk-taking and controversial, at least within its own relatively marginal milieu, *Polyurethane* evoked multiple associations with the war on terror. The cowling of the Iraqis and the incarceration of their bodies made the art critic Adrian Searle think of women wearing the burka or chador, and of chemical attacks. He also thought 'inevitably' of Americans committing torture, 'those terrible dehumanised and degrading images from Abu Ghraib jail, and the shackled, manacled prisoners shuffling and humiliated at Guantánamo. People treated as objects' (Searle 2004). *Polyurethane Sprayed on the Backs of 10 Workers* also located human rights abuses at Abu Ghraib in a much broader narrative about the exploitation of Iraqi resources by Western agencies, partly by making such exploitation integral to the construction of the installation itself. Sierra's Iraqi workers were paid casual rates – 'as little as possible', Sierra said (in Herbert 2004: 211) – and given only minimal information as to the nature of the work that they would be asked to undertake (a literal performance of their own humiliating exploitation as immigrant labour in Britain, as well as an allusive performance of Abu Ghraib).

In order to 'perform' its exploitations the more thoroughly, in other words, *Polyurethane Sprayed on the Backs of 10 Workers* was itself exploitative. By becoming what it addressed, the better to distil and dissect it, *Polyurethane* was highly confrontational, positioning viewers as consumers of a commodity produced by exploitation (the installation), making viewers themselves complicit in the broader imperial relationships of power embodied in the Abu Ghraib prison scandal 'quoted' in the art. *Polyurethane*'s real political punch derived from this conflation of neocolonialism in Iraq with the everyday exploitations of labour and resources in Western markets (even art markets, right here, in this gallery). By merging these worlds, Sierra encouraged viewers to contextualise the abuses and torture at Abu Ghraib in the functioning of markets, the objectifications and commodifications of capitalism, and the complex patterns of class and ethnic exploitation evoked in *Polyurethane*'s statements about imperialism in Iraq. Sierra's choice of materials also allowed *Polyurethane Sprayed on the Backs of 10 Workers* to demystify description of the Iraq war as a humanitarian intervention (Bush's and Blair's defence of the war after the search for Iraqi WMD proved fruitless). Sierra had used polyurethane foam before, notably in Italy in 2002 when he sprayed it over a group of prostitutes from Eastern Europe. He returned to it at the Lisson 'because I wanted to bring the guns used to apply it together with the system of protection from it – a dual way of administering power: with love and hate'. Using the polyutherane foam, Sierra suggested, allowed him to evoke this neocolonial duality to particularly good effect, because it 'protects aggressively', releasing 'toxic fumes' as it solidifies around its subject (in Herbert 2004: 211).

One reason the Abu Ghraib photographs were described by contemporaries as 'ubiquitous and unforgettable' (Wallis 2004), 'indelible' (Griffin 2004c), 'a logo for the war itself' and 'iconic' (Apel 2005: 97) was because of their profound resonance with Bush Doctrine commitments to unilateral policy-making and pre-emptive war in pursuit of an expanded American hegemony. As suggested in Chapter 2, Abu Ghraib, Guantánamo Bay and the storm over CIA 'rendition' flights became scandals of such magnitude because the issues they raised went to the very heart of contemporary debates about war on terror governance and empire. As Susan Sontag put it, in one of her final essays, when history remembers the Iraq war 'the defining association of people everywhere will be photographs of the torture of Iraqi prisoners by Americans in the most infamous of Saddam Hussein's prisons' (Sontag 2004). Holzer, Serra and Sierra represented just one leading edge of a massive cultural appropriation of Abu Ghraib imagery that took place across diverse forms of visual and material culture, from the high-end 'high art' of Santiago Sierra at the Lisson, to the bumper stickers, T-shirts, posters, cartoons and other items of torture kitsch flooding Western markets.

Another reason the Abu Ghraib photos became so instantly iconic was that they seemed so familiar, evoking and activating numerous other traditions, texts and fragments of everyday American visual culture through which Americans encountering the images could filter the implications of what was happening in Iraq. Contemporary responses compared the Abu Ghraib pictures to imagery from Vietnam and the Second World War, and to genres that included sports 'trophy' photos, lynching photos, photos from concentration camps, media imagery of 'hazing' rituals, the commodified eroticism and gendered subjugations of pornography, and holiday snaps – a reference the conservative pundit Rush Limbaugh may have had in mind when he described the acts of torture and abuse that the images depicted as leisure, or recreation, soldiers who 'are being fired at every day' blowing off some steam, just 'people having a good time' (in Sontag 2004). Among the many images activated in the infamous photograph of the hooded man standing on a box, his arms outstretched in a cruciform pose, his body trailing electric wires, one of the most powerful associations for commentators at the time was the passion and crucifixion of Christ, the camera's forceful inscription of Christian imagery on the cowled body of the Iraqi placing both the American soldiers who made the photo and viewers who looked at it in the imperial position of 'Roman torturers, crucifiers, persecutors of the humble and holy' (Apel 2005: 92). In this respect, the photographs and the acts they depicted were not so much 'about' imperialism as they were imperialism in action, part of the imperialist process of 'marking difference through violence' (Philpott 2005: 232), with a colonial gaze that turned Iraqi bodies into raw material for the production of 'actionable intelligence' or leisure. As Sontag noted, the sexual humiliation that featured prominently in the Abu Ghraib photographs had a recognisably colonialist pedigree, the French and the Belgians having practised sexual torture on 'despised recalcitrant natives' in Algeria and the Congo (Sontag 2004).[4]

Cultural appropriation of Abu Ghraib imagery, and its redeployment in art that addressed a broader nexus of 'imperialist' relations and flows of power, was also a telling theme for artists in the Middle East. Reworkings of the more famous images, including the hooded man on a box, and the photograph of Private Lynndie England holding a male prisoner on a leash, appeared as murals protesting the occupation of Iraq in Baghdad and Tehran (Figure 6.5). The hooded man on the box was also turned into sculpture exhibited by the Iraqi artists Abdel-Karim Khalil and Qassim al-Sabti in a show curated by al-Sabti at the Hewar Gallery, Baghdad in 2004. One of three exhibits Khalil showed

Figure 6.5 In June 2004, an Iranian couple walks past mural paintings depicting scenes of the torture of Iraqi prisoners by US soldiers at the Abu Ghraib prison near Baghdad, on a major highway in the Iranian capital Tehran. This photo was part of the exhibition *Inconvenient Evidence: Iraqi Prison Photographs from Abu Ghraib*.
© epa/Corbis.

at the Hewar depicted a hooded prisoner carved in white marble, a medium associated with classical Greek sculpture and the 'rational civilisation' of imperial antiquity, but which Khalil used, via his borrowings from the Abu Ghraib photographs, as 'the symbol of a barbarian oppressor' (Apel 2005: 99).

As part of their embodiment of empire, the photos also dramatised flows of hierarchical power within the hegemonic culture of Americanism itself. Lynndie England's defence was that she was following orders and had been instructed to pose for the photograph. In the image itself, as one commentator observed at the time, 'her discomfort is palpable as she looks away from the camera toward the human being at the end of the leash she holds. Linked to the prone figure both by her gaze and by the physical line of connection [the leash], we might believe that the youthful England is trapped in a descending spiral of victimization produced by the pressure to conform to the demands of prison culture' (ibid.: 91). As well as a gendered exploitation (a woman ordered to participate in acts of sexual abuse and humiliation by male superiors), Lynndie England's 'victimisation' by the military culture and political administration she served also made Abu Ghraib and empire intelligible as *class* exploitations. England, it was widely noted at the time, was 'poor white trash', from the same working-class constituencies with narrowing prospects that Michael Moore's *Fahrenheit 9/11* argued were most victimised by Bush's dereliction of republican duty in Iraq (see Chapter 4). Like the lynching photos to which they were widely compared, as images containing shameful truths about power and exploitation in the culture of the 'homelands', as well as in Iraq, the Abu Ghraib pictures quickly came to function 'as sites of resistance against the very acts they represent[ed]', their emergence into the public realm transforming them 'from private souvenirs of American supremacy into blistering anti-American pictures' (ibid.: 89, 95).

It would be a mistake, however, to assume that liberal or dissenting narratives about the Iraq war were the only stories that became attached to the Abu Ghraib photos. As noted in Chapter 2, supporters of the occupation also 'span' the scandal vigorously, turning the prison 'crisis' into stories about the 'remarkable grace and courage' of the US military and 'the moral purpose' of the war (Krauthammer 2004a; 2004b). One reason they were able to do this was that the cropping of the photos for public display by TV networks and newspapers often served the 'few rotten apples' explanation for Abu Ghraib promoted by the White House, countering claims that a culture of abuse existed in US military prisons by removing from the frame the presence of groups of soldiers 'hanging out' while detainees were tortured around them. In a less well known, uncropped version of the famous hooded man on a box image, for example, a soldier in the right-hand side of the image stands cleaning his nails. He was cropped from the version broadcast by CBS on *60 Minutes II*, the show that broke the Abu Ghraib story in April 2004, and he didn't appear in the canonical version of the photo that was recycled around the world (which focused instead on the image of torture itself), profoundly altering the stories the image could tell.

Another reason the Abu Ghraib photographs were able to accommodate and recycle such divergent political readings of the Iraq war were that the photos themselves, as aesthetic objects, embraced so enthusiastically the neoconservative 'values' shaping both the prosecution of the war and its doctrinal defence. For Slavoj Žižek and Susan Sontag, the key to the photos was the very openness with which they displayed the acts they recorded; a 'culture of shamelessness', as Sontag put it, that Allen Feldman may also have had in mind when he cited the photographs as leading examples of the 'actuarial gaze' that he felt was characteristic of early war on terror aesthetics (Žižek 2004; Sontag

2004; Feldman 2005). Feldman's 'actuarial gaze', by which he meant visual culture's fostering of American-centric perspectives that were designed to intimidate by the use of threatening, often ethnocentric, visual imagery (Feldman 2005), raised questions about the role of visual culture in the construction and administration of empire. David Wallis, curator of *Inconvenient Evidence: Iraqi Prison Photographs from Abu Ghraib* – an exhibition of seventeen of the photos shown in New York at the International Center of Photography (September–November 2004), and at the Warhol Museum, Pittsburgh (October 2004–January 2005) – agreed with Feldman, arguing that the photos raised important questions about the uses of photography 'to assert cultural dominance locally and . . . racial and political hierarchies globally' (in Philpott 2005: 34). In the contexts in which the photographs were made and first 'used', and in accounts by conservative pundits like Charles Krauthammer and Rush Limbaugh, the photographs told stories that meant affirming Americanism, not challenging it. Liberal disgust at a regime of torture and abuse was by no means the only politics read off the Abu Ghraib photographs by Americans. It seemed ironic, then, that Arthur Danto should describe the photographs as 'art' in the September 2004 *ArtForum* because they struck him as 'powerful examples of how images can change what we are', adding that there was nothing capable of doing this at the 2004 Whitney Biennial. Perhaps what he meant was that the photos were 'art' because they acted as nodal points through which the conflicting ideological cross-currents of the time all seemed to converge, allowing the images to dramatise such diverse political narratives that they captured their time and place, figuratively at least, in something approaching its totality.[5]

In some ways, the crisis the Abu Ghraib prison photographs represented for the Bush administration and the Pentagon in 2004 was also a perfect microcosm of the broader 'republican crisis' of the time, in that the Abu Ghraib scandal seemed self-correcting to some degree, under the terms of republican adversarial review (see Chapter 2). Critics of the administration, and soldiers on the ground at Abu Ghraib, argued that guilty parties higher up the chain of command escaped unpunished. As soon as they were made public, however, the Abu Ghraib photographs were also locked into a therapeutic counternarrative in which covert acts of torture became subject to civic and judicial scrutiny, and thus to processes of republican accountability. Transfigured from their private origins by their ubiquity in global media and reconstructed as objects of civic discourse, the photographs showed smiling soldiers who freely admitted their crimes and seemed eager to share the evidence with us. In tandem with cropping that tended to bolster the Bush administration's argument that a few 'rotten apples' were responsible for Abu Ghraib, the 'theatricality' of their confession, as Žižek termed it, allowed the photographs to 'perform' in advance the narratives of democratic accountability that followed – in the courts martial, prison sentences and dismissals from service dealt out to privates and low-ranking officers involved in the scandal. Viewed in this light, far from a narrative of liberal disgust, the story of the Abu Ghraib photographs had an impressively Straussian ring to it, an authoritarian fable for the New American Century, in which citizen-soldiers were flawed, but state power was moral, just and redemptive.

1. One thrilling exception to this was the Chilean photographer Camilo José Vergara's *Twin Towers Remembered* (2001), a collection of images of the World Trade Center stretching back from 9/11 to the towers' construction in the early 1970s. In Vergara's photographs the towers often appeared as an exercise in architectural brutalism, class inequalities and corporate neglect, echoing the social criticism of Eric Darton and Marshall Berman, and the independent film-making of Sean Penn in *11'09"01*, each of whom described the buildings as a blight on the communities of lower Manhattan (Darton 2002; Berman 2002; *11'09"01* 2002).

2. Reviewing a touring version of the collection, the *San Diego Union-Tribune* noted that the exhibition 'holds 9/11 in suspension, so we can think, not just see', because 'by turning the rush of incidents into [still] pictures, we can begin to shape our thoughts about them' (Pincus 2002).

3. Among the exhibits *ArtForum* contributors referred to as evidence of a post-9/11 politicising of art were *Documenta 11* (2002), the 100-day festival of international art held every five years in the German town of Kassel, and *Manifesta 5* (2004) held in Spain, a European biennial staged in different cities to promote 'new forms of artistic expression . . . at one remove from the operations of the market'. Curated by individuals 'with a bent toward geopolitics' (Rosler 2004: 218), *Documenta 11* was transformed by 9/11 into 'a history lesson' and 'a raising of questions about margins and centre, globalisation, postcolonialism and individual and group efforts to make sense of the world' (Searle 2002).

4. *The Arab Mind* (1973) by Raphael Patai, a classic of late twentieth-century orientalist anthropology, whose claim that 'Arabs' were particularly vulnerable to sexual humiliation, was widely cited as a direct influence on military prison culture during the 'crisis' years. Seymour Hersh called *The Arab Mind* a neocon 'bible' (Hersh 2004: 39).

5. The Abu Ghraib photographs' 'actuarial' depiction of homosexuality as torture and humiliation meant that the photos also spoke allusively to American audiences about contemporary 'culture wars' controversies in the

US (the Abu Ghraib scandal coincided with vigorous debates in America about gay marriage, for example). Reports that the torture photographs were juxtaposed with images of American soldiers having heterosexual sex highlight the extent to which the pictures were used, in their original military context, to affirm the heterosexual norms against which 'homosexual deviance' was measured. This aggressively heterosexual cultural politics was also overtly masculinist in its 'actuarial' suggestion that to be 'feminised' by being mastered by a woman was as grave a humiliation as being 'feminised' by being penetrated by a man (see Apel 2005: 95).

Conclusion

One of the more remarkable early representations of 9/11 was an independent portmanteau film, *11'09"01* (2002) – a film comprising eleven segments by eleven different directors, from Iran, France, Egypt, Bosnia-Herzegovina, Burkina Faso, Britain, Mexico, Israel, India, the US and Japan, sequenced in that order. Five of the films, including the American submission directed by Sean Penn, were set wholly or partly in New York, with the rest set in diverse locations around the world. The film's publicity materials emphasised that every director had enjoyed complete freedom of expression to explore what 9/11 meant to them in the contexts of their own cultures and backgrounds. The only stipulation was that each film should be eleven minutes and nine seconds long – a requirement dismissed as a tasteless gimmick by hostile reviewers in the US, but one that allowed *11'09"01* to make the same formal claims to a democratic representation of events as a photography collection like *here is new york*. Where *here is new york* seemed stuck in the interiority of an American trauma, though, *11'09"01*'s cosmopolitan crew of directors from around the world forged a powerful, relativist aesthetic, multiplying the international contexts in which the attacks could be gauged – historically, politically, socially, culturally, emotionally, linguistically, geographically, aesthetically – and restoring in the process a series of critical distances on contemporary events that seemed largely missing from *here is new york*'s iterative return to the traumatic primal scene. In this respect, *11'09"01* was also the antithesis of the discourse that grew up around powerful eyewitness documentaries shot in and around the World Trade Center as it burned and fell – films like *9/11* (2001) by Jules and Gédéon Naudet, or Etienne Sauret's *WTC: The First 24 Hours* (2001), which was originally sold from the *here is new york* exhibition space in SoHo – where the idea that such films provided 'authentic' representations of 9/11 was closely linked to the fact that they were made by first-hand participants whose gaze was directed 'inward' at Ground Zero.

Formally, *11'09"01* looked like an aesthetic approximation of the historical narrative mooted in Chapter 1, an account of 9/11 and the war on terror capable of engaging the multiplicity of interlocking conflicts and contexts shaping the event, while granting each a 'relative autonomy' by acknowledging the meanings and histories those contexts enjoyed outside and beyond their part in the shaping of 'American' history. *11'09"01* included one film, directed by Youssef Chahine, that reversed the Hollywood norm whereby even 'foreign' characters speak English, making even American characters speak Arabic. This worked as a metaphor for *11'09"01* as a whole, where the multiple reinscriptions of the attacks asserted the authenticity and legitimacy of each director's response by allocating exactly the same amount of screen time to each segment. In a profound sense, *11'09"01* implied that 9/11 and the war on terror would only become knowable events if knowledge about them was de-Americanised, or at least stripped of its American-centrism.

To this effect, the film included two segments, one directed by the British director Ken Loach, the other by Danis Tanovic from Bosnia-Herzegovina, structured on the significance of the date, September 11, in other cultures and political histories. (Loach's segment, about the CIA-sponsored coup in Chile, on September 11 1973, won the prize for best short film at the 2002 Venice Film Festival.) *11'09"01* also included segments that echoed Jonathan Safran Foer's emphasis on private tragedies so intense that, though some of them were set in New York on September 11, 9/11 was simply blotted out or made meaningless in the experience of characters. Several segments touched on the wider implications of the Arab/Israeli conflict. Others evoked the central role played by electronic mass media in the construction and proliferation of 9/11 as trauma. One, an extraordinary contribution from the Mexican director Alejandro González Iñárritu, alternately withheld either sound or vision from the viewer, using a blank screen, fragmented images of the World Trade Center and an incoherent babble of electronic voices rising to a crescendo of white noise, to evoke both the saturation of 9/11 in media and the shutting down of coherent vision that this entailed (certainly for commentators on corporate media coverage of 9/11 in the US).

What sealed *11'09"01*'s significance as a cultural and historical artefact was the way it encouraged audiences to establish connections between and among its different segments, allowing audiences to build, layer and consolidate meaning across the film as a whole, so that the plurality of meanings attributed to the attacks was holistic and coherent, and felt empowering, not disorienting or traumatic. This gathering together of the multiplicity presented to the viewer was achieved by a poetic framing of the film within contemporary debates about 'empire';

a manoeuvre which meant that, while *11'09"01* was able to attribute an open-ended and 'semi-autonomous' plurality of meanings to 9/11, it was also able to contain those meanings, aesthetically and politically, in a broader implied narrative about American imperial power. This narrative figured prominently in both the opening and closing segments of the film, framing *11'09"01* as a 'whole' as a story about empire. The opening segment, from the Iranian director Samira Makhmalbaf, showed a young teacher in an impoverished rural community in the Middle East struggling to convey to a class of infants the magnitude of what 9/11 might mean for them. References to American 'atom bombs' and the visual image anchoring the segment – a tall chimney billowing smoke, shot from close to its base looking steeply up – suggested the likelihood of a 9/11-scale event here, in this community, a new massacre of the innocents in retaliation for the destruction in America. The film's stunning final segment, by the Japanese director Shohei Imamura, a modern folktale with magical realist trimmings, told the story of a soldier who fought for the Japanese empire in the Second World War, but who returned to his village so disgusted by imperialism that he preferred to live as a snake, having surrendered his humanity in the service of empire. With a knowing nod to the timeline of American empire under discussion in revisionist currents of contemporary intellectual history, and a cautionary allusion to broader historical cycles of imperial decline and fall, Imamura concluded *11'09"01* by taking viewers back to a very precise moment at the end of the Second World War – the days between the atom bombing of Hiroshima on 6 August 1945 and Nagasaki on 9 August, the precise historical moment, poetically at least, when one empire ended and another came to pass.

11'09"01's description of contemporary events as a multiplicity of semi-autonomous contexts and conflicts, contained, wrapped around or overdetermined by a narrative of American empire, made it the closest thing to an aesthetic realisation of the story this book has tried to tell about 9/11 and the war on terror. In certain respects, the post-9/11 period saw a new reconfiguring of margins and centres, a shifting of 'forbidden', tabooed or repressed historical narratives – about empire, about anti-American resentments, about foreign policy and national security strategy, and about the nature of American 'civilisation' itself – from the periphery of public discussion into the mainstream of American daily life. Traditional ideologies about nationhood, belonging and identity reasserted themselves powerfully as well. Yet there was also a centrifugal energy at work in American culture that did significant damage to traditional myths already reeling from a generation of domestic 'culture wars' conflicts over the meanings of American history and 'values'.

Sometimes this took the form of penetrating analyses of malign or corrosive forces at work in American and Western modernity. Paul Virilio's *Ground Zero* (2002) described Western 'progress' as a collection of destructive, and self-destructive, practices and ideologies. John Gray's *Al Qaeda and What it Means to be Modern* (2003) traced the roots of al-Qaeda terrorism to Western models of revolutionary terror, not Islamic ones. Elaine Scarry warned that a bureaucratic centralisation of 'homeland' defence initiatives made Americans more, not less, vulnerable to terrorism (Scarry 2006). A number of accounts described the World Trade Center as a blight on lower Manhattan, because its treatment of the environment around it, the communities cleared to make way for it and the workers it eventually housed, expressed in architectural form a brutalism that had deep roots in the values and mores of capitalist modernity. One of the better known instances of this, Eric Darton's 'The Janus Face of Architectural Terrorism' (2002), even compared the architectural vision of Minoru Yamasaki, the chief designer of the Trade Center, to the political vision of the men who demolished it. The World Trade Center's monumental design, Darton suggested, disguised the fact that the towers were full of people, allowing both the architect and the terrorist to envisage them, and the people inside, as abstractions – in twinned logics that were equally disdainful of 'the human material' the buildings contained (Darton 2002: 91). The building of the World Trade Center and its knocking down were 'polarized daydreams of domination', the very creation of the Towers 'a destructive act' (ibid.: 91).

In some respects the cultural crisis exemplified in Darton, Scarry and Gray was more troubling than the time-limited, self-correcting political 'crisis' represented by Bush, because it was more profound, more rooted in the values and practices that mainstream narratives about America described as good and desirable. One of the most affecting statements of this cultural entropy was the American segment of *11'09"01*, directed by Sean Penn, which introduced viewers to the almost unbearably sad world of an elderly New York widower, played by eighty-five-year-old Ernest Borgnine. In the film it is morning. Penn shoots Borgnine shaving in close-up, filling the screen with a slow motion cascade of water droplets splashed off the craggy architecture of Borgnine's ageing face, a disarming visual echo of the debris storms that rained from the Trade Center as the towers collapsed. The apartment is dark, dank. A pot of dead flowers is on the sill. Borgnine looks broke. He seems to be deaf and, at times, demented, talking aloud to himself, to his dead wife, to no one in particular, with Penn's 'cut-up' shot sequencing disrupting the segment's central section, conveying the man's disorientation, the narrowness of his world, his remoteness from events happening outside his window. Penn's film reveals itself slowly, but in the closing moments it becomes clear that Borgnine's apartment lies within the shadow cast over lower Manhattan by the South Tower of the World Trade Center. The old man, exhausted, sleeps like Rip Van Winkle through the attacks, and is only woken when the collapse of the South Tower removes the building's shadow and floods the room with light, awakening the flowers on the sill. Given complete freedom of expression to describe what 9/11 meant to him, Penn showed audiences a vulnerable old man drifting towards death in poverty in New York, to whom 9/11 meant nothing. When the Trade Center falls, flowers bloom. In the febrile political climate of the time, Penn's film was provocative, to say the least.

Penn's film was also representative, in the sense that it exemplified so cogently the narrative of a new American dissensus that represented 9/11 by intensifying existing 'culture wars' conflicts in contemporary American society. These conflicts underwrote the post-9/11 period in sometimes seismic ways. Yet, as in the 1960s, it was the narratives emanating from state agencies and institutions, particularly the White House and the Pentagon, that remained the most literally power*ful*, in the sense that they occupied the 'centres' of power around which the conflicts of the time substantially revolved, retaining a capacity to intervene in world affairs that comfortably exceeded external competitors and dissenting opinion at home. The post-9/11 period also saw the reassertion, and a new hegemony, of traditional power bases – conservative Republicans, the Christian Right, the elite political, military and corporate interests still sometimes referred to, in a quaint echo of the early Cold War, as 'the military-industrial complex'. To some degree 9/11 and the war on terror did reconfigure 'margins' and 'centres' in contemporary American life. Yet the 'crisis' years of the early war on terror were also a period when old hegemonies renewed themselves forcefully in the rubble of 9/11. The story of how 9/11 was represented by and to Americans, and the story of the wars that followed, belonged substantially to that hegemony. If one thing was clear after 9/11, it was the continued appeal of versions of American nationalism that were aggressively affirmative of existing American institutions and political/economic structures – an appeal that was particularly powerful, this book has argued, because it was embraced almost as widely by Americans who dissented from the hegemonic narrative, as by those who signed up to it.

Appendix A: Timeline

1945

February
President Roosevelt meets King Abdul Aziz Al-Saud of Saudi Arabia aboard *USS Quincy* in the Suez Canal, forging an alliance said to guarantee US access to Saudi oil.

1948

May
State of Israel declared.

1953

August
CIA-assisted coup in Iran.

1979

December
Islamic revolution in Iran.
USSR invades Afghanistan.

1980

September
Iran-Iraq war starts (ends August 1988).

1989

February
Last Soviet troops leave Afghanistan.

1990

August
Iraq invades Kuwait. US troops stationed in Saudi Arabia for first
time.

1990–91

January–February
Gulf War. US-led 'Operation Desert Storm' expels Iraq from Kuwait.
Saddam Hussein remains in power.

1993

February
Islamist terrorists bomb World Trade Center.

July
Foreign Affairs publishes Huntington's 'The Clash of Civilizations?'.

1996

August
Osama Bin Laden declares *jihad* against the US.

1998

February
Bin Laden and co-signatories issue 'World Islamic Front' declaration
of *jihad* against 'Jews and Crusaders'.

May
Brenner's 'The Economics of Global Turbulence' published in *New
Left Review*.

August
Al-Qaeda bomb US embassies in Kenya and Tanzania.

1999

June
US closes six embassies in Africa due to bin-Laden related threats.

August
UN report says 500,000 Iraqi infants killed by sanctions on Iraq since
Gulf War.

2000

March
Chalmers Johnson's *Blowback*.

September
Second *Intifada* begins.

October
Blum's *Rogue State*.
Suicide bombers attack *USS Cole*.

2001

August
Bush receives CIA report entitled 'Bin Laden Determined to Attack America'.

September
9/11 attacks on New York and Washington.
Bush tells Congress al-Qaeda hates America's 'way of life'.
here is new york opens.

October
US attacks Afghanistan.
Chomsky's *9/11*.
USA Patriot Act.

November
Taliban flee Kabul.

December
Bin Laden escapes Afghanistan in Battle of Tora Bora.

2002

January
First prisoners arrive from Afghanistan at Guantánamo Bay.
Bush's 'Axis of Evil' State of the Union address.
Joe McNally's *Faces of Ground Zero* exhibits at Grand Central Station.
WTC – The First 24 Hours shown at Sundance film festival.

February
Bush signs statement saying Geneva Conventions do not apply to war with al-Qaeda.

March
Defense Department analysis asserts president's right to override federal and international torture laws.
Nye's *The Paradox of American Power*.
9/11 (Naudets) released in US.
Tribute in Light shown at Ground Zero.

May
Darton's 'The Janus Face of Architectural Terrorism'.

June
Bush's West Point address.
'Anonymous' (Michael Scheuer) publishes *Through Our Enemies' Eyes*.

August
Jay Bybee's torture memo to Alberto Gonzales.
Zelizer and Allan's *Journalism After September 11*.

September
Rumsfeld institutes Office of Special Plans to bypass CIA.
White House publishes *National Security Strategy*.
11'09"01 opens in Europe.
Meyerowitz's *After September 11: Images from Ground Zero* opens on Capitol Hill.

October
Virilio's *Ground Zero*.
First Bali bombing.

November
Bacevich's *American Empire*.
Congress establishes 9/11 Commission.
Homeland Security Act.
Sachs' *Presidential Seal*, at the Bohen Foundation.

2003

January
Knight Ridder poll says 44 per cent Americans believe 9/11 hijackers were Iraqis.
Ignatieff's 'The American Empire (Get Used to It)' published in *New York Times*.
Kagan's *Paradise and Power*.
North Korea withdraws from Nuclear Non-Proliferation Treaty.

February
Kaplan and Kristol's *The War Over Iraq*.
Antiwar demonstrations in 800 cities worldwide (150 cities in US). Two million protest in London.

March
Richard A. Clarke resigns as Bush's anti-terrorism 'czar'.
France, Russia, Germany say they will block US/UK attempts to secure UN resolution authorising war in Iraq. US and Britain withdraw resolution seeking authorisation.
New York Times/CBS poll says 45 per cent Americans believe Saddam 'personally involved' in 9/11.
Dixie Chicks vilified for criticising Bush.
Invasion of Iraq begins, without UN authorisation.
Michael Moore vilified for speaking against Bush at the Oscars Award ceremony.

April
CentCom breaks Jessica Lynch story.
US planes bomb Al Jazeera and Abu Dhabi TV in Baghdad. US tank shells Palestine Hotel.
Saddam's statue toppled in Firdus Square.

May
Bush announces 'mission accomplished' in Iraq on USS *Abraham Lincoln*.

July
White House leaks identity of covert CIA agent, Valerie Plame ('Plamegate').
Gray's *Al Qaeda and What it Means to be Modern*.

August
Washington Post poll says 69 per cent Americans believe Saddam involved in 9/11.

October
Harvey's *The New Imperialism*.

December
Saddam captured.

2004

January
Iraq Survey Group reports no weapons of mass destruction found in Iraq.

March
Madrid train bombings.
Hans Blix, former chief UN weapons inspector, says Iraq war was illegal.
Richard A. Clarke's *Against All Enemies*.
The Alamo premiere.

April
Ferguson's *Colossus*.
60 Minutes II (CBS) and *New Yorker* (Hersh) break Abu Ghraib story.
Ignatieff's *The Lesser Evil*.

May
New York Times retracts its pre-war coverage of Iraqi weapons of mass destruction.
Bush/Rumsfeld condemn 'un-American' conduct by 'a few American troops' at Abu Ghraib.

June
Supreme Court rules in *Rasul v. Bush*.
Fahrenheit 9/11 released in US.

July
9/11 Commission Report published.
Serra's *Stop Bush*.
The Village premiere.
The Manchurian Candidate premiere.
Sierra's *Polyurethane Sprayed on the Backs of 10 Workers*, at Lisson Gallery.

September
UN Secretary General, Kofi Annan, says Iraq war was illegal.
'Art of Politics' *ArtForum*.
Inconvenient Evidence exhibit opens at International Center of Photography.
Roth's *The Plot Against America*.
Beigbeder's *Windows on the World* (translation).
Hersh's *Chain of Command*.

October
CIA Report says Iraq had no weapons of mass destruction.
Elections in Afghanistan.

November
Bush re-elected.

2005

January
Search for weapons of mass destruction in Iraq declared over.

June
Foer's *Extremely Loud and Incredibly Close*.
War of the Worlds premieres worldwide.

July
'7/7' bombings in London.

August
Antiwar camp ('Camp Casey') established outside Bush's ranch in Crawford, Texas.
Iran resumes uranium conversion in violation of Nuclear Non-Proliferation Treaty.

September
Holzer's *For the City*, New York.

October
Second Bali bombing.
Saddam goes on trial.

November
Syriana released in US.

December
Iraqi Assembly elections.
Detainee Treatment Act.

2006

January
Four thousand locked out of Noam Chomsky's lecture on torture in Dublin.

March
David Hicks becomes first Guantánamo prisoner brought before military tribunal.
New *National Security Strategy* issued.

April
Amnesty's 'Below the Radar' report on CIA 'rendition'.
United 93 released.

July
3438 Iraqi civilians killed this month (Wong and Cave 2006).
War between Israel and Hezbollah in Lebanon (ends September).

August
Bush admits Iraq and 9/11 are unconnected.
World Trade Center released, implies connection between Iraq and 9/11.

September
National Intelligence Estimate says Iraq war has increased threat from terrorism.
Cormac McCarthy's *The Road*.

October
Military Commissions Act.
Lancet report says 650,000 Iraqi deaths directly caused by US invasion.
Fifty-eight per cent Americans believe Bush administration lied to American public about Iraq (CNN).
Only 19 per cent Americans believe US is winning war in Iraq (USA Today).

November
Catastrophic losses for Republican Party in Congressional midterm elections.
Rumsfeld resigns.
Saddam sentenced to death.

December
Iraq Study Group report.
AP-Ipsos poll says 71 per cent Americans disapprove of Bush's handling of Iraq war.

Appendix B: Synoptic Biographies

Bin Laden, Osama

(Born 10 March 1957, Riyadh, Saudi Arabia). Raised in a powerful family with close ties to Saudi elites, Osama bin Laden became a co-ordinating influence, spokesman and figurehead for the loose and devolved insurgent Islamist network known as al-Qaeda, and was a key architect of the 9/11 attacks. Bin Laden made his name as a military leader, trainer, engineer and fighter in the anti-Soviet *jihad* waged by Afghan Muslims, and by the brigades of international Islamic fighters that he trained and led, in Afghanistan during the 1980s. Placed under house arrest by the Saudi regime when US troops were stationed in the kingdom during the Gulf War, bin Laden left Saudi Arabia in 1991, travelling first to Afghanistan, then Sudan (1992–96), which was identified by the US as a state sponsor of terrorism. Following several assassination attempts by Saudi agents in Sudan, bin Laden returned to Afghanistan in 1996, where he remained on 9/11, prompting the US war in Afghanistan which began on 7 October 2001. He is understood to have escaped US troops in the Tora Bora mountains in eastern Afghanistan in December 2001. Bin Laden is credited with a central role in the switch to an 'America-first' targeting strategy among radical Islamists during the mid-late 1990s and in the creation of a transnational Islamist insurgency motivated by the Koranic theme of 'defensive' *jihad*.

Bacevich, Andrew J.

(Born 1947, Normal, Illinois). Former US Army lieutenant colonel, and professor of history and international relations at Boston University. Bacevich served in Vietnam (1970–71), having graduated from West Point in 1969. An opponent of the Iraq war, his son was killed there in May 2007.

Bush, George W.

(Born 6 July 1946, New Haven, Connecticut). Forty-third President of the United States. Bush was elected in 2000 in controversial circumstances with a minority of the popular vote, following allegations of voting irregularities in Florida, and a presidential election that was eventually settled in the Supreme Court. He was re-elected in 2004. Previously held office as Republican Governor of Texas (1994–2000), where he developed further his close ties with powerful US energy interests. Bush is part of a political dynasty. His father, George H. W. Bush, was the forty-first president (1989–93); his brother, Jeb, was Republican Governor of Florida (1998–2006).

Cheney, Richard (Dick)

(Born 30 January 1941, Lincoln, Nebraska). Vice President to George W. Bush in both Bush junior administrations. Cheney worked in the Nixon administration at the Cost of Living Council, the Office of Economic Opportunity, and in the White House (1969–73). He was President Ford's White House Chief of Staff between 1975 and 1977. Cheney was elected a Republican member of the House of Representatives for Wyoming in 1978, and successively re-elected until 1989, when President Bush senior made him Secretary of Defense (1989–93). In the 1990s, Cheney was a senior fellow at the American Enterprise Institute, and president and CEO of the Halliburton Company. Described as the most powerful vice president in American history, in October 2005 the *Washington Post* called him 'Vice President for Torture'.

Clarke, Richard A.

(Born 1951, Dorchester, Massachusetts). White House counterterrorism expert for Presidents Bush senior, Clinton and Bush junior, Clarke resigned in March 2003, protesting that Bush was diverting resources from the fight against al-Qaeda into a war in Iraq that had no connection with 9/11. Before working in the White House, Clarke worked in the US intelligence community, the Department of State and the Pentagon. His *Against All Enemies* (2004) was a sensational attack on the Bush administration.

Foer, Jonathan Safran

(Born 1977, Washington, DC). Before *Extremely Loud and Incredibly Close* (2005), Foer's bestselling first novel, *Everything Is Illuminated* (2002), won numerous awards, including Book of the Year from *the Los Angeles Times*, the National Jewish Book Award and the *Guardian* First Book Award. He also won the Zoetrope All Fiction Story Prize in 2000.

Harvey, David

(Born 31 October 1935, Gillingham, Kent). Prominent Marxist geographer and professor of anthropology at the Graduate Center of the City University of New York. Before *The New Imperialism* (2003), Harvey wrote a number of influential books bridging geography, economics and social/critical theory, the best known of which include *The Limits to Capital* (1982, with a revised edition in 2006) and *The Condition of Postmodernity* (1989).

Huntington, Samuel P.

(Born 18 April 1927, New York). Harvard political scientist, specialising in national security strategy and civil/military relations. Author of 'The Clash of Civilizations?' (2003). Served in the Carter administration as coordinator of security planning for National Security Council (1977–78). Founder and early co-editor of journal *Foreign Policy*.

Ignatieff, Michael

(Born 12 May 1947, Toronto). Prominent Canadian liberal intellectual and former Director of Harvard's Carr Center for Human Rights Policy, Ignatieff has also been a journalist, broadcaster, novelist, TV dramatist and political pundit. He has taught at the universities of Harvard, California, Oxford, Cambridge and London School of Economics. Ignatieff was elected a Member of the Canadian parliament in 2006, and became Deputy Leader of the Liberal Opposition. According to the *New Internationalist*, Ignatieff, 'has helped turn human rights into a disreputable slogan, posing as their standard-bearer while condoning imperialism and equivocating on torture. His politics amount to a slippery slope, with nuanced arguments at the top and the horror chambers of Abu Ghraib below' (*New Internationalist* 2005).

Moore, Michael

(Born 23 April 1954, Flint, Michigan). Liberal filmmaker, writer, TV presenter and prominent anti-Bush political activist, Moore directed the key film of the early war on terror, political documentary *Fahrenheit 9/11* (2004), which played to huge audiences around the world and won the *Palme d'Or* at the 2004 Cannes Film Festival. Moore was already well known for earlier documentaries *Bowling for Columbine* (2002), which won the 2003 Oscar for Best Documentary, and *Roger & Me* (1989). In the 1990s he also hosted the popular TV shows *TV Nation* and *The Awful Truth*.

Rice, Condoleezza

(Born 14 November 1954, Birmingham, Alabama). Stanford University political scientist, specialising in Russia and Eastern Europe. National Security Adviser to the president during Bush junior's first term, Rice was promoted to Secretary of State in January 2005 at the start of Bush's second term, where she succeeded Colin Powell. In the 1980s, Rice was an international affairs fellow of the Council on Foreign Relations, Special Assistant to the Director of the Joint Chiefs of Staff, and a foreign policy adviser to President Bush senior (1989–91). She advised Bush junior during his first campaign for president (1999–2000). She has been a member of the board of directors of the Chevron Corporation, the Charles Schwab Corporation, the Transamerica Corporation, Hewlett Packard, the Carnegie Corporation, the RAND Corporation and the International Advisory Council of J. P. Morgan.

Rumsfeld, Donald

(Born 9 July 1932, Chicago). As Bush junior's Secretary of Defense (2001–6), Rumsfeld directed the wars in Afghanistan and Iraq, until forced to resign in December 2006. A former Navy pilot (1954–57) and reservist until 1975, Rumsfeld was elected as a Republican member of the House of Representatives for Illinois in 1962, and then successively re-elected until 1969, when he took up the first of several posts in the Nixon administration. He was US Ambassador to NATO (1973–74), White House Chief of Staff to President Ford (1974–75), then Ford's Secretary of Defense (1975–77). A signatory of the Project for the New American Century's letter to Clinton on Iraq (1998), Rumsfeld also has strong ties to the intelligence community and to American business, particularly the pharmaceuticals industry. He has been on the boards of

General Instrument Corporation, Gilead Sciences, Pfizer Inc., Amylin Pharmaceuticals, ABB Ltd, Gulfstream Aerospace, Motorola, General Dynamics, Allstate, Kellogg, Sears, Roebuck and Company, Tribune Company and the RAND Corporation.

Scheuer, Michael

Founder and chief of the bin Laden unit at the CIA Counterterrorist Center (1996–99), Scheuer resigned from the CIA in 2004. He wrote two books, *Through Our Enemies' Eyes* (2002) and *Imperial Hubris* (2004) as 'Anonymous', attacking Bush's stewardship of the war on terror. After he resigned from the CIA, Scheuer appeared widely in highbrow print and broadcast media in the US and around the world as a national security pundit. As Clinton's anti-terrorism chief, Scheuer oversaw the introduction of the CIA 'renditions' programme in 1995. He is Adjunct Professor of Security Studies at Georgetown University.

Serra, Richard

(Born 2 November 1939, San Francisco). American artist best known for his minimalist public sculpture, who has exhibited around the world since the early 1970s, including at the Venice Biennales of 1984 and 2001, seven Whitney Museum Annual and Biennial exhibitions between 1968 and 1995, and successive *Documenta* festivals – the 100-day exhibition of international art held every five years in the German town of Kassel – between 1972 and 1987. Major retrospective exhibitions of Serra's work were displayed at the Museum of Contemporary Art in Los Angeles (1998), and Museum of Modern Art in New York (1986 and 2007).

Annotated bibliography of further reading and texts cited

Readers looking for targeted further reading might usefully begin with the contemporary sources discussed in this book. For additional further reading, a good place to begin is Booth and Dunne (2002), Denzin and Lincoln (2003), Dudziak (2003), Kellner (2003), Martin and Petro (2006) and Simpson (2006).

For further discussion of issues raised in contemporary 'empire' debates, see Brenner (1998), Chomsky (2001, 2004), Buchanan (2002), Ignatieff (2003b), Klare (2002 and 2004), Kleveman (2003), Kupchan (2003), Kagan (2003), Zunes (2003), Burbach and Tarbell (2004) and Johnson (2004). On the Bush Doctrine specifically, see Kaplan and Kristol (2003), Gaddis (2004), Bacevich (2005), Gurtov (2006) and the June 2005 issue of *Diplomatic History*, which featured Leffler (2005), and a range of responses to Leffler. For a good introduction to contemporary neoconservatism see Frum and Perle (2003), Kaplan and Kristol (2003), Norton (2004) and Stelzer (2004). See also Fukuyama (2006). On the wider contemporary conservative movement in the US, see Frank (2004), Micklethwait and Wooldridge (2004) and Hedges (2007).

On legal issues thrown up by 9/11 and the war on terror, see Cole and Dempsey (2002), Chang (2002), Schulhofer (2002), Strawson (2002), Van Krieken (2002) and Dudziak (2003). On Abu Ghraib, Guantánamo Bay and torture, Greenberg and Gratel (2005) is indispensable. See also Hersh (2004), Krauthammer (2004a and 2004b), Ratner (2004), Rose (2004) and Karpinsky (2005).

For an indicative sample of approaches to Islamism in the West, see Anonymous (2002), Benjamin and Simon (2002), Baudrillard (2003), Burke (2003), Gray (2003), Lewis (2003) and Devji (2005). Laqueur (2004) includes a substantial section of Islamist documents. The best introduction to the political statements of Osama bin Laden is Lawrence (2005).

For contemporary criticism of film and TV treatments of 9/11 and the war on terror, see Dixon (2004), Spigel (2004), Stanley (2006, 2007a,

2007b) and Mayer (2007) and relevant sections in McCrisken and Pepper (2005) and Dickenson (2006). For collections of 9/11 photography in book-form, see Magnum Photographers (2001), Vergara (2001), Feldschuh (2002), McNally (2002) and Shulan (2002) and Meyerowitz (2006). For contemporary critical essays on 9/11 photography and other war on terror visual culture, see Frascina (2003), Kennedy (2003), Apel (2005) and Feldman (2005). On attempts to control photography at Ground Zero, in a compelling account of what it meant to make art there, see Josyph (2006). Other '9/11 novels' not discussed in detail or at all in this book, include Auster (2005), Beard (2005), Kunkel (2005), McDonnell (2005), McGrath (2005), McInerney (2006), Messud (2006), Updike (2006), DeLillo (2007) and Shriver (2007). For an array of approaches taken and issues raised in 9/11 and war on terror Media Studies, begin with Zelizer and Allan (2002), Chermak et al. (2003), Katovsky and Carlson (2003), Miller (2003), Snow (2003), Seib (2004) and Ben-Shaul (2006), and relevant sections in Kellner (2003), Allan and Zelizer (2004) and Hoskins (2005). On Al Jazeera, see El-Nawawy (2003) and Miles (2005).

11'09"01 – September 11, film, directed by Youssef Chahine et al. UK et al.: CIH Shorts, 2002.

ACLU [American Civil Liberties Union] (2003), 'The USA PATRIOT ACT and Government Actions that Threaten Our Civil Liberties': http://www.aclu.org/safefree/resources/17343res20031114.html

Adorno, Theodor W. and Horkheimer, Max (1997), *Dialectic of Enlightenment* [1944], London: Verso.

Ahmed, Nafeez M. (2003), *Behind the War on Terror*, Forest Row: Clairview.

Ajami, F. (1996), 'The Summoning', in S. P. Huntington et al., *The Clash of Civilizations: The Debate*. New York: Norton, pp. 26–35.

Alamo, The, film, directed by John Lee Hancock. USA: Touchstone/Imagine Entertainment, 2004.

Aletti, V. (2001), 'Start Making Sense: Eyewitness Photographers at Ground Zero', *Village Voice* (10–16 October); http://www.villagevoice.com/art/0141, aletti,28863,13.html.

Allan, S. (2002), 'Reweaving the Internet: Online News of September 11', in B. Zelizer and S. Allan (eds), *Journalism After September 11*, New York: Routledge, pp. 119–40.

Allan, Stuart and Zelizer, Barbie (eds) (2004), *Reporting War: Journalism in Wartime*, London: Routledge.

Amnesty International (2006), 'Below the Radar: Secret Flights to Torture and Disappearance'; http://web.amnesty.org/library/pdf/AMR510512006-ENGLISH/$File/AMR5105106.pdf.

Anonymous [Michael Scheuer] (2002), *Through Our Enemies' Eyes: Osama bin Lade, Radical Islam, and the Future of America*, Washington: Brassey's.

Anonymous [Michael Scheuer] (2004), *Imperial Hubris: Why the West is Losing the War on Terror*, Washington: Brassey's.

Apel, D. (2005), 'Torture Culture: Lynching Photographs and the Images of Abu Ghraib', *Art Journal*, 64(2): 88–100.

Arrighi, Giovanni (1994), *The Long Twentieth Century: Money, Power, and the Origins of Our Times*, London: Verso.

Arrighi, Giovanni and Silver, Beverly J. (1999), *Chaos and Governance in the Modern World System*, Minneapolis, MN: University of Minnesota Press.

Auster, Paul (2005), *The Brooklyn Follies*, New York: Faber.

Bacevich, Andrew J. (2002), *American Empire: The Realities and Consequences of US Diplomacy*, Cambridge, MA: Harvard University Press.

Bacevich, Andrew J. (2005), 'Requiem for the Bush Doctrine', *Current History*, December: 411–17.

Bamford, James (2004), *A Pretext for War: 9/11, Iraq, and the Abuse of America's Intelligence Agencies*, New York: Doubleday.

Bartley, R. L. (1996), 'The Case for Optimism', in S. P. Huntington et al., *The Clash of Civilizations: The Debate*, New York: Norton, pp. 41–5.

Baudrillard, Jean (2003), *The Spirit of Terrorism*, London, Verso.

BBC (2006), 'Spooks, Episode Synopsis' (Series 5, Episode 10), bbc.co.uk: http://www.bbc.co.uk/drama/spooks/series5_ep10.shtml.

Beard, Charles A. (1935), *The Open Door at Home*, New York: Macmillan.

Beard, Philip (2005), *Dear Zoe*, New York: Penguin Books.

Beigbeder, Frédéric (2004), *Windows on the World*, London: Fourth Estate.

Ben-Shaul, Nitzan (2006), *A Violent World: TV News Images of Middle Eastern Terror and War*, Lanham, MD: Rowman and Littlefield.

Benjamin, Daniel and Simon, Steven (2002), *The Age of Sacred Terror*, New York: Random House.

Berger, J. (2004), 'The Beginning of History', *Guardian*, 24 August: http://www.guardian.co.uk/comment/story/0,,1289430,00.html.

Berman, M. (2002), 'When Bad Buildings Happen to Good People', in M. Sorkin and S. Zukin (eds), *After the World Trade Center: Rethinking New York City*, New York: Routledge, pp. 1–12.

Billig, M. (1995), *Banal Nationalism*, London: Sage.

bin Laden, Osama (2005), 'Declaration of Jihad' [23 August 1996], in B. Lawrence (ed.), *Messages to the World: The Statements of Osama bin Laden*, London: Verso, pp. 23–30.

bin Laden, Osama et al. (2005), 'The World Islamic Front' [23 February 1998], in B. Lawrence (ed.), *Messages to the World: The Statements of Osama bin Laden*, London: Verso, pp. 58–62.

Binyan, L. (1996), 'Civilization Grafting', in S. P. Huntington et al., *The Clash of Civilizations: The Debate*, New York: Norton, pp. 46–9.

Bird, S. Elizabeth (2002), 'Taking it Personally: Supermarket Tabloids after September 11', in B. Zelizer and S. Allan (eds), *Journalism after September 11*, New York: Routledge, pp. 141–59.

Black Hawk Down, film, directed by Ridley Scott. USA: Jerry Bruckheimer Films/Revolution Studios, 2001.

Blum, William (2002), *Rogue State: A Guide to the World's Only Superpower*, London: Zed Books.

Blumenthal, S. (2006a), 'The Neocons Last Stand', *Guardian*, 16 November: 33.

Blumenthal, Sidney (2006b), *How Bush Rules: Chronicles of a Radical Regime*, Princeton, NJ: Princeton University Press.

Booth, Ken and Dunne, Tim (eds) (2002), *Worlds in Collision: Terror and the Future of Global Order*, New York: Palgrave Macmillan.

Bordowitz, G. (2004), 'Tactics Inside and Out: Critical Art Ensemble', *ArtForum* (September): 212–15, 292.

Borger, J. (2005), 'Cheney "may be guilty of war crime"', *Guardian*, 30 November: 22.

Bradshaw, P. (2006), 'Syriana', *The Guardian*, 3 March: http://film.guardian. co.uk/News_Story/Critic_Review/Guardian_review/0,,1721669,00.html.

Breithaupt, F. (2003), 'Rituals of Trauma: How the Media Fabricated September 11', in Chermak et al. (eds), *Media Representations of September 11*, Westport, CT: Praeger, pp. 67–81.

Brenner, Robert (1998), 'The Economics of Global Turbulence: A Special Report on the World Economy, 1950–98', *New Left Review* (whole issue) 229, May/June.

Brenner, Robert (2002), *The Boom and the Bubble: The US in the World Economy*, London: Verso.

Brown, M. et al. (2003), 'Internet News Representations of September 11: Archival Impulse in the Age of Information', in S. Chermak et al. (eds), *Media Representations of September 11*, Westport, CT: Praeger, pp. 103–16.

Bruzzi, Stella (2000), *New Documentary: A Critical Introduction*, London: Routledge.

Buchanan, Patrick J. (2002), *A Republic, Not an Empire: Reclaiming America's Destiny*, Washington: Regnery [revised edn].

Burbach, R. and Tarbell, J. (2004), *Imperial Overstretch: George W. Bush and the Hubris of Empire*, London: Zed.

Burke, Jason (2003), *Al Qaeda*, London: Penguin Books.

Bush, G. W. (2001), 'Address to a Joint Session of Congress and the American People', 20 September: http://www.whitehouse.gov/news/releases/2001/09/20010920-8.html

Bush, G. W. (2002), 'President Bush Delivers Graduation Speech at West Point', 1 June: http://www.whitehouse.gov/news/releases/2002/06/20020601-3.html.

Bush, G. W. (2003), 'President Delivers "State of the Union"', 28 January: http://www.whitehouse.gov/news/releases/2003/01/20030128-19.html.

Bush, G. W. (2004), 'Remarks by the President at Victory 2004 Luncheon. The River Club, New York, New York', 20 April; http://www.whitehouse.gov/news/releases/2004/04/20040420-4.html.

Bush, G. W. (2005), 'President Outlines Steps to Help Iraq Achieve Democracy and Freedom. Remarks by the President on Iraq and the War on Terror', 24 May: http://www.whitehouse.gov/news/releases/2004/05/20040524-10.html.

Bush, G. W. (2006), 'President Discusses Creation of Military Commissions to Try Suspected Terrorists', 6 September: http://www.whitehouse.gov/news/releases/2006/09/20060906-3.html.

Byars, Jackie (1991), *All That Hollywood Allows: Re-Reading Gender in 1950s Melodrama*, Chapel Hill, NC: University of North Carolina Press.

Campagna, J. and Roumani, R. (2003), 'Permission to Fire: CPJ Investigates the Attack on the Palestine Hotel': http://www.cpj.org/Briefings/2003/palestine_hotel/palestine_hotel.html.

Carnegie International (2004), 'Artists' Bios: Isa Genzken'; http://www.cmoa.org/international/the_exhibition/artist.asp?genzken.

CBS (2005), 'Former POW Lynch Starts College: Jessica Lynch Tries To Keep Low Profile At West Virginia University', *CBS News*, 22 August: http://www.cbsnews.com/stories/2005/08/22/national/main791087.shtml.

Chang, N. (2002), *Silencing Political Dissent: How Post-September 11 Anti-Terrorism Measures Threaten Our Civil Liberties*, New York: Seven Stories.

Chermak, Steven et al. (eds) (2003), *Media Representations of September 11*, Westport, CT: Praeger.

Chomsky, Noam (2001), *9/11*, New York: Seven Stories.

Chomsky, Noam (2004), *Hegemony or Survival: America's Quest for Global Dominance*, London: Penguin Books.

Chrisafis, A. (2006), 'Concerns Grow in Ireland over Use of Shannon Airport as US Military Stopover', *Guardian*, January 21: 20.

Clarke, Richard (2004), *Against All Enemies: Inside America's War on Terror*, New York: Free Press.

Cole, D. and Dempsey, J. X. (2002), *Terrorism and the Constitution*, New York: New Press.

Control Room, DVD, directed by Jihane Noujaim. USA: Magnolia Pictures, 2004.

Corcoran Gallery (2002), *here is new york: a democracy of photographs* [press release]: http://www.corcoran.org/exhibitions/press_results.asp?Exhib_ID=52.

Council of Europe (2006a), 'Secretary General's report under Article 52 ECHR on the question of secret detention and transport of detainees suspected of terrorist acts, notably by or at the instigation of foreign agencies'; https://wcd.coe.int/ViewDoc.jsp?Ref=SG/Inf(2006)5&Sector=secPrivateOffice&Language=lanEnglish&Ver=original&BackColorInternet=9999CC&BackColorIntranet=FFBB55&BackColorLogged=FFAC75.

Council of Europe (2006b), 'Secretary General's supplementary report under Article 52 ECHR on the question of secret detention and transport of detainees suspected of terrorist acts, notably by or at the instigation of foreign agencies': http://www.coe.int/t/E/Com/Press/Source/SG_Inf(2006).doc.

CPJ [Committee to Protect Journalists] (2004), 'Army Finds No Fault in Palestine Hotel Shelling: CPJ Questions Findings in Long-Awaited Probe', 5 November: http://www.cpj.org/news/2004/Iraq05nov04na.html.

CPJ [Committee to Protect Journalists] (2006), 'Journalists in Danger: Facts on Iraq': http://www.cpj.org/Briefings/2003/gulf03/iraq_stats.html.

Creative Time (2005), 'Creative Time: History', http://www.creativetime.org/about/history.html.

Daalder, I. H. and Lindsay, J. M. (2003), 'Bush's Revolution', *Current History: A Journal of Contemporary World Affairs*, November: 367–76.

Danto, A. C. (2004), 'American Self-Consciousness in Politics and Art', *ArtForum* (September): 206–9.

Darton, W. (2002), 'The Janus Face of Architectural Terrorism; Minoru Yamasaki, Mohammed Atta, and Our World Trade Center', in M. Sorkin and S. Zukin (eds), *After the World Trade Center: Rethinking New York City*, New York: Routledge, pp. 87–95.

Davis, Mike (1990), *City of Quartz: Excavating the Future in Los Angeles*, London: Verso.

DeLillo, Don (2007), *Falling Man*, London: Picador.

Denzin N. and Lincoln, Y. (2003), *9/11 in American Culture*, Lanham, MD: Altamira.

Devji, F. (2005), *Landscapes of the Jihad: Militancy, Morality, Modernity*, London: Hurst and Company.

Dickenson, Ben (2006), *Hollywood's New Radicalism: War, Globalisation and the Movies from Reagan to George W. Bush*, London: I. B. Tauris.

Dixon, W. W. (2004), *Film and Television After 9/11*, Carbondale, IL: Southern Illinois University Press.

Doward, J. (2005), 'Muslim Anger at Terror Plot in TV Drama *24*: New Series of Hit Sky Show Accused of Islamophobia', *The Observer*, 30 January: http://www.guardian.co.uk/religion/Story/0,,1401755,00.html.

Drezner, D. W. (2005), 'Values, Interests, and American Grand Strategy', *Diplomatic History* 29(3), June: 429–32.

Dudziak, Mary L. (ed.) (2003), *September 11 in History: A Watershed Moment?* Durham, NC: Duke University Press.

Earle, S. (2004), liner notes to 'The Revolution Starts . . . Now', CD, recorded by Steve Earle. UK: Rykodisc, 2004.

Eisenberg, C. (2005), 'The New Cold War', *Diplomatic History* 29(3), June: 423–7.

Elbies, J. (2002), 'A Grassroots Memorial Turns into a Big Cultural Story', *American Photo* (January/February): 14.

El-Nawawy, M. (2003), *Al-Jazeera*, Boulder, CO: Westview.

Fahrenheit 9/11, film, directed by Michael Moore. USA, Lion Gate Films/Fellowship Adventure Group, 2004.

Feldman, A. (2005), 'On the Actuarial Gaze', *Cultural Studies*, 19(2), (March): 203–26.

Feldmann, L. (2003), 'The Impact of Bush Linking 9/11 and Iraq', *Christian Science Monitor*, 14 March: http://www.csmonitor.com/2003/0314/p02s01-woiq.html.

Feldschuh, M. (ed.) (2002), *The September 11th Photo Project*. New York: HarperCollins.

Ferguson, Niall (2004), *Colossus: The Rise and Fall of the American Empire*, London: Allen Lane.

Ferguson, N. (2006), 'The Crash of Civilizations', *Los Angeles Times*, 27 February: http://uniset.ca/terr/news/lat_huntingtonclash.html.

Foer, Jonathan Safran (2005), *Extremely Loud and Incredibly Close*, London: Hamish Hamilton.

Fog of War: Eleven Lessons from the Life of Robert S. McNamara, The, film (2003), directed by Errol Morris. USA: Radical Media/Sony Pictures Classics, 2003.

Follman, M. (2003), 'The White House War with the CIA', *Salon.com*, 8 November: http://dir.salon.com/story/news/feature/2003/11/08/powers/index.html.

Frank, Thomas (2004), *What's the Matter with America: The Resistible Rise of the American Right*, London: Secker and Warburg.

Frascina, F. (2003), 'Inventing and Sustaining a Visible Resistance', *Peace Review* 15(4): 491–8.

Friedman, Thomas L. (1999), *The Lexus and the Olive Tree*, New York: Farrar Straus Giroux.

Frum, David and Perle, Richard (2003), *An End to Evil: How to Win the War on Terror*, New York: Random House.

Fukuyama, Francis (1992), *The End of History and the Last Man*, London: Hamish Hamilton.

Fukuyama, Francis (2006), *After the Neocons: America at the Crossroads*, London: Profile.

Gaddis, John L. (2004), *Surprise, Security and the American Experience*, Cambridge, MA: Harvard University Press.

Genzken, I. and Tillmans, W. (2005), 'Who Do You Love? Isa Genzken and Wolfgang Tillmans in Conversation', *ArtForum*: http://www.*ArtForum*.com/inprint/id=9739.

Gladman, R. (2003), 'Tom Sachs; A Visit to Nutsy's', *C International Contemporary Art* 77 (Spring): http://www.akrylic.com/contemporary_art_article32.htm.

Gledhill, Christine (ed.) (1987), *Home Is Where the Heart Is: Studies in Melodrama and the Woman's Film*, London: British Film Institute.

Goldenberg, S. and Harding, L. (2005), 'Detainee Flights Have Saved European Lives, says Rice', *Guardian*, 6 December: 5.

Good Night, and Good Luck, film, directed by George Clooney. USA: Participant/Warner Independent Pictures, 2005.

Greenberg, Karen J and Dratel, Joshua L. (2005), *The Torture Papers: The Road to Abu Ghraib*, Cambridge: Cambridge University Press.

Grey, S. and Cobain, I. (2006), 'From Logistics to Turning a Blind Eye: Europe's Role in Terror Abductions', *Guardian*, 7 June: 3.

Griffin, T. (2004a), 'The Art of Politics: Introduction', *ArtForum* (September): 204–5.

Griffin, T. (2004b), 'Historical Survey: An Interview with Hans Haacke', *ArtForum* (September): 224–7.

Griffin, T. (2004c), Untitled introduction to 'Electoral Collage: A Portfolio', *ArtForum*, September: 227.

Gurtov, Melvin (2006), *Superpower on Crusade: The Bush Doctrine in US Foreign Policy*, Boulder, CO: Lynne Rienner.

Harding, L. (2005), 'EU Threat to Countries with Secret CIA Prisons', *Guardian*, 29 November: 13.

Harmon, A. (2003), 'Weblogs: Facts Are In, Spin Is Out', *New York Times*, 25 March: http://query.nytimes.com/gst/fullpage.html?res=9F00E6DA1230-F936A15750C0A9659C8B63&sec=&spon=&pagewanted=print.

Harvard College (2006), 'Recent Developments: Detainee Treatment Act of 2005', *Harvard Human Rights Journal* (19: Spring): http://www.law.harvard.edu/students/orgs/hrj/iss19/suleman.shtml#Heading41.

Harvey, David (2003), *The New Imperialism*, Oxford: Oxford University Press.

Hayes, S. F. (2004), 'The CIA Fights Back', *The Weekly Standard*, 15 November: http://www.weeklystandard.com/Content/Public/Articles/000/000/004/925wciab.asp.

Hearts and Minds, film, directed by Peter Davis. USA: BBS Productions, 1974.

Hedges, C. (2007), *American Fascists: The Christian Right and the War on America*, Free Press: New York.

Herbert, M. (2004), 'Material Witness', *ArtForum*, September: 210–11.

Hersh, Seymour M. (2004), *Chain of Command: The Road from 9/11 to Abu Ghraib*, London: Allen Lane.

Hixson, W. L. (2005), 'Leffler Takes a Linguistic Turn', *Diplomatic History* 29(3), June: 419–21.

Hoberman, J. (2004), 'Sleeper in the White House', *The Guardian*, 30 October: http://books.guardian.co.uk/review/story/0,,1338293,00.html.

Hofstadter, R. (1964), 'The Paranoid Style in American Politics', *Harper's Magazine*, November: 77–86.

Holloway, David (2002), *The Late Modernism of Cormac McCarthy*, Westport, CT: Greenwood.

Holloway, David and Beck, John (eds) (2005), *American Visual Cultures*, New York: Continuum.

Hoskins, Andrew (2004), *Televising War: From Vietnam to Iraq*, London: Continuum.

Hoskins, A. (2005), 'Constructing History in TV News from Clinton to 9/11: Flashframes of History – American Visual Memories', in D. Holloway and J. Beck (eds), *American Visual Cultures*, New York: Continuum, pp. 299–305.

Human Rights Watch (2002), *Human Rights Watch World Report 2002*: http://www.hrw.org/wr2k2/

Huntington, S. P. (1996a), 'The Clash of Civilizations?', in S. P. Huntington et al., *The Clash of Civilizations: The Debate*, New York: Norton, pp. 1–25.

Huntington, S. P. (1996b), 'If Not Civilizations, What? Paradigms of the Post-Cold War World', in S. P. Huntington et al., *The Clash of Civilizations: The Debate*, New York: Norton, pp. 56–67.

Huntington, Samuel P. (1998), *The Clash of Civilizations and the Remaking of World Order*, London: Touchstone.

Huntington, S. P. (2001), 'The Age of Muslim Wars', *Newsweek*, 138(25): 42–7.

Huntington, Samuel P. (2004), *Who Are We? America's Great Debate*, London: Free.

Ignatieff, M. (2003a), 'The American Empire (Get Used to It)', Sunday *New York Times* Magazine, 5 January; http://www.wehaitians.com/the%20american%20empire.html.

Ignatieff, Michael (2003b), *Empire Lite: Nation Building in Bosnia, Kosovo, Afghanistan*, New York: Vintage.

Ignatieff, Michael (2005), *The Lesser Evil: Political Ethics in an Age of Terror*, Edinburgh: Edinburgh University Press.

Ikenberry, G. J. (2005), 'The Strange Triumph of Unilateralism', *Current History: A Journal of Contemporary World Affairs*, December: 414–15.

Jarhead, film, directed by Sam Mendes. USA: Universal Pictures, 2005.

Johnson, Chalmers (2002), *Blowback: The Costs and Consequences of American Empire*, London: Timewarner [revised edn; 1st edn 2000].

Johnson, Chalmers (2004), *The Sorrows of Empire: Militarism, Secrecy and the End of the Republic*, London: Verso.

Josyph, Peter (2006), *Liberty Street: Encounters at Ground Zero*, Hanover: University Press of New England.

Kagan, Robert (2003), *Paradise and Power: America and Europe in the New World Order*, London: Atlantic.

Kagan, R. (2005), 'Between Wisdom and Foolishness', *Diplomatic History* 29(3), June: 415–17.

Kampfner, J. (2003), 'The Truth about Jessica', *Guardian*, 15 May: http://www.guardian.co.uk/Iraq/Story/0,2763,956255,00.html.

Kaplan, Lawrence F. and Kristol, William (2003), *The War over Iraq: Saddam's Tyranny and America's Mission*, San Francisco: Encounter.

Karpinski, Janis (2005), *One Woman's Army: The Commanding General of Abu Ghraib Tells Her Story*, New York: Hyperion.

Katovsky, Bill and Carlson, Timothy (eds) (2003), *Embedded: The Media at War in Iraq*, Guilford: Windsor.

Kellner, Douglas (2003), *9/11 and Terror War: The Dangers of the Bush Legacy*, Lanham, MD: Rowman and Littlefield.

Kelman, James (2004), *You Have to be Careful in the Land of the Free*, New York: Harcourt.

Kennedy, L. (2003), 'Framing September 11: Photography After the Fall', *History of Photography* 27(3): 272–83.

Kennedy, Paul (1990), *The Rise and Fall of the Great Powers: Economic Change and Military Conflict from 1500 to 2000*, London: Fontana.

Kingdom of Heaven, film, directed by Ridley Scott. USA: 20th Century Fox, 2005.

Kirkpatrick, J. J. (1996), 'The Modernizing Imperative', in S. P. Huntington et al., *The Clash of Civilizations: The Debate*. New York: Norton, pp. 50–3.

Klare, Michael T. (2002), *Resource Wars: The New Landscape of Global Conflict*, New York: Owl Books.

Klare, Michael T. (2004), *Blood and Oil: The Dangers and Consequences of America's Growing Petroleum Dependency*, New York: Metropolitan Books.

Kleveman, Lutz (2003), *The New Great Game: Blood and Oil in Central Asia*, London: Atlantic.

Kornblut, A. E. and Bender, B. (2003), 'Cheney Link of Iraq, 9/11 Challenged', *The Boston Globe*, 16 September; http://www.boston.com/news/nation/articles/2003/09/16/cheney_link_of_iraq_911_challenged/.

Krauthammer, C. (2004a), 'Abu Ghraib as Symbol', *Washington Post*, 7 May: A33.

Krauthammer, C. (2004b), 'The Abu Ghraib Panic', *Washington Post*, 14 May: A25.

Kunkel, Benjamin (2005), *Indecision*, New York: Random House.

Kupchan, Charles A. (2003), *The End of the American Era*, New York: Knopf.

Kurtz, H. (2006), 'ABC to Alter Show on Pre-9/11 Run-Up', *Washington Post*, 8 September: A02.

Lal, Deepak (2004), *In Praise of Empires: Globalization and Order*, New York: Palgrave Macmillan.

Laqueur, Walter (ed.) (2004), *Voice of Terror*, New York: Reed Press.

Lawrence, Bruce (ed.) (2005), *Messages to the World: The Statements of Osama bin Laden*, London: Verso.

Leffler, M. P. (2005), '9/11 and American Foreign Policy', *Diplomatic History* 29(3), June: 395–413.

Lewis, Bernard (2003), *The Crisis of Islam: Holy War and Unholy Terror*, London: Phoenix.

Lewis, J. and Brookes, R. (2004), 'How British Television News Represented the Case for the War in Iraq', in S. Allan and B. Zelizer, *Reporting War: Journalism in Wartime*, London: Routledge, pp. 283–300.

Lewis, J. et al. (2004), 'Too Close for Comfort? The Role of Embedded Reporting during the 2003 Iraq War. Report Summary', Cardiff: Cardiff School of Journalism, Media and Cultural Studies. http://www.warandmedia.org/documents/research/comfort_summary.doc.

Lost, TV Series. USA: ABC, 2004–

Magnum Photographers (2001), *New York September 11 By Magnum Photographers*, New York: Powerhouse Books.

Mahbubani, K. (1996), 'The Dangers of Decadence', in S. P. Huntington et al., *The Clash of Civilizations: The Debate*. New York: Norton, pp. 36–40.

Maltby, Richard (2003), *Hollywood Cinema* [2nd edition], Oxford: Blackwell.

Manchurian Candidate, The, film, directed by John Frankenheimer. USA: M.C. Productions, 1962.

Manchurian Candidate, The, film, directed by Jonathan Demme. USA: Paramount, 2004.

Mann, Michael (2003), *Incoherent Empire*, New York: Verso.

Martin, Andrew, and Petro, Patrice (eds) (2006), *Rethinking Global Security: Media, Popular Culture and the War on Terror*, New Brunswick: Rutgers University Press.

Mayer, J. (2007), 'Whatever It Takes: The Politics of the Man Behind "24"', *The New Yorker*, 19 February; http://www.newyorker.com/reporting/2007/02/19/070219fa_fact_mayer.

McCarthy, Cormac (2006), *The Road*, London: Picador.

McChesney, R. W. (2002), 'September 11 and the Structural Limitations of US Journalism', in B. Zelizer and S. Allan (eds), *Journalism After September 11*, New York: Routledge, pp. 91–100.

McCrisken, Trevor and Pepper, Andrew (2005), *American History and Contemporary Hollywood Film*, Edinburgh: Edinburgh University Press.

McDonnell, Nick (2005), *The Third Brother*, New York: Grove Press.

McEwan, Ian (2005), *Saturday*, London: Random House.

McGrath, Patrick (2005), *Ghost Town*, London: Bloomsbury.

McInerney, Jay (2006), *The Good Life*, London: Bloomsbury.

McNally, Joe (2002), *Faces of Ground Zero: Portraits of the Heroes of September 11, 2001*, Boston, MA: Little, Brown.

Messud, Claire (2006), *The Emperor's Children*, New York: Knopf.

Meyerowitz, Joel (2006), *Aftermath: World Trade Center Archive*, London: Phaidon.

Micklethwait, J. and Wooldridge, A. (2004), *The Right Nation: Why America is Different*, London: Allen Lane.

Miles, H. (2005), *Al Jazeera*. London: Abacus.

Miller, David (ed.) (2003), *Tell Me Lies: Propaganda and Media Distortion in the Attack on Iraq*, London: Pluto.

Mittell, J. (2005), 'The Value of *Lost* Part Two', *Flow* 2(10); http://jot.communication.utexas.edu/flow/?jot=view&id=902.

Monbiot, G. (2005), 'Behind the Phosphorus Clouds are War Crimes within War Crimes', *Guardian*, 22 November: 31.

Montgomery, D. (2006), 'The Author Who Got A Big Boost from bin Laden', *Washington Post*, January 21 (Saturday): C01. http://www.washingtonpost.com/wp-dyn/content/article/2006/01/20/AR2006012001971.html.

Moore, Michael (2002), *Stupid White Men . . . And Other Sorry Excuses for the State of the Nation*, London: Penguin Books.

Moore, Michael (2003), *Dude, Where's My Country*. London: Allen Lane.

Mortenson, D. (2004), 'Violence subsides for Marines in Fallujah', *North County Times*, 10 April; http://www.nctimes.com/articles/2004/04/11/military/iraq/19_30_504_10_04.txt.

Nadelson, R. (2002a), 'In Pictures: The People's Pictures', *Guardian* (10 September): 12.

Nadelson, R. (2002b), 'One Year Ago', *ArtReview* (September): 66–9.

National Commission on Terrorist Attacks Upon the United States (2004a), *The 9/11 Commission Report*, New York: W. W. Norton.

National Commission on Terrorist Attacks Upon the United States (2004b), *The 9/11 Commission Report: Executive Summary*; http://www.9-11commission.gov/report/911Report_Exec.pdf.

National Security Strategy of the United States of America (2002); http://www.whitehouse.gov/nsc/nss.pdf.

Navasky, V. (2002), 'Foreword', in B. Zelizer and S. Allan (eds), *Journalism After September 11*, New York: Routledge, pp. xiii–xviii.

Nelson, A. K. (2005), 'Continuity and Change in the Age of Unlimited Power', *Diplomatic History* 29(3), June: 437–9.

New Internationalist (2005), 'Michael Ignatieff, Who Calls Himself a Liberal and a Human Rights Campainer, is a Wolf in Sheep's Clothing', December; http://findarticles.com/p/articles/mi_m0JQP/is_385/ai_n15970734.

New York Times (2004), 'The *Times* and Iraq' [editorial], *New York Times*, 26 May; http://www.nytimes.com/2004/05/26/international/middleeast/26FTE_NOTE.html?ex=1400990400&en=94c17fcffad92ca9&ei=5007&partner=USERLAND.

Norton, Anne (2004), *Leo Strauss and the Politics of American Empire*, New Haven, CT: Yale University Press.

Norton-Taylor, R. (2002), 'Terror Crackdown "Encourages Repression"', *Guardian*, 17 January: 4.

Nye, Joseph S. Jr (2002), *The Paradox of American Power: Why the World's Only Superpower Can't Go It Alone*, Oxford: Oxford University Press.

Offner, A. A. (2005), 'Rogue President, Rogue Nation: Bush and US National Security', *Diplomatic History*, 29(3), (June): 433–5.

Outfoxed: Rupert Murdoch's War on Journalism, film, directed by Robert Greenwald. USA: Carolina Productions, 2004.

Paradise Now, film, directed by Hany Abu-Assad. Palestine: Augustus Film, 2005.

Participate.net (2005a), 'PARTICIPATE: Movies have the power to inspire. You have the power to act. Participate!': http://www.participate.net/about.

Participate.net (2005b), 'GOOD NIGHT, AND GOOD LUCK. Take the media into your own hands': http://www.participate.net/reportitnow/issue.

Pax, Salam (2003–4), *Where is Raed?*, weblog: http://dear_raed.blogspot.com/.

Pax, Salam (2003), *The Baghdad Blog*, London: Atlantic.

PBS (2007a), *Frontline* – 'News War'; http://www.pbs.org/wgbh/pages/frontline/newswar/.

PBS (2007b), *Frontline* – 'Interview, Carl Bernstein'; http://www.pbs.org/wgbh/pages/frontline/newswar/interviews/bernstein.html.

Philpott, S. (2005), 'A Controversy of Faces: Images from Bali and Abu Ghraib', *Journal for Cultural Research*, 9(3), July: 227–44.

Piel, G. (1996), 'The West is the Best', in S. P. Huntington et al., *The Clash of Civilizations: The Debate*. New York: Norton, p. 55.

Pincus, R. L. (2002), 'Time Stopped: 'New York' holds 9/11 in suspension, so we can think, not just see', *San Diego Union-Tribune* (12 September): http://entertainment.signonsandiego.com/profile/249185/?p=1.

PollingReport.com (2007), 'President Bush – Overall Job Rating in Recent Polls': http://www.pollingreport.com/BushJob.htm.

Powers, Thomas (2004), *Intelligence Wars: American Secret History from Hitler to Al-Qaeda*, New York: New York Review of Books.

Price, Reynolds (2005), *The Good Priest's Son*, New York: Scribner.

Publishers Weekly (2004), review of *9/11 Commission Report*, *in* 'From our editors: the Barnes & Noble Review'; http://search.barnesandnoble.com/booksearch/isbninquiry.asp?z=y&isbn=0393326713.

Ratner, M. et al. (2004), *Guantánamo: What the World Should Know*, Moreton-in-Marsh: Arris Books.

Reynolds, A. and Barnett, B. (2003), ' "America under Attack": CNN's Verbal and Visual Framing of September 11', in S. Chermak et al. (eds), *Media Representations of September 11*, Westport, CT: Praeger, pp. 85–101.

Ritchin, F. (2002), 'Photo Redux', *Print* 56(3) (July/August): 41–7.

Road to Guantánamo, The, film, directed by Michael Winterbottom. UK: FilmFour, 2006.

Rose, D. (2004), *Guantánamo: America's War on Human Rights*. New York: Faber and Faber.

Rosen, J. (2002), 'September 11 in the Mind of American Journalism', in B. Zelizer and S. Allan (eds), *Journalism After September 11*, New York: Routledge, pp. 27–35.

Rosler, M. (2004), 'Out of the Vox: Art's Activist Potential', *ArtForum* (September): 218–19.

Roth, Philip (2004), *The Plot Against America*, London: Jonathan Cape.

Rumsfeld, D. (2004), 'Transcript: Rumsfeld's Opening Statement'. Defense Secretary Offers "My Deepest Apology" to Iraqi Prisoners', *Washington Post*, 7 May: http://www.washingtonpost.com/ac2/wp-dyn?pagename=article& contentId=A8098–2004May7&notFound=true.

Sardar, Ziauddin and Davies, Merryl Wyn (2003), *Why Do People Hate America?* London: Icon.

Scarry, E. (2006), 'Who Defended the Country?', in D. J. Sherman and T. Nardin (eds), *Terror, Culture, Politics: Rethinking 9/11*, Bloomington, IN: Indiana University Press, pp. 184–205.

Schudson, M. (2002), 'What's Unusual about Covering Politics as Usual?', in B. Zelizer and S. Allan (eds), *Journalism After September 11*, London: Routledge. pp. 36–47.

Schulhofer, S. J. (2002), *The Enemy Within: Intelligence Gathering, Law Enforcement, and Civil Liberties in the Wake of September 11*, New York: Century Foundation Press.

Searle, A. (2002), 'Being Here Now', *Guardian* (23 July); http://www.guardian. co.uk/arts/features/story/0,11710,766127,00.html.

Searle, A. (2004), 'Buried Alive', *Guardian*, 13 July; http://arts.guardian.co.uk/ critic/feature/0,,1260091,00.html.

Seib, Philip (2004), *Beyond the Front Lines: How the News Media Cover a World Shaped by War*, New York: Palgrave Macmillan.

Sherwell, P. (2004), 'The CIA "Old Guard" Goes to War with Bush', *Daily Telegraph*, 10 October; http://www.telegraph.co.uk/news/main.jhtml?xml=/ news/2004/10/10/wbush10.xml&sSheet=/news/2004/10/10/ixnewstop.html.

Shriver, Lionel (2007), *The Post-Birthday World*, London: HarperCollins.

Shulan, M. (2002), untitled introduction, in M. Shulan et al. (eds), *here is new york: a democracy of photographs*, New York: Scalo, pp. 7–10.

Simpson, B. (2004), 'Techniques of Today: Bernadette Corporation', *ArtForum* (September): 220–23.

Simpson, David (2006), *9/11: The Culture of Commemoration*, Chicago: University of Chicago Press.

Sleeper Cell, TV series. USA: Showtime, 2005–

Smith, J. (2003), 'Missing a Beat: Story-making and the Absent President on September 11', *European Journal of American Culture*, 22(2): 85–102.

Snow, Nancy (2003), *Information War: American Propaganda, Free Speech and Opinion Control Since 9/11*, New York: Seven Stories.

Sontag, S. (2004), 'Regarding the Torture of Others', http://southerncrossreview. org/35/sontag.htm.

Spiegelman, Art (2004), *In the Shadow of No Towers*, London: Viking.

Spigel, L. (2004), 'Entertainment Wars: Television Culture after 9/11', *American Quarterly*, 56(2) (June): 235–70.

Stanley, A. (2006), 'Inside Terrorism's Tangled Web', *New York Times*, 8 December: http://www.nytimes.com/2006/12/08/arts/television/08slee. html?ex=1178424000&en=0d141b8197286c98&ei=5070.

Stanley, A. (2007a), 'Abu Ghraib and Its Multiple Failures', *New York Times*, 22 February; http://www.nytimes.com/2007/02/22/arts/television/22stan. html?ex=1329800400&en=2fd16bdec0aadebc&ei=5088&partner=rssnyt& emc=rss.

Stanley, A. (2007b), 'Beyond the News, Reminders of War', *New York Times*, 20 March: E1.

Stelzer, Irwin (ed.) (2004), *Neoconservatism*, London: Atlantic.

Strawson, J. (ed.) (2002), *Law After Ground Zero*, London: Glasshouse Press.

Syriana, film, directed by Stephen Gaghan. USA: Participant/Warner Bros. Pictures, 2005.

Taylor, P. M. (2004), 'The World Wide Web Goes to War: From Kosovo to the "War" Against Terrorism', in D. Gauntlett and R. Horsley (eds), *Web.Studies* [2nd edition], London: Arnold, pp. 230–42.

The Revolution Starts Now, CD, recorded by Steve Earle. USA: Artemis, 2004.

Truman, H. (1947), 'The Truman Doctrine: President Harry S Truman's Address Before a Joint Session of Congress', 12 March; http://www.yale. edu/lawweb/avalon/trudoc.htm.

Tumber, H. (2002), 'Reporting Under Fire: The Physical Safety and Emotional Welfare of Journalists', in B. Zelizer and S. Allan (eds), *Journalism After September 11*, New York: Routledge, pp. 247–62.

Tumber, H. (2004), 'Prisoners of News Values? Journalists, Professionalism, and Identification in Times of War', in S. Allan and B. Zelizer, *Reporting War: Journalism in Wartime*, London: Routledge, pp. 190–205.

Uncovered: The War on Iraq, film, directed by Robert Greenwald. USA: Cinema Libre Studio, 2004.

United 93, film, directed by Paul Greengrass. USA: Sidney Kimmel Entertainment, 2006.

Updike, John (2006) *Terrorist*, London: Hamish Hamilton.

USAFCC [United States Army Forces Central Command] (2004), Report on Shelling of Palestine Hotel [untitled]; http://www.cpj.org/Briefings/2003/ palestine_hotel/Army_rep_Pal_hotel.pdf.

USA Today (2006), 'Former POW Jessica Lynch expecting baby', *USA Today*, 24 August: http://www.usatoday.com/news/nation/2006-08-24- lynch-pregnant_x.htm.

US Department of State (2004), 'What did Secretary Powell say about the film *Osama?*' Question Taken at February 19, 2004 Daily Press Briefing. Office of the Spokesman, Washington DC; http://www.state.gov/r/pa/prs/ps/2004/29698.htm.

Van Krieken, P. J. (ed.) (2002), *Terrorism and the International Legal Order*. The Hague: TMC Asser.

Vergara, C. J. (2001), *Twin Towers Remembered*, Princeton, NJ: Princeton Architectural Press.

Vidal, Gore (2003), *Dreaming War: Blood for Oil and the Cheney–Bush Junta*, London: Clairview.

Village, The, film, directed by M. Night Shyamalan. USA: Touchstone Pictures, 2004.

Waisbord, S. (2002), 'Journalism, Risk, and Patriotism', in B. Zelizer and S. Allan (eds), *Journalism After September 11*, New York: Routledge, pp. 201–19.

Wallach, A. (2005), 'New "Truisms" In Words And Light', *New York Times*, 28 September: E1.

Wallis, D. (2004), *Inconvenient Evidence: Iraqi Prison Photographs from Abu Ghraib*; http://museum.icp.org/museum/exhibitions/abu_ghraib/introduction.html.

War of the Worlds, film, directed by Steven Spielberg. USA: Paramount, 2005.

Washington Post (2005), 'Vice President for Torture' [editorial], *Washington Post*, 26 October: A18.

Weeks, A. L. (1996), 'Do Civilizations Hold?', in S. P. Huntington et al., *The Clash of Civilizations: The Debate*. New York: Norton, pp. 53–4.

Wells, H. G. (2005), *The War of the Worlds* [1898], Harmondsworth: Penguin Books.

Williams, L. (1998), 'Melodrama Revised', in N. Browne (ed.), *Refiguring American Film Genres: Theory and History*, pp. 42–88.

Wilson, J. (2003), 'What I Didn't Find in Africa', *New York Times*, 6 July; http://www.nytimes.com/2003/07/06/opinion/06WILS.html?ex=1372824000&en=6c6aeb1ce960dec0&ei=5007&partner=USERLAND.

Winter Soldier, film, no director. USA: Winterfilm Collective, 1972.

Wong, E. and Cave, D. (2006), 'Iraqi Death Toll Rose Above 3,400 in July', New York Times, 15 August; http://www.nytimes.com/2006/08/15/world/middleeast/15cnd-iraq.html?ex=1313294400&en=791fbf910f54ab2f&ei=5088&partner=rssnyt&emc=rss.

Wood, G. (2006), 'Hollywood's new politics', *The Observer*, 8 January; http://observer.guardian.co.uk/review/story/0,6903,1681324,00.html.

World Trade Center, film, directed by Oliver Stone. USA: Paramount, 2006.

Young, D. (2006), 'The Road to Guantánamo' [review], *Variety.com*, 14 February; http://www.variety.com/index.asp?layout=features2006&content=jump&jump=review&head=berlin&nav=RBerlin&articleid=VE1117929622&cs=1&p=0.

Zelizer, B. (2002), 'Photography, Journalism and Trauma', in B. Zelizer and S. Allan (eds), *Journalism After September 11*, New York: Routledge, pp. 48–68.

Zelizer, Barbie and Allan, Stuart (eds) (2002a), *Journalism After September 11*, New York: Routledge.

Zelizer, B. and Allan, S. (2002b), 'Introduction: When Trauma Shapes the News', in B. Zelizer and S. Allan (eds), *Journalism After September 11*, New York: Routledge, pp. 1–24.

Žižek, S. (2004), 'What Rumsfeld Doesn't Know that He Knows about Abu Ghraib', *In These Times*, 21 May; http://www.inthesetimes.com/article/747/.

Zunes, S. (2003), *Tinderbox: US Foreign Policy and the Roots of Terrorism*, London: Zed.

Zwirner Gallery (2005), Press release. Isa Genzken: New Work (15 January): http://www.davidzwirner.com/resources/16940/IG_DZ2005.pdf.

Index

ABC (American Broadcasting Company), 61, 74, 75
Abu-Assad, Hany, 84
Abu Dhabi TV, 68, 71, 163
Abu Ghraib, 42, 46–8, 52–3, 77, 84, 137, 142–4, 146–52, 152–3n, 164, 169
Actuarial gaze, 65–6, 150–1
Adams, John Quincy, 37
Adelman, Kenneth, 36
Adversarial review, 38, 46–7, 53, 151
Afghanistan, 2, 4, 10, 15, 19, 20, 27, 31, 32, 35, 41, 45, 48, 49, 55, 57n, 62, 94, 95, 159, 161, 164, 167, 170
After September 11: Images from Ground Zero, 132, 162
Against All Enemies, 31–2, 34, 164, 168
Al-Aqsa mosque, 18
Al-Gama'at Al-Islamiyah (IG), 21
Al Jazeera, 66, 68, 71, 73, 85, 95, 163
Al-Qaeda, 1, 2, 8, 19, 20, 21, 31, 40, 42, 48, 51, 75, 157, 160, 161, 167, 168
Al-Qaeda and What it Means to be Modern, 157, 163
Al-Sabti, Qassim, 148
Al-Saud, Abdul Aziz, 18, 159
Alamo, The (1960), 87
Alamo, The (2004), 83, 86–8, 92, 96, 164
Algeria, 2
Ali, Laylah, 137, 140

Allan, Stuart, 59, 60, 162
Allegory lite, 80, 83–99, 108, 109, 110, 112, 129
American Civil Liberties Union (ACLU), 34, 57n
'American Empire (Get Used to It), The', 14–17, 37, 162
American Empire: The Realities and Consequences of US Diplomacy, 22–4, 162
American Flag, 138
Amnesty International, 49, 165
Anna, Santa, 87, 96
Annan, Kofi, 164
Anonymous *see* Scheuer, Michael
Anti-war demonstrations, 33–4, 113, 163, 165
AOL Time Warner, 73
Arab Mind, The, 152n
Arendt, Hannah, 24–5
Arrighi, Giovanni, 24–5
ArtForum, 129, 137–43, 151, 152n, 164
Ashcroft, John, 99
Axis of evil, 55, 161
Ayyoub, Tareq, 68

Ba'ath Party, 74
Bacevich, Andrew J., 4, 22–4, 162, 167
Baghdad Blog, The, 74
Baker, James, 36
Bali (bombs in), 162, 165
Balkans, 2

Baudrillard, Jean, 120
BBC (British Broadcasting
    Corporation), 56n, 67, 74
Beard, Charles, 23–5
Beard, Philip, 108
Beigbeder, Frédéric, 108, 119–25,
    164
Bennett, John, 145
Berman, Marshall, 122, 152n
Bernstein, Carl, 72–3
Big Noise Tactical Media, 131
Billig, Michael, 62
Bin Laden, Osama, 1, 5, 18–21, 40,
    60, 66, 96, 160, 161, 167
Black Hawk Down, 83, 84, 86
Blair, Tony, 56n, 147
Blix, Hans, 164
Blowback, 6, 17–22, 27, 37, 97,
    117
*Blowback: The Costs and Consequences
    of American Empire*, 17, 161
Blum, William, 17–18, 22, 161
Blumenthal, Sidney, 36–7
Bohen Foundation, 141, 162
Bonevardi, Gustavo, 145
Borgnine, Ernest, 157–8
Bosnia-Herzegovina, 154, 155
Bourne, Randolph, 38
Brenner, Robert, 26, 160
Britain, 13, 14, 15, 28, 56n, 75–6, 97,
    154, 155, 163
Brothers and Sisters, 75
Burkina Faso, 154
Bush, George H. W., 22, 36, 168,
    170
Bush, George W., 5, 8, 19, 23, 33,
    35, 36, 37, 38, 47, 48, 53, 55,
    56, 57n, 61, 66, 71, 75, 78, 82,
    85, 99, 100, 147, 150, 157, 161,
    162, 163, 164, 165, 166, 168,
    171
Bush, Jeb, 168
Bush administration, 4, 5, 6, 12, 15,
    22, 23, 25, 26, 27, 29, 31, 32,
    34–9, 41–57, 65–6, 71–3, 77,
    83, 85, 99, 102, 104, 108, 150,
    152, 158, 162, 163, 166, 168,
    170
Bush Doctrine, 4, 35, 38, 43–57, 74,
    78, 143, 147
Bybee, Jay, 50, 57n, 162

Camp Casey, 165
Cannes Film Festival (2004), 170
Carnegie International (2004/5), 138
Carter, Jimmy, 169
CBS (CBS Broadcasting Inc), 32,
    60–1, 150, 163, 164
CentCom (United States Central
    Command), 69–72, 163
Chahine, Youssef, 155
Chain of Command, 47–8, 50, 164
Chechnya, 2
Cheney, Richard (Dick), 35, 43, 51,
    99, 168
Chermak, Steven, 59
Chicago Convention *see* Convention
    on International Civil Aviation
Chile, 155
China, 2, 27, 44, 55
Chomsky, Noam, 17, 22, 23, 46, 161,
    165
CIA (Central Intelligence Agency),
    5, 6, 17, 18, 19, 20, 22, 34, 40,
    41, 42, 46, 48, 49, 51, 74, 98,
    147, 155, 159, 161, 162, 163,
    164, 165, 171
Clarke, Richard A., 5, 31–2, 34, 38,
    163, 164, 168
Clash of civilisations
    *Clash of Civilizations and the
    Remaking of World Order, The*, 7
    'Clash of Civilizations?, The',
    7–12, 21, 28, 160, 169
    clash of civilisations thesis, 7–12,
    17, 43, 94
Clinton, Bill, 22, 25, 26, 35, 36, 75,
    82, 168, 170
Clinton, Hillary, 83
CNN (Cable News Network), 61,
    62–4, 74, 166
Coalitions of the willing, 45, 52

Cold War, 8, 9, 11, 12, 24, 27, 43, 81, 86, 92
Colossus: The Rise and Fall of the American Empire, 13, 164
Committee to Protect Journalists (CPJ), 68, 80n
Congress, US House of, 6, 8, 15, 23, 32, 34, 39–40, 46–7, 51, 57n, 75, 103, 161, 162
Congressional midterm elections (2006), 5, 32, 34, 36, 54–5, 57n, 166
Conscience Liberalism, 83, 90, 112
Constitution of the United States of America, 6, 31, 34, 38, 51, 97, 104
Control Room, 71, 84–5
Convention on International Civil Aviation ('Chicago Convention'), 49
Council of Europe, 49
Couso, José, 68
Creative Time, 144–5
Creedence Clearwater Revival, 81
Criminal Minds, 75
Culture wars, 7, 10, 12, 28, 152–3n, 156, 158

Dagestan, 2
Danto, Arthur, 137, 141, 151
Danzig, David, 76
Darton, Eric, 122, 152n, 157, 162
Darwinism, 93–4, 113–14
Davies, Merryl Wyn, 17
Davis, Mike, 126
DC 9/11: Time of Crisis, 75
Defense Department *see* Department of Defense
Defense Policy Board (DPB), 36
Deller, Jeremy, 140
Demme, Jonathan, 81
Democratic Party, 32, 34, 64
Department of Defense, 1, 40, 41–2, 47–8, 50, 51, 57n, 65–73, 85, 95, 151, 158, 162, 168

Department of Homeland Security, 41
Department of State, 1, 42, 132, 168
Detainee Treatment Act (2005), 51, 165
Dewey, John, 38
Disney *see* Walt Disney Company
Dixie Chicks, 33–4, 163
Documenta 11 (2002), 152n
Donnelly, Trisha, 140

Earle, Steve, 38
Economist, The, 74
Edwards, Bob, 61
Egypt, 2, 15, 49, 154
Egyptian Islamic Jihad (EIJ), 21
Eisner, Michael, 86–7
11'09"01, 84, 152n, 154–8, 162
Embedded journalism, 66–8
Emma Booker Elementary School, 99
Empire, 12–30, 37, 43–4, 51, 54–5, 81, 117, 136, 137, 141, 155–6; *see also* Bush Doctrine, imperialism
Empire denial, 13, 16, 28, 127
Empire lite, 15–16, 28, 40; *see also* empire, empire denial, Michael Ignatieff, imperialism
Empire/Vampire, Who Kills Death, 138–40, 141, 142
End of History and the Last Man, The, 14
England, Lynndie, 148–50
ER, 75
Eritrea, 2
Ethiopia, 2
European Convention on Human Rights (1950), 49
European Union (EU), 44, 49
Extremely Loud and Incredibly Close, 114–19, 125, 165

Faces of Ground Zero, 130, 131, 161
Fahrenheit 9/11, 82, 84, 99–104, 135, 150, 164, 170
Failed states, 13–14, 16–17

Fallujah, 57, 84
FBI (Federal Bureau of Investigation), 40
Federal Anti-torture statute (1994), 57n
Federal Aviation Administration (FAA), 40
Feldman, Allen, 65, 150–1
Fellowship Adventure Group, 99
Ferguson, Niall, 8, 13, 27, 28, 164
Finnegan, Patrick, 76
Firdus Square, 71, 163
Foer, Jonathan Safran, 108, 114–19, 121, 123, 124, 155, 165, 169
Fog of War, The, 85
For the City, 144–5, 165
Ford, Gerald, 36, 168, 170
Foreign Affairs, 7, 9, 160
Fox TV, 80n, 84; see also 24
France, 154, 163
Frascina, Francis, 131
Friedman, Thomas, 14
Frontline, 72–3
Fukuyama, Francis, 14

Geneva Conventions (1949), 48, 161
Genzken, Isa, 137–40, 141, 142
George, Alice Rose, 132
Germany, 26, 50, 163
Globalisation, 14, 23, 25, 26, 82
Gonzales, Alberto, 50, 162
Good Night, and Good Luck, 82, 83, 96–7, 102
Good Priest's Son, The, 111–13
Gould, Richard Nash, 145
Grand Central Station, 139
Gray, John, 157, 163
Great Depression (1930s), 23
Greengrass, Paul, 86
Greenwald, Robert, 84
Grey's Anatomy, 75
Grid, The, 76
Griffin, Tim, 138, 140–1, 143
Ground Zero, 3, 78, 86, 122, 123, 132, 145, 154, 162
Ground Zero, 157, 162

Guantánamo Bay, 42, 46–51, 84, 144, 161
Guardian, the, 74
Gulf War, 11, 18, 81, 160, 167

Haacke, Hans, 129–30
Habeas corpus, 50–1
Hamdan v. Rumsfeld, 51
Hancock, John Lee, 86–7
Harvey, David, 24–9, 104, 163, 169
Hawaii, 79
Hearts and Minds, 85
Hegemony or Survival, 17
here is new york: a democracy of photographs, 130–7, 154, 161
Hersh, Seymour, 41, 47–8, 50, 152n, 164
Hewar Gallery, 148–9
Hezbollah, 166
Hicks, David, 51, 165
Hiroshima, 156
Hofstadter, Richard, 53
Holzer, Jenny, 130, 144–5, 147, 165
Homeland Security Act (2002), 41, 162
Horowitz, Jonathan, 137
Howard, Bryce Dallas, 89
Hulton, Kurt, 139
Human Rights First, 76
Human Rights Watch, 48
Huntington, Samuel P., 7–12, 21, 28, 30n, 43, 160, 169
Hussein, Saddam, 5, 30, 31, 35, 41, 66, 71, 74, 77, 96, 140, 147, 160, 163, 165, 166
Hutton Inquiry, 56n

Ignatieff, Michael, 14–17, 19, 26, 27, 28, 30n, 37, 38–9, 40, 46, 55, 162, 164, 169
Ikenberry, John, 55–6
Imamura, Shohei, 156
Imperial Hubris, 19, 20, 171
Imperialism, 4, 6, 11, 12–30, 51, 76, 81, 100, 104, 146–8; see also Bush Doctrine, empire

In Praise of Empires, 14
In The Shadow of No Towers, 109, 115
Iñárritu, Alejandro González, 155
Inconvenient Evidence: Iraqi Prison Photographs from Abu Ghraib, 151, 164
India, 2, 27, 55, 154
Indonesia, 2
Indymedia, 131
Institute of Contemporary Art, 137
International Center of Photography, 151, 164
International Criminal Court, 45
Intifada, 84, 161
Iran, 2, 5, 17, 27, 55, 97, 148, 154, 156, 159, 165
Iraq, 2, 4, 5, 6, 10, 15, 18, 26, 27, 30, 31–4, 35–6, 37, 41, 42, 45, 46, 47, 49, 52, 55, 56, 56n, 58, 65–71, 73, 74, 77, 82, 85, 86, 92, 94, 95, 99–100, 104, 113, 129, 142–3, 147–52, 159, 160, 163, 164, 165, 166, 167, 168, 170
Iraq Study Group (ISG), 32, 34, 36, 166
Iraq Survey Group (ISG), 163
Islamist insurgency, 1–2, 11, 19, 20–1, 167
Israel, 11, 18, 21, 55, 84, 154, 155, 156, 159, 166

Japan, 26, 154, 156
Jarhead, 84
Jennings, Peter, 61
Jerusalem, 18
Jihad, 1, 18, 19, 20, 55, 160, 167
Johnson, Chalmers, 17, 19, 22
Johnson, Lyndon B., 85
Jordan, 49
Journalism After September 11, 59–60

Kagan, Robert, 28, 54, 162
Kaplan, Lawrence, 36, 163

Karpinski, Janis, 47, 52–3
Kashmir, 2
Kellner, Douglas, 59
Kelly, David, 56
Kelman, James, 108, 125–7
Kennan, George, 8
Kennedy, John F., 85
Kennedy, Paul, 27
Kenya (bomb at US embassy in), 1, 160
Kerry, John, 82, 105–6n
Khalil, Abdel-Karim, 148–9
Khobar Towers, 1
Kingdom of Heaven, 83, 86, 96
Knight Ridder, 5, 162
Krauthammer, Charles, 52–3, 151
Kristol, William, 36, 163
Kruger, Barbara, 140
Kupchan, Charles, 27
Kuwait, 160
Kyrgyzstan, 2

Lal, Deepak, 14, 23, 26, 28
Lancet, The, 55, 95, 166
Lansing, Sherry, 105n
Late Show With David Letterman, The, 60–1
LaVerdiere, Julian, 145
Law
    federal, 4, 42, 46, 48–51, 56n, 162
    international, 4, 6, 13, 29, 45, 48–52, 55–6, 56–7n, 161, 162, 164
Law & Order, 75
Lebanon, 2, 166
Leffler, Melvyn, 53
Lesser Evil, The, 38, 164
Lexus and the Olive Tree, The, 14
Libby, Lewis ('Scooter'), 42–3
Liberal International Economic Order (LIEO), 14, 28
Liberty, 49
Libya, 2, 49
Limbaugh, Rush, 148, 151
Lipscomb, Lila, 99, 101, 103
Lisson Gallery, 146–7, 164

Loach, Ken, 155
London (bombs in), 165
Los Angeles Times, 8
Lost, 77–80, 94
Lost generation, 108, 120, 128n
Luxemburg, Rosa, 26
Lynch, Jessica, 69–71, 163

McCarthy, Cormac, 107, 108,
    110–11, 123, 166
McCarthyism, 81, 96
McChesney, Robert, 58–60, 63
McDonnell, Nick, 108
McEwan, Ian, 94, 108, 113–14, 125
McGrath, Patrick, 108
McNally, Joe, 130, 131, 161
McNamara, Robert S., 85
Madagascar, 2
Madrid (train bombs), 164
Magnum photo agency, 131, 132
Makhmalbaf, Samira, 156
Malaysia, 2
Maltby, Richard, 83
Manchurian Candidate, The (1962),
    81
Manchurian Candidate, The (2004),
    81–3, 85, 88, 164
Manifesta 5 (2004), 152n
Mapplethorpe, Robert, 138
Marantz, Paul, 145
Marx, Karl, 24, 26
Mauritania, 2
Mecca, 18
Media Representations of 9/11, 59
Medina, 18
Mexico, 154, 155
Meyerowitz, Joel, 131–2, 162
Military commissions, 48, 51
Military Commissions Act (2006),
    51, 166
Miramax, 99
Moore, Michael, 34, 36, 38, 82, 84,
    99–104, 105, 135, 150, 163,
    170
Morocco, 2, 49
Morris, Errol, 85

Mossadegh, Mohammad, 17, 97, 98
Murrow, Edward R., 97
Museum of the City of New York,
    132
Muslim Council of Britain, 80n
Myoda, Paul, 145

Nagasaki, 156
National Commission on Terrorist
    Attacks Upon the United States
    see The 9/11 Commission
National Endowment for the Arts
    (NEA), 144
National Public Radio (NPR), 61
National Security Strategy (NSS)
    (2002), 4, 19, 26, 35, 43–6, 50,
    52, 56, 162
National Security Strategy (NSS)
    (2006), 56, 165
NATO, 6, 44
Naudet, Gédéon, 154, 162
Naudet, Jules, 154, 162
Neoconservatism, 5, 14, 22, 26, 28,
    35, 36, 43, 44, 45, 78, 92, 98,
    111, 152n
Neoliberalism, 25–6
New Imperialism, The, 24–8, 29, 163,
    169
New Internationalist, 169
New Left, 103
New Left Review, 160
New York City Independent Media
    Center, 131
New York Municipal Art Society,
    145
New York September 11, 131
New Yorker, The, 76, 164
New York Times, 5, 15, 19, 31, 42, 58,
    74, 76, 131, 162, 163, 164
Niger, 42, 56n
Nigeria, 2
9.11, 131
9/11 (Chomsky), 17, 161
9/11 (Naudet and Naudet), 154, 162
9/11 Commission Report, The, 39–41,
    75, 164

9/11 Commission, The, 5, 39–41, 42, 75, 162
9/11 Photo Archive, 131–2
9/12 (Omar), 131
Nixon, Richard, 37, 72–3, 81, 168, 170
Non Governmental Organisations (NGOs), 34, 48, 49, 95
North American Aerospace Defense Command (NORAD), 40
North Korea, 55, 162
Noujaim, Jehane, 71, 84
Nuclear Non-Proliferation Treaty (1968), 162, 165
Nye, Joseph S. Jr., 162

Observer, The, 74
Office of Special Plans, 41, 162
Oil, 15, 17, 18, 26, 27, 55, 97, 98; see also resource wars
Omar, Dega, 131
Outfoxed: Rupert Murdoch's War on Journalism, 84
Overstretch, 27, 28
Over There, 75, 76

Pakistan, 2, 27, 55
Palestine, 2, 84
Palestine Hotel, 68, 71, 163
Paradise and Power, 28, 162
Paradise Now, 84
Paradox of American Power, The, 162
Participant Productions, 82, 83, 84, 96–9
Path to 9/11, The, 75
Patriot Act see USA Patriot Act
Pax, Salam, 74
Pearl Harbor, 5, 62
Penn, Sean, 152n, 154, 157–8
Pentagon see Department of Defense
Peress, Gilles, 132, 133
Perle, Richard, 36
Philippines, 2
Phoenix, Joaquin, 89
Pinewood Studios, 86
Plame, Valerie, 42–3, 163

Plot Against America, The, 107–11, 125, 164
Poland, 49
Polyurethane Sprayed on the Backs of 10 Workers, 146–7, 164
Postmasters Gallery, 129
Powell, Colin, 35, 42, 170
Powers, Thomas, 41, 42
Pre-emptive war, 4, 45–6, 50, 52, 53–4, 56, 147; see also Bush Doctrine, preventive war
Presidential Seal, 141–3, 162
Preventive war, 45–6; see also Bush Doctrine, pre-emptive war
Price, Reynolds, 108, 111–13, 116
Project for the New American Century, 35, 170
Protsyuk, Taras, 68
Public Broadcasting Service (PBS), 72

Qatar, 66, 69, 72

Rasul v. Bush, 51, 164
Rather, Dan, 60–1
Reagan, Ronald, 42, 59, 140
Regime change, 4, 5, 35, 53, 81; see also Bush Doctrine
Rendition, 46, 48–52, 147, 165
Republican 'crisis', 5, 6, 29, 31–56, 58–60, 63, 68, 72, 81, 83, 85, 88, 99–100, 107, 108, 110, 127n, 129, 150–2, 157–8; see also Constitution of the United States of America
Republican Party, 32, 64, 105n, 166
Rescue Me, 75
Resource wars, 27; see also oil
Reuters, 68
Revisionism, 4, 12–30, 81, 87, 158
Rice, Condoleezza, 35, 41, 42, 50, 60, 170
Rise and Fall of the Great Powers, The, 27
Road, The, 107, 110–11, 166

Road to Guantánamo, The, 84
Rockwell, Norman, 131
Rogue State, 17–18, 161
Rogue states, 4, 5, 13–14, 16–17, 35, 43
Romania, 49
Rome, 13, 28, 76, 148
Rome, 76
Roosevelt, Franklin Delano, 18, 108, 159
Rosenquist, James, 137
Rosler, Martha, 137–8, 140
Roth, Kenneth, 48
Roth, Philip, 36, 107–11, 125, 164
Rudin, Scott, 104n
Rumsfeld, Donald, 35, 41, 47, 103, 140, 162, 164, 166, 170–1
Russia, 27, 44, 55, 163

Sachs, Tom, 130, 137, 141–3, 162
Sacranie, Iqbal, 80n
San Diego Union-Tribune, 133
Sardar, Ziauddin, 17
Saturday, 94, 113–14
Saudi Arabia, 2, 18, 55, 159, 160, 167
Sauret, Etienne, 154
Scarry, Elaine, 41, 157
Scheuer, Michael (Anonymous), 2, 17, 18–22, 40, 162, 171
Schreiber, Liev, 82
Scott, Ridley, 86, 96
Scowcroft, Brent, 36
Searle, Adrian, 146
Second World War, 11, 12, 16, 25, 54, 137, 148, 156
September 11 Photo Project, The, 131, 133
September Dossier, 56n
Serra, Richard, 130–1, 135, 137, 143–4, 147, 164, 171
7/7 *see* London (bombs in)
Shulan, Michael, 132–5
Shyamalan, M. Night, 88–91
Sidney Kimmel Entertainment, 86

Sierra, Santiago, 130, 137, 146–7, 164
Simpson, Bennett, 137, 141
60 Minutes II, 150, 164
Skol, Jeff, 96
Sleeper Cell, 75, 84
Somalia, 2
Sontag, Susan, 147–8, 150
'Sources of Soviet Conduct, The', 8
South Africa, 2
Soviet Union, 2, 8, 19, 20, 159, 167
Spears, Britney, 102
Spiegelman, Art, 109, 115, 121
Spielberg, Steven, 92–5
Spooks, 75–6
Staehle, Wolfgang, 129
Stanley, Alessandra, 76
State Department *see* Department of State
Stone, Oliver, 86
Stop Bush, 130–1, 135, 137, 143–4, 164
Strauss, Leo, 88, 90, 106n, 152
Streep, Meryl, 82
Stupid White Men, 102
Sudan, 2, 167
Sundance Film Festival (2002), 161
Supreme Court, 6, 41, 46–7, 51, 164, 168
Swift Boat Veterans for Truth, 105–6n
Syria, 49
Syriana, 82, 84, 97–9, 102, 165

Tajikistan, 2
Taliban, 161
Tanovic, Danis, 155
Tanzania (bomb at US embassy in), 1, 160
Taylor, Philip, 67
Telecinco, 68
Terrorist, 84
Through Our Enemies' Eyes, 17, 19–22, 162, 171
Tipton Three, 84
Tora Bora, 84, 161, 167

Torture, 42, 46–53, 56–7n, 76–8, 80,
    146, 148, 162, 165, 168, 169
Traub, Charles, 131–2
Trauma, 6, 60–2, 64–5, 88, 116–18,
    121, 127n, 136–7, 140, 154,
    155
Treaty of Nice, 49
Tribute in Light, 145, 162
Truman, Harry, 43
24, 76–7, 80n
Twin Towers Remembered, 152

Uganda, 2
Uncovered: The War on Iraq, 84
Unilateralism, 4, 27, 44–51, 53, 55,
    147; see also Bush Doctrine
Unit, The, 75
Unitary executive, 37, 43, 46, 49, 50
United Kingdom (UK) see Britain
United Nations (UN), 6, 13–14, 15,
    18, 44–6, 54, 160, 163, 164
United Nations Charter (1945), 46
United Nations Convention Against
    Torture and Other Cruel,
    Inhuman or Degrading
    Treatment or Punishment
    (1984), 51, 56–7n
United Nations Protocol on
    Incendiary Weapons (1980),
    57n
United Nations Universal
    Declaration of Human Rights
    (1948), 49
United 93, 86, 165
United States Central Command see
    CentCom
Updike, John, 84, 108
USA Patriot Act, 34, 57n, 103, 117,
    161
USS Abraham Lincoln, 71, 72, 163
USS Cole, 1, 161
USSR see Soviet Union
Uzbekistan, 2
Venice Film Festival (2002), 155
Vergara, Camilo José, 152n
Vidal, Gore, 36

Vietnam War, 23, 65, 81, 85, 129,
    148, 167
Village, The, 83, 88–92, 164
Village Voice, 133
Virilio, Paul, 157, 162
Voight, Jon, 82
Vote rigging, 168

Waisbord, Silvio, 62
Walt Disney Company, 73, 86, 99
War crimes, 42, 46, 48, 57n; see also
    torture
War of the Worlds, 83, 92–5, 165
War over Iraq: Saddam's Tyranny and
    America's Mission, The, 35–6,
    163
Warhol Museum, 151
Washington, Denzel, 82
Washington Post, 5, 28, 48, 51, 52, 74,
    163, 168
Wayne, John, 87
Weapons of mass destruction
    (WMD), 6, 30, 56n, 58, 84, 89,
    95, 147, 163, 164, 165
Weiner, Lawrence, 137, 140
Wells, H. G., 93–5
West Wing, The, 75
Where is Raed?, 74
Whitney Biennial (2004), 130, 151
Why Do People Hate America?, 17
Wilkerson, Lawrence, 42
Williams, William Appleman,
    23–5
Wilson, Joseph, 42
Wilson, Woodrow, 36
Windows on the World, 119–25,
    164
Winter Soldier, 85
Winterbottom, Michael, 84
Wisconsin School, 24–5, 100
Without a Trace, 75
Wolfowitz, Paul, 35, 99
World Trade Center, 1, 2, 10, 65, 73,
    78, 114, 116–19, 121–3, 129,
    132, 136, 152n, 154, 155,
    157–8, 160

World Trade Center, 86, 166
WTC: The First 24 Hours, 154, 161
Yamasaki, Minoru, 157
Yemen, 2

You Have to be Careful in the Land of the Free, 125–7

Zelizer, Barbie, 59–60, 137, 162
Žižek, Slavoj, 150, 152

DATE DUE